Business Feel

Business Feel

From the Science of Management to the Philosophy of Leadership

Dr Steven Segal

First published 2004 by
PALGRAVE MACMILLAN
Houndmills, Basingstoke, Hampshire RG21 6XS and
175 Fifth Avenue, New York, N. Y. 10010
Companies and representatives throughout the world

PALGRAVE MACMILLAN is the global academic imprint of the Palgrave Macmillan division of St. Martin's Press, LLC and of Palgrave Macmillan Ltd. Macmillan® is a registered trademark in the United States, United Kingdom and other countries. Palgrave is a registered trademark in the European Union and other countries.

ISBN 1–4039–3592–0

This book is printed on paper suitable for recycling and made from fully managed and sustained forest sources.

A catalogue record for this book is available from the British Library.

Library of Congress Cataloging-in-Publication Data
Segal, Steven, 1959–
    Business feel : from the science of management to the philosophy of leadership / Steven Segal.
        p. cm.
    Includes bibliographical references and index.
    ISBN 1–4039–3592–0 (cloth)
    1. Industrial management. 2. Leadership. I. Title.

HD31.S438 2004
658′.001–dc22   2004048579

10   9   8   7   6   5   4   3   2   1
13   12   11   10   09   08   07   06   05   04

Printed and bound in Great Britain by
Antony Rowe Ltd, Chippenham and Eastbourne

*To Margot, my wife, Di, my sister-in-law and Annette,
my mother-in-law
Whose love and support have liberated me.*

Contents

1

In the Cracks of Conventions

Jack Welch is recognised as one of the great corporate leaders of the modern world. It is natural that many managers and leaders would want to learn from him. To this end a number of books have been written on Jack Welch, many of which outline the "Jack Welch way" of leadership and organisational management. Yet one of the outstanding features of Welch is that his way of doing things cannot be reduced to a set of techniques or formulas. Business, he maintains, is not a great science. It is underpinned by being able to trust in "one's gut." His success lies in his uncanny business feel.

Welch is not alone in exemplifying the importance of business feel. It is central to the leadership practice of, for example, Andrew Grove of Intel. Worry is the primary form of business feel that underpins Grove's technical expertise in a number of areas. As we inquire more into the practices of other leaders we see business feel playing a central role in their leadership styles. George Soros, for example, talks of the central role that anxiety has played in his management style. Anita Roddick speaks of herself as having the passion of an obsessive. Ricardo Semler has written of the role of stress in transforming his understanding of organisations. Mort Meyerson identifies the role of uncertainty and despair in leading him to rethink leadership. And Lou Gerstner in his time at IBM came to recognise the role of emotions in leadership.

The interesting thing about business feel is that it cannot be learnt in a purely cognitive way. It relies on a feeling for the situation, on being able to make instinctive or intuitive judgements in the situation, judgements in which we feel that we are doing is correct without necessarily being able to explain in abstract and rule-like terms why it is correct. If we try to follow principles of "business feel" in too conscious and rational way, we lose the very feel that is the most vital element of business feel.

How, then, can we talk and learn about business feel?

What we shall see during the course of this book is that these leaders discovered the importance of business feel in a "philosophical experience," an experience in which they could no longer take their habitual or conventional ways of thinking about management for granted. Their day to day experiences as managers challenged them to think about their practices as managers in new ways. As they questioned their habitual ways of doing things, they began to see their own practices and the practice of management in general in a new light.

All the leaders mentioned in this book experienced themselves, at one time or another, as being outside of the socially approved habitual way of doing things. Ricardo Semler, for example, thought of himself as a maverick. Jack Welch says that one needs to be "crazy" to be a leader. Andrew Grove sees himself as "paranoid," while Anita Roddick sees a sense of being an "outsider" as central for her entrepreneurial attunement. Perhaps the only one who does not fit this mould clearly is Lou Gerstner but it was as an "outsider" who was invited inside to lead GE from its old way of doing things into a new way of being. And CEO's like Mort Meyerson have shown how their experience of depression and anxiety opened up opportunities for moving from old but stale ways of doing things to new and invigorating ways of leading.

Yet none of these leaders is or was so crazy that they were out of touch with the world in which they worked. Far from being out of touch with the world, their view from the outside gave them a perspective on the inside that those who were on the inside could not see. For like a fish in water we do not see the water that we are in. Only when we are deprived of water do we begin to see the water that we are in.

The experience of gaining perspective on a situation by being an outsider is an "existential experience." Generally speaking existential philosophers have developed a framework in which to show how experiences of "craziness," "paranoia," "stress" and being an "outsider" enable us to see the world in new ways. Existential philosophers were both part of but unhappy with the society in which they found themselves. Fredric Nietzsche, for example, felt very alone and isolated from the mainstream. Soren Kierkegaard was tormented by a sense of profound alienation from the Christianity of his childhood. Jean Paul Sartre writes of intense feelings of alienation generated by mass culture and Martin Heidegger's early life was spent caught between the familiarity of his Catholic upbringing and the uncertainty of the unfamiliar new and modern world. Martin Buber speaks about a "holy insecurity" which linked him to the traditions from which he felt estranged.

In all cases they were able to turn this experience of being on the margins of society into opportunities to reflect on society and to develop philosophies which have inspired both scholars and those grappling with the question of the meaning of existence. In this book we shall see how some of those recognised as outstanding corporate leaders have been able to turn existential experiences into opportunities for leading and managing in new ways.

Both the existential thinkers and the leaders used in this book operate in what will be called the "cracks of convention," where the stability of the old and familiar habits for doing things has broken down, the new is on the horizon but has not yet been firmly established. They are able to thrive in the space between the collapse of the certainty of the old and the uncertainty of the not yet new. Indeed, they are able to turn the experience of disruption into opportunities for new possibilities. For the existential philosophers, the uncertainty experienced in being in the cracks of conventions provides the dynamic energy for philosophical thought. Outside of the cracks of convention, philosophical thought, from the existential perspective, is sterile. Where life is simply routine, philosophy becomes abstract and empty. Similarly the leaders who operate in the cracks of convention are able to thrive and inspire others to thrive in the movement through the cracks of convention.

The aim of the book is to enable managers to achieve excellence in their practice by learning how to turn disruptive management experiences into learning opportunities. The key to doing this is learning the philosophical skills of management. The outline of these skills is the central theme of the book. These skills will be developed by situating the management experiences of recognised corporate leaders such as Jack Welch of GE, and Andrew Grove of Intel in the context of the views of recognised figures in the history of philosophy such as Socrates, Plato, Jean Paul Sartre and Martin Heidegger.

The way in which managers and management theorists think about management is currently undergoing a transition. Historically management was rooted in the scientific management account of Fredric Taylor. Today there is increasing dissatisfaction with this approach. Yet management still holds onto the idea of being a science. Because management discourse and practice is so embedded in a scientific approach, movement beyond it is fraught with difficulty. As Jack Welch says to change an embedded tradition such as scientific management is a hundred-year project.

This book examines the process of moving beyond the scientific approach to management. It will do this on three levels: firstly, as has already been stated, it will show the movement from scientific to philosophical conceptions of management as exemplified in a number of corporate leaders. Secondly, it will show some contemporary trends in management theory imply a philosophical rather than a scientific framework. Thirdly, it will develop a concept of education appropriate for the transition from a scientific to a philosophical notion of management.

Regarding the first level, the book will demonstrate how the philosophical skills of those corporate leaders mentioned above have enabled them to move beyond scientific accounts of management. Based on their experience, it will also suggest that a philosophical rather than a scientific base is more appropriate to the changing world in which managers find themselves, and thus that managers need to complement their scientific understanding with a philosophical attunement.

In this sense the book will develop in rich ways some of the themes that emerge in the Emotional Intelligence literature. However, this book will argue that the conventional literature on emotional intelligence does not do justice to the experience of business feel, that we need to go back to notions of practical wisdom or practical reasoning situated within the philosophical tradition in order to fully appreciate the notion of "business feel." Situating the notion of "business feel" in the context of the history of philosophy will also make the notion more accessible to business people who habitually are averse to any talk of feel. It will also allow us to integrate feeling and cognition in a way that does not privilege one over the other.

In terms of the second level, the book will also show how a number of contemporary trends in management theory presuppose a philosophical rather than a scientific disciplinary framework. It will show how Hammer and Champy's concept of re-engineering, how Clayton Christensen's concept of the innovator's dilemma, how Fernando Flores' idea of the "entrepreneurial life," how the concept of creative destruction put forward by Kaplan and Foster in their work on creative destruction and how Boleman and Deal's concept of organisational frames presuppose a philosophical framework.

It is important to point out that the book is not a critical look at the philosophies of leaders. Rather, its aim is to bring out the philosophies that are implicit in the experiences and practices of leaders. The central thrust of the book is to make clear that managers and leaders are philosophical in their practices but that the significance and their being philosophical is not always apparent and needs to be made apparent. The process of bringing out or making explicit that which is implicit in the experiences of the leaders is called an "existential hermeneutic" form of inquiry. As expressed in this work, it is derived from the philosophy of Martin Heidegger who provides a framework for developing the philosophies that are implicit in the way we experience the world.

The book is also concerned with the changing process of education implied in changing from a scientific to a philosophical conception of management. It will outline an existential hermeneutic account of management education in which theories and case studies are situated within the context of the experiences of managers and not discussed in a way that is detached from the experiences of managers. Situating the theories and case studies in the context of the experience of managers makes it possible for managers to not only learn the theories and the case studies but to explicitly examine their own hidden and taken for granted assumptions of management – something that is not necessarily achieved through studying either theories or case studies.

The book is addressed to a number of audiences:

Managers who need the skills to turn negative experiences into learning opportunities and who are also engaged in a transition from a scientific management to a philosophical style of management, **management theoreticians** concerned with articulating the transition from a scientific management to a philosophical conception of management, **management educators** frustrated with traditional forms of management education and open to an existential hermeneutic account of management education, **management consultants** working at the interface between theory and practice and to **philosophers** who believe that philosophy is a practical activity.

The book is written in an "existential hermeneutic" style. This means that it situates theory in the context of the experiences of managers. It begins with the experience of managers who, in transforming negative management experiences into learning opportunities, also find themselves in a shift from a scientific to a philosophical account of management. The theoretical expression of their experiences is then built on to their journey. In this way theory is not imposed on but emerges out of experience. This ensures that the theory is always discussed in the context of experience and so it ensures that theory is accessible to those who have no background in the particular theories or philosophies developed in the book.

The book is written in such a way that it can be read on a number of levels: for the practising manager it can be read as a series of skills that allow him or her to reflect on their practices. For the management theorist it provides a framework to examine the transition from a scientific to a philosophical account of management. For the management educator it provides an educational process for learning from experience. For the consultant, it provides a framework to integrate theory and practice and for the philosopher it opens up the realm of the practical.

2
Philosophical Experiences

I

Anita Roddick tells us that she learnt from experience. She also tells us that to learn from experience means to "never stop asking questions, and knock on doors to seek as many different opinions as exist. Then you have to make up your own mind." (Roddick, 2000, p. 39) Surely, as practical people, we cannot always be asking questions. For the most part we need to get the work done. In getting the work done we need to be goal focused. Asking questions is not always a good idea when we need to be goal focused rather than question focused. Indeed, we tend to get irritated with people who come asking questions whilst we are on the job.

There is, as Solomon told us, a time for all seasons, for all activities. There is a time for getting the work done and there is a time for questioning the way in which we get the work done. The question then is, when is the time for questioning? When, in the context of our practices, do we come to ask questions? What are the occasions in our experience that invite us to question our experiences? And what, in our practices, leads us to ask questions?

It is this question that will be answered in this chapter. The answer that will be given in this chapter is as follows: when our experiences are flowing smoothly there is no need to question our experiences. Indeed when in the flow of experience, our mind is not even aware of the questioning process. It is only when things are not going as planned, when there is a disturbance or disruption in our experience that we begin to question our experience. As will be shown, disturbance or disruption in the flow of experience leads us to be emotionally detached from our experiences in such a way that we enter a questioning rather than simply doing mindset.

The crucial issue is the ability to turn a disruption or disturbance into a questioning of experience. For it can also happen that rather than being open to question, we can in moments of disruption be overwhelmed by experiences of being threatened and thus become defensive. When things get too much, we tend to "sweep them under the carpet," blame other people or try and avoid the issue as best we can. We need what shall be called the Socratic dynamic of humility and strong determination in order to turn a potentially threatening disruption into a learning opportunity.

The idea of learning through the disruption of experience has a long history in the discipline of philosophy. For brevity's sake, we shall call the philosophical model of experience the convention-disruption-disclosure model of learning. Based on the work of Jean-Marie Dru, this is a model that suggests that we develop new visions or insights through the disruption of our habitual or conventional modes of experience. It is the disruption of our experience that allows us to see things in a new light. The philosophical history of this model will be presupposed in this chapter and spelt out in chapter 6.

II

The theme of developing new conventions in the experience of the disruption of old conventions is not an historically new phenomenon but can be traced back to the recorded beginnings of humanity. For example, it can be found in the biblical vision of Moses leaving the familiarity of Egypt wondering through the desert for forty years and receiving the Ten Commandments which were to become the basis of Western and Middle Eastern religion. Although Egypt was a place of oppression for Moses and the Israelites, it was also a place of familiarity. They knew how things got done. In entering the desert, they entered the strange and unfamiliar. In this way they lost sense of all their old habits and customs. But it was precisely the experience of being divested of their old ways of doing things that opened them up to the possibility of new ways of doing things and thus to receiving the Ten Commandments.

It can be found in the experience of Socrates, recognised as the archetype of the philosophical life. Socrates lived in a state of almost permanent disruption, having no job, no secure routine, nothing definite to hold onto. Yet out of this disruption came the underpinnings for the traditions of Western thought. For Socrates is seen as the turning point in the development of Western rationality. The same kind of experience was had by Christ who left the security of his Jewish upbringing and conventions, wondered through the wilderness and emerged with a new vision for humanity. Buddha also had the same set of experiences. Having grown up in the security of his father's kingdom, he rejected the way of life of his parents, went into the wilderness of the unknown and emerged as the archetype of Eastern spiritual enlightenment.

Together it can be said that these different perspectives cover some of the major wisdom traditions of humanity. Whatever the differences of their language and practices it seems that all of them reflect the central process underlying this book; namely the disruption of habitual conventions opens up the possibility of new visions or new ways of being. Each develops in terms of the conventions of their society. Each comes to have a critical perspective on the conventions of the society. Each is able to handle the uncertainty of a critical perspective of their society; each is also able to embrace being estranged from the mainstream way of dealing with things. And each is able to come back offering humanity a new vision.

Today there is enough evidence to indicate that management is in the grips of a transformation that could benefit from an appreciation of the process underpinning the wisdom traditions. There are many writers in the field of management who acknowledge that management is undergoing changes in which many of the old conventions are falling away but no new, well-established conventions have yet come to take their place. Describing the experience of being caught in the grips of disruption AOL Time Warner Chairman Stephen M. Case says: "I sometimes feel like I'm behind the wheel of a race car..." he said. "One of the biggest challenges is there are no road signs to help navigate. And in fact...no one has yet determined which side of the road we're supposed to be on." (Garten, 2001)

Case is referring to the blindness in the experience of being caught between the collapse of an old way of doing things and the not-yet of a new set of conventions or habits. A question that we need to ask is: how do we operate when we do not have road signs to guide us? Indeed how do we begin to establish new road signs? It is in this context that philosophy becomes significant. For it is where our conventional language fails us, where we do not have a framework to describe our experiences that the passion and "motive" for being philosophical begins. As will be developed later in more detail, the emotional basis for philosophy begins where words and concepts fail us.

The experience of the form of learning through the disruption of conventions is quite explicitly addressed by Andrew Grove who wrote the book "Only the Paranoid Survive" for this purpose: "What this book is about is the impact of changing rules. It's about finding your way through uncharted territories. Through examples and reflections on my own and others' experiences, I hope to raise your awareness of what it is like to go through cataclysmic changes and to provide a framework in which to deal with them." (Grove, 1997, p. 7)

It is not only CEO's who have been articulating the experience of being caught in disruption. So too have management theorists. For example, Gary Hamel has said: "Continuous improvement is an industrial-age concept, and while it is better than no improvement at, it is of marginal value in the age of revolution. Radical, non-linear innovation is the only way to escape the ruthless hypercompetition that has been hammering down margins in industry after industry. Non-linear innovation requires a company to escape the shackles of precedent and imagine entirely novel solutions to customer needs." (Hamel, 2000)

John Kotter has added his voice to the need for an understanding of disruption: "Changes driven by powerful forces associated with technology, the globalisation of competition and markets, and workforce demographics ... have been destroying the mid-twentieth century stability and pushing up the speed of so much, demanding from managers both incremental change and bigger leaps. ... In the mid twentieth century ... industries changed more slowly, demanding less in turn less organizational change."

Although the old has broken down, no new language or "roadmap" has come to replace it. Indeed it is reasonable to suggest that we still do not know how to name the new way of doing things. There are so many fads that come and go. Nothing sticks as well as and for as long as scientific management has. Thus we have quality assurance, re-engineering philosophies, disruptive technologies, each of which is insightful but none of which has taken route in the same way as scientific management has. They may stimulate some people for some of the time but it seems that disillusionment begins to set in. Similarly we have new metaphors for organisations; no longer conceived as machines, they are now seen as "organic" entities or "learning" organisations full of "spirit" and "culture" but, again there is just as much scepticism of each metaphor as there is support for it.

Management education has also been caught between the collapse of an old way of doing things and the not yet of a new way of educating. Indeed there has been a shift away from disengaged academic processes of education to a case study approach to education. The belief here is that case studies give us access to the issues in a non-theoretical and practical way. And even more than this there have been shifts away from university-centred education to education at the coal face of the workplace, underpinned by the belief that to study cases in the ideal time conditions of the university is not the same as thinking and questioning under the real life conditions of the workplace. Theoreticians have also been concerned with developing new concepts of the relationship between practice and theory that parallel the shift from disengaged to engaged educational practices. Practitioners have themselves been calling for a new model of the relation between theory and practice. An example is Jack Welch who developed the concept of "work-out" to integrate theory and practice in a new kind of way. It will be very interesting to look at the congruence between theorists who are looking, from a theoretical perspective, at a new relation between theory and practice, and practitioners who, from the perspective of practice are looking at a new kind of relationship between theory and practice.

In the context of being caught between the collapse of the old and the not yet of the new, "business as usual" is in question. We do not have the road signs or conventions to guide us. We are forced to take a step back and examine the conventions and assumptions underpinning our way of doing things. This is the moment of philosophy, a moment in which philosophy is practical and not just an abstract activity. This is the point that I am about to develop. It will be embodied in the process of philosophy as convention-disruption-vision (CDV).

III

In contrast to the popular image of philosophy as something abstract and unintelligible, philosophy is actually a very concrete activity when it is engaged in its appropriate context. The context for philosophy is a disruption in our conventional ways of doing things. For the most part, when things are running smoothly, we do not need to be philosophical. In order to achieve our ends, we need to get on with the demands of everyday living. To be philosophical when we should be "efficient" or practical would be self-destructive.

However, there are times in all of our lives when we do experience a disruption to our conventional or habitual ways of doing things. For example, in the experience of the death of a loved one, our everyday lives are disrupted in such a way that we cannot help but start to question the meaning of life. Our whole mood shifts in such experiences. We move out of the mood of everyday efficiency into a mood of contemplative reflection. In the face of death life feels strange and in the face of the haunting strangeness of life, we find ourselves asking the question of meaning. In the mood of death, the question of meaning does not seem to be an abstract question but a very concrete question. Indeed it is often experienced as chilling. It is something that grabs us. We find ourselves asking and exploring questions that we never thought we would ask. It offers us the opportunity to evaluate the way we have lived our lives and examine our projects for the future. In such an experience what we have been doing is exploring our own assumptions about life. These assumptions are usually implicit in our experiences. They guide our way of experiencing the world without us being aware of the way in which they guide us. It is at times of death that our life assumptions become explicit. These moments of explicitness can be used as occasions upon which to rethink or reaffirm our life assumptions.

Death is not the only disruption that places the human being in the mood of philosophy. Divorce is another kind of disruption which often places people into a reflective mode. It is often the case, that divorce becomes an occasion upon which people come to recognise the values underpinning their way of life and either recommit to the old values or begin a search for new habits or styles of living. This is demonstrated in the case of Brian who in the face of a divorce began to take notice and examine in a critical way the values that had been implicit in his actions: "Mostly it was asking myself the question of why I am behaving in such and such a way. Why am I doing this at work? Why was I doing this at home? The answer was that I was operating as though a certain value was of the utmost importance to me. Perhaps it was success. Perhaps it was fear of failure, but I was extremely success orientated." (Bellah, 1985, p. 6)

Prior to the divorce, he had assumed success as a value that underpinned his striving. He did not question it but acted in terms of it. He was success driven without thinking about the "meaning" of being success driven. As he says: "I didn't even question [success]. I just went out and did it." It was in the face of the divorce that he came to see the way in which the value of success functioned in his life and how it had affected his relationship. In the face of the divorce, instead of simply acting in terms of the success ethic, he came to question the orientation around success. And when he saw the way in which the ethic of success governed his life, he did not like it and began to open up new ways of relating. As he put it: "Bullshit. That aint the way it is supposed to be. ... To be able to receive affection and give it..." became important values in terms of which he structured his activities. (Bellah, 1985, pp. 6 and 76)

Divorce was able to disrupt Brian's conventions or flow of experience because it shocked him out of his complacency. He began to see things about himself that he had always taken for granted. The shock of divorce disrupted his everyday way of doing things in such a way that he came to notice and question the conventions that structured his life.

So too do midlife crises in which lives are disrupted in such a way that the question of the meaning of life becomes a central preoccupation – even for those who had historically experienced the question of life as a meaningless question. This, for example, was the experience of Leo Tolstoy, famous author, businessman, farmer and philanthropist. Seeing himself as a practical man, he just wanted to get on with the demands of everyday living which for him included writing, looking after his farms and businesses. Yet, as is typical in a middle life crisis, he was overwhelmed by feelings of emptiness which deprived his everyday activities of meaning. As he says: "Amidst my thoughts of farming, which interested me very much during that time, there would suddenly pass through my head a question like this: 'Alright, you are going to have six hundred desyatinas of land in the Government of Samara, and three hundred horses – and then?' And I completely lost my senses and did not know what to think further". (Hanflig, 1988, p. 10)

These feelings of meaningless were stronger than his commitment to his pragmatism. No matter how much he tried to "get on with the job," the questions of the meaning of existence kept disturbing his thinking. They disturbed him to such an extent that they became his central preoccupation. Instead of finding meaning in his work, he began to find that the question of the search for meaning became his central concern: ""I searched painfully and for a long time, and I searched not from idle curiosity, not in a limp manner, but painfully and stubbornly, day and night – I searched as a perishing man searches for his salvation..." (Hanflig, 1988, p. 13)

He became the very "unpragmatic" reflective person that he never dreamed of becoming. He became enchanted by the practice of questioning. Questioning became his passion. This may sound strange to common sense but it has long been known in philosophy that intense questioning is a passion that grips and enthrals us. As Bertrand Russell, the famous English philosopher says: "There is nothing to compare to passion for giving one [philosophical] insight. Most of my best work has been done in the inspiration of remorse, but any passion will do if it is strong. Philosophy is a reluctant mistress – one can only reach her heart with [reflective thought] in the hands of passion."

The comparison of philosophy to a mistress suggests the role of passion in philosophy. It also suggests that we are seduced into the experience of philosophy. Indeed, as another philosopher, Colin McGinness remarks, he found himself being "seized" by the power of thought. It was in the joy of being seized by thought that encouraged him to make a career out of philosophy. However, it is important to note that remorse is not the only – nor is it the customary passion of philosophy. In the history of philosophy both wonder and dread are articulated as the moods in which we come to philosophy. For in the state of wonder, the conventions of a society have lost their grip on us and we come to see things through fresh eyes. As Terry Eagelton notes: "Children make the best theorists, since they have not yet been educated into accepting our routine social practices as "**natural**," and so insist on posing to those practices the most embarrassingly general and fundamental questions, regarding them with a wondering estrangement which we adults have long forgotten. Since they do not grasp our social practices as inevitable, they do not see why we might not do things differently." (Eagleton, 1990)

Eagelton's quotation also allows us to re-iterate the model of the philosophical process: wonder is a moment in which the experience of conventions are disrupted in such a way that we come to experience things through fresh eyes. In adulthood such experiences of wonder are rare. It is usually in anxiety that the conventions of society cease to hold their grip on us and so open up the possibility of philosophical thinking. This kind of experience is described by bell hooks who says: "I came to theory because I was hurting – the pain within me was so intense that I could not go on living. I came to theory desperate, wanting to comprehend – to grasp what was happening around and within me." (hooks, 1994, p. 59)

The hurt was a specific kind of hurt. It was the experience of being estranged from the very family(iar) environment in which she lived: "I did not feel truly connected to these strange people, to these familial folks who could not only fail to grasp my worldview but who just simply did not want to hear it. As a child, I didn't know where I had come from. ... I was desperately trying to discover the place of my belonging. I was desperately trying to find my way home." (1994, p. 60) It was in the context of her estrangement that the norms and standards of the way of life into which she had been thrown became explicit themes of questioning. She began to challenge male authority, "rebelling against the very patriarchal norm" of her parental house.

Even though it was through the pain of a disruption of her everyday experiences that she came to theorise or philosophise, bell hooks commitment to philosophising was unshakable. The same can be said in the case of Tolstoy. His pain became a passion which gave his life a central purpose and focus that he could not set aside but in fact affected all his other activities.

It is important to highlight the way in which Tolstoy's pain became his passion. A term to describe the way in which a pain becomes the underpinning force of a passion is the notion of a "philosophical fever." A philosophical fever occurs where we are seized by questions which even if we do not want to ask, cannot help but asking and pursuing. It is almost as if our minds are overcome by the passion of questioning. In the grips of his philosophical fever, Tolstoy began to question science, rationality and all conventional wisdom. What was interesting is that he began to question these things not in an abstract way, not as an armchair philosopher in an ivory tower but in an intensely emotional way. His very life depended on being able to understand the limits of science and rationality. He was involved in these questions in a way that a sports person or spectator may be engaged in a sports event.

It is important to emphasise that Tolstoy's philosophical fever arose not because he was an intellectual but because he was seized by a question, was able to turn a pain into a passion. In subsequent chapters we will also see how leaders in the grips of leadership crises ask the question "what does it mean to be a leader?" not as a theoretical question but in an intensely personal or existential way, in a way that their very life depends on how they grapple with and answer the question.

For Tolstoy the search for meaning was always an examination of the conventions through which he had made sense of experience. He came to examine the rational, scientific and religious conventions which had framed his experience. He came to see that his rationality was not so rational, that his scientific ways of thinking were very limited and that a reinterpretation of the conventions of religion were needed. His crisis of meaning opened up the possibility of a different way of life for him. It led him into new possibilities, possibilities that he had not expected for himself. He found himself entering what to him was the strange territory of religion and finding it incongruous to find himself there.

IV

What we see in the case of the death of a loved one, the experience of divorce and in the example of Tolstoy is the structure of the process of philosophising. This is a process in which the disruption of existing con-ventions, opens up the mood of philosophy in a practical way, allows us to reflect on our conventions that we have habitually taken for granted, and makes it possible to either affirm our existing conventions or entertain new assumptions and ways of doing things. The destruction of existing conven-tions opens up new horizons of possibilities.

This conception of the philosophical process has its roots in Socrates, recognised by many as the father of philosophy and thus of rational think-ing in the Western world. In accounting for his own process of thinking, Socrates often says that he came to philosophy not because he was more intelligent than anyone else but because he was confused – or as he puts it, perplexed. As he puts it: "I perplex others, not because I am clear, but because I am utterly perplexed myself." (Plato, 1976, p. 128)

Because he was confused and perplexed and because he accepted rather than denied his confusion, he was able to ask questions of those things that most people took for granted. He did not believe that he was necessar-ily wiser than other people – only that he knew that he did not know and because he knew that he did not know he could see that which most people took for granted, that is, the conventions of the society. Because he was perplexed in this way he was constantly thinking about the conven-tions of the society and challenging others to think about them. Socrates' aim in this regard was to help people examine their lives because he believed that the dangers of an unexamined life created a pervasive sense of meaninglessness. Or as he put it, the unexamined life is not worth living. Without examining the conventions that guide us, we lose sense of why we do whatever it is that we do. We tend to live in an automatic way without having an embedded sense of the purpose for achieving the particular ends that we are striving to achieve or of the relation between the means and ends, that is, whether our means are in fact achieving the ends.

Indeed, from a Socratic perspective, without examining our lives we have no way of knowing whether the things that we do are not self-destructive. For example, it might well be the case that in striving after pleasure or hap-piness we might be enslaving ourselves to our desires. Socrates gives the example of a drug addict who in constantly satisfying the desire does not release himself from the desire but needs more and more fixes to satisfy himself. He thus becomes a greater slave to his desire. So too the need to satisfy our consumer desires does not necessarily bring satisfaction but an increasing enslavement to the desire. For Socrates, only by examining our lives are we able to understand the place of happiness and pleasure in our lives.

What we see in Socrates is that it was the way in which he engaged with his perplexity that allowed him to question the conventions of the society in which he lived. The role of disruption in opening up the mood of philosophy is not limited to Socrates. To be sure, the form of disruption differs from philosopher to philosopher. For example, in the case of Montaigne, it was melancholia rather than a sense of being perplexed that led him into the mood and activity of philosophy. In the philosophy of Descartes, it was doubt that led him into reflecting on the conventions which had shaped society and to begin to develop new conventions for philosophical activity. An interesting case is that of the philosopher John Stuart Mill. His disruption in the form of overwhelming anxiety and uncertainty led him from one style of doing philosophy to another. It led him away from a reliance on rationality to an appreciation of the role of emotion in thinking. And in modern times existential philosophers have emphasised the role of disruption in philosophy. In Nietzsche, for example, nihilism comes to be the basis for examining and challenging the conventions of society. In the writing of Sartre, the confrontation with the nature of existence is made possible by the experience of nausea and in the philosophy of Martin Heidegger it is through the experience of anxiety that the question of Being is raised as a meaningful question.

V

But it is not only formal philosophers who have emerged through a process of disruption. The philosophical process can be seen at work in non-philosophers. A good example is the following experience of Nelson Mandela: "We put down briefly in Khartoum, where we changed to an Ethiopian Airways flight to Addis. Here I experienced a rather strange sensation. As I was boarding the plane I saw that the pilot was black. I had never seen a black pilot before, and the instant I did I had to quell my panic. How could a black man fly a plane? But a moment later I caught myself: I had fallen into the apartheid mind-set, thinking Africans were inferior and that flying was a white man's job. I sat back in my seat, and chided myself for such thoughts." (Mandela, 1995, p. 281)

In the context of the philosophical process what Mandela is saying is that he had a certain experience or perception of black men being unable to fly. However, instead of simply taking this belief for granted, he stood back from it and questioned it. The basis upon which he came to stand back and question it was a moment of disruption, or, as he puts it, an experience of a "strange sensation." This strange sensation was the disruptive mood which allowed him to question and then to free himself from his assumption. Without the experience of the "strange sensation" it is doubtful that he would have questioned the convention of black men being unable to fly. The strange sensation was the mood that alerted him to his own dis-ease. Perhaps what is crucial in the case of Mandela is that he was highly attuned to the disruption, to the moment of a "strange sensation." And because he was attuned to it, he was able to ask the question that was begging him to ask.

It is important to emphasise the relationship between questioning and the mood of a "strange sensation." Mandela questioned his assumption because he experienced a "sensation" that invited him to question the assumption. Without this sensation of strangeness he would not have even noticed that there was a question to be asked. Rather he would not have even known that he had a prejudice. For by definition we do not simply notice our blind spots: we cannot even make an effort to see what we are blind to, for we do not know that we are blind to it. We need to be alerted to our blind spots. One way of being alerted is through the experience of strange sensations.

Our habits and conventions are very much like blind spots. They affect and influence us without us even being aware of them having an influence on us. Hubert Dreyfus provides an example of how in the experience of people of other cultures our own taken for granted conventions becomes explicit to us. When we meet people who do things differently from us, not only do we notice their way of doing things but we notice our own way of doing things as well. He gives the example of physical proximity in friendship and says that in different cultures people stand at different distances from each other. In some cultures people stand close to each other while in other cultures people stand at a greater distance from each other. For the most part we do not notice our patterns of social proximity. We only begin to notice our own patterns of physical proximity when we meet people of other cultures. Thus he says: "We do not even know we have such know-how until we go to another culture and find, for example, that in North Africa strangers seem to be oppressively close while in Scandinavia friends seem to stand too far away. This makes us uneasy, and we cannot help backing away or moving closer." (Dreyfus, 1993, p. 294)

It is in the face of the stranger that our own conventions for social proximity become explicit through the ways in which we are "paralysed" or feel uneasy in situation. As Dreyfus is suggesting, without the unease experienced in the face of the stranger we would not even have a need to become aware of our conventions for social distancing. It would not be an issue at all. It is in the experience of the disruption of our conventions that our conventions become explicit. And this disruption is experienced as a mood state.

The same point can be made in terms of culture in a more general sense. For the most part we operate in terms of the conventions of our culture without thinking about them. Indeed we need to. If we spent our time thinking about the conventions we would not act. In order to act, we need to take the conventions of our culture for granted. It is when there is a disruption to the conventions that they become explicit. An example of this is to be found in the experience of Gregg, an Australian manager working in Taiwan. He tells of an experience in which a female employee came to tell him that she was pregnant. This was in the 1980's. Based on 1980's

Australian management assumptions, he expected her to resign, and so quite naturally asked her to help him find a replacement for her position. She was shocked at his expectation. In Taiwan, pregnancy does not mean the need to resign. She burst into tears. Gregg articulates his response: "I suddenly realised – how dumb is that – the norm in Taiwan is that you have the baby and you're home within three hours and back within a few weeks. The baby goes to the grandparent and life goes on...I had absolutely no concept. I didn't even think about it." (Sinclair, 2002, p. 7)

So embedded was the connection between pregnancy and resignation in Gregg that he did not even know that he needed to think about it. It was the response of the female employee which made him feel dumb and, on the basis of feeling dumb, he began to take notice of and question his cultural assumptions. In this process of questioning new ways of seeing things and engaging with other people opened up to him: "The incident enabled me to dig down ... and we all became comfortable about talking about differences that are not obvious ..." (Sinclair, 2002, p. 7)

The process that Gregg underwent is no different from the process that Socrates underwent. For Socrates it is in the moment of our own ignorance that the possibility of questioning assumptions arises. As Gregg says: "I found I had to start making these really stupid errors to start understanding differences." In a similar way Socrates often said that it was only when he realised that he did not know anything that he could begin the process of questioning the assumptions of a set of conventions. Those who did not realise their ignorance did not realise the need to question their conventions.

We need, however, to be able to accept our own ignorance – or in the words of Gregg, our own experience of being dumb in order to question the assumptions. For it is not the disruption itself that allows us to question the assumptions. It is our attitude towards our own experience of dumbness or ignorance that is crucial. It could well be that we seek to hide, out of shame or embarrassment our experience of our own ignorance or dumbness. This is a theme that we will turn to again and again in the book: how to turn disruptions into occasions for questioning and opening up new possibilities rather than into occasions for defensive closing up.

All of this may seem irrelevant to management which has historically been conceived as an exclusively rational activity. Is this, however, the case?

3
Managers and Leaders: The Unnamed Philosophers

The philosophical experience described in the last chapter is vital in the world of management. Without calling it by name, managers do engage in the activity of the philosophical process. They have experiences which can be described as philosophical. These experiences are central to their practices as managers. These are experiences in which managers are concerned with gaining and giving perspective on situations in which they find themselves. This chapter will show how central philosophical experiences are to the practices of leaders.

The last chapter allows us to identify certain features of the philosophical experience. It is not an everyday experience. It is an experience which becomes significant when we cannot take our habits of practice or our everyday way of doing things for granted. It disrupts or jolts us out of our everyday complacency. In the experience of disruption we come to see the assumptions which have guided our way of experiencing the world but have for the most part been implicit. We are challenged to question our taken for granted ways of seeing things. The philosophical experience opens up the possibility of seeing and experiencing the world in new ways.

How does this description of the philosophical experience relate to management? It is a common observation that we live in a world of change. The more things change, the less we can rely on our habitual ways of doing things. The more things change, the more we need to be able to think "outside of our boxes." The original image for thinking outside of our boxes is in fact derived from the philosopher Plato who says that philosophy begins in the moment of learning to think outside of "our caves." For Plato philosophy begins where we leave the "comfort zone" of the familiar.

Historically, as John Kotter tells us, managers have not been trained for thinking outside of our caves or boxes. Rather managers have been trained to think under conditions of stability: "too many people have been trained for and raised in a more stable world, a world that for the most part no longer exists. Too many people have been trained only to manage the

18

current system or to make incremental shifts. They have not been shown how to provide the leadership necessary to make bigger leaps." (1999)

Yet as, amongst others Jack Welch tells us, we are living in times where we cannot take the conventions of management for granted. In the context of arguing for the limitations of scientific rationalist approaches to management Welch has said: "We have to undo a 100-year old concept [of scientific management] and convince managers that their role is not to control people and stay 'on top' of things, but rather to guide, energize, and excite." (Lowe, 1998, 15)

Welch is suggesting that we cannot take the traditional assumptions of management for granted. These assumptions informed by the scientific tradition in management are no longer appropriate to the everyday reality in which managers, leaders and people in organisations find themselves. As Kotter suggests in the above quotation, managers and leaders find themselves in a position of questioning their habitual assumptions and conventions. In the terms of this book, they find themselves in the middle of a philosophical experience in which the old assumptions are no longer valid but no new ones have yet taken root – if anything there are a number of fads, none of which have been affirmed as an enduring foundation for management.

Whether they like it or not, those managers and leaders who experience the collapse of the old assumptions are in a process of questioning the assumptions of management. It may not be something they asked for. It may not be something that they wish to do. Indeed they may simply wish to carry on with their job. But once having experienced the unviability of the traditional way of doing things, they are thrown into the uncertainty of questioning. They are thrown into a philosophical mode. In this space we need to embrace and engage in the art of questioning. This is why Lou Gerstner of IBM can say: "Once you think you're at the point that it's time to write it down, build the manual, and document the formula, you're no longer exploring, questioning, the status quo. We are constantly challenging what we do – building a culture of restless self-renewal." (Neff, 1999)

It is in the space between the collapse of the old management assumptions and the not yet of the new that we engage in such questioning. The idea of building a culture of restless renewal through constantly questioning the status quo lies at the heart of philosophy. Socrates, the archetypal philosopher of the Western world is famous for his process of constantly questioning everything, not for the sake of being clever but because it always opened up new possibilities and ways of seeing things – just as in the case of Gerstner. Socrates is identified as a philosopher because of his process of constantly questioning the status quo. Furthermore, he questioned in the experience of being between the collapse of Athens traditional image of itself as a military empire and the not yet of a new way of being for Athens, one in which Athens would become a seat of learning that would influence Western thought for at least the next two thousand years.

Although it may come as a surprise to many, philosophy is not an abstract but a very concrete activity. Its concreteness is to be found in the mood of uncertainty that is experienced when caught between the collapse of the old and the not yet of the new way of doing things. The insecurity and uncertainty experienced in the between is the mood that makes philosophy concrete and relevant. Philosophy is based on the ability to tolerate and embrace the uncertainty. Instead of withdrawing or becoming paralysed in the face of the uncertainty, philosophy is the willingness to turn that uncertainty into a dynamic energy of questioning and finding direction. This is why Jack Welch says that his success as a manager and leader lay in the development of a philosophy. Writing about his experience as CEO of GE he says that what came out of his experience is "no gospel or management handbook.... There is a philosophy that came out of my journey." (Welch, 2001, p. xv) It was through a philosophy that Jack Welch found direction in the face of the uncertainty of being caught between the collapse of the old conventions and the not yet of the new management conventions.

It is important not to miss the significance of Welch's point. It is not good enough for a manager to have only a manual or a technique. They must also have a philosophy. For it is a philosophy which gives the flexibility of thought and vision to be able to respond in proactive ways to the often unanticipated changes in conventions or ways of doing things. Because we cannot always predict what changes will take place, we cannot always have "the plan" to deal with change. Rather we need to have the flexibility of mind that is able to adjust to changes. This flexibility comes from engaging in the activity of philosophising.

Agreeing with Welch also means shifting the emphasis of management education away from an exclusive reliance on technique and formula to one that takes the discipline of philosophy seriously. Welch did develop practices in GE for thinking in the face of disruption. His educational style is based on the ability to turn what he calls experiences of the "Vortex" into learning opportunities. "Vortex" experiences are those experiences in which a manager, because of a crisis in their practice begins to doubt their management style. They lose confidence in their way of doing things. These experiences are from Welch's perspective, opportunities to reflect on and challenge our habitual ways of doing things so as to develop new possibilities for our management practices.

Questioning the status quo was essential to Welch's management style. He often stood outside of the conventional or habitual ways of doing things, challenged people to see things in new ways and was more than able to withstand the pressure to conform coming from the herd. Referring to the first time in which he spoke to the Wall Street market analysts he says that he did not give them the message that they wanted to hear. In fact he challenged the very terms in which they analysed the financial data of organisations. Instead of giving them hard facts, he gave them a lecture on the value of soft skills in organisations. They could not make sense of anything that he was saying. He experienced them as looking at him as though he was crazy. Yet rather than turning away from his position, it made him more determined to challenge their assumptions by clarifying his position: "Over a 20 minute speech, I gave [Wall Street analysts] little of what they wanted and quickly launched into a qualitative discussion around the vision for the company. ... At the end this crowd thought they were getting more hot air than substance. One of our staffers overheard one analyst moan, "We don't know what the hell he's talking about.' I left the hotel ballroom knowing there had to be a better way to tell our story. Wall Street had listened, and Wall Street had yawned." (Welch, 2001, p. 105)

The idea of being able to withstand the pressure of standing outside of the status quo has always been at the centre of philosophy. Socrates saw his role in ancient Greece as that of a gadfly to the state, constantly interrogating it in order that it would be aware of the assumptions guiding its way of doing things. No matter how much he was pressurised into adopting a conformist position, he had the will and resolve to stand outside of the herd – to the extent of being put to death for his commitment.

A corporate CEO who learnt the art of philosophical questioning in a painful disruption is Andrew Grove of Intel. For Grove the process of "philosophical questioning" became part of his leadership "toolkit" or approach. When confronted with situations that threw his habitual assumptions into question, he was not overwhelmed or flumexed but turned these experiences into opportunities for seeing things in a new way. An example that he gives concerns the significance of Netscape: "I remember being shocked by the Netscape IPO. I was quite familiar with Netscape, and for that company to be valued at $4 billion or $5 billion after it came out – that stunned me. But that shock had a positive impact, because it made me think, Hey, you better rethink your prejudices, because people are seeing something here that you are not seeing. I mean, I thought the browser was an interesting piece of software, but not a life-altering or strategy-altering technology." (Heilemann, 2001)

Here we see how Grove is able to turn an experience of being shocked into an opportunity for questioning his assumptions and how through questioning his assumptions he is able to see something in a new way, that is, he begins to see the browser in a completely new way as a strategy-altering technology. This is philosophy. Philosophy is that activity of questioning assumptions. Existential philosophy is that activity of questioning assumptions in the face of a shocking, disturbing or jarring experience, in those moments that we experience that reality is not the way we thought it was. Crucial to this practice of philosophising is the willingness to turn moments of shock into educational opportunities, that is opportunities for questioning and seeing things in new ways. It is not inevitable that shock will lead to an educational attunement. It can and often does lead to a sense of defensiveness where we remain blinded by our inability to move beyond our habitual ways of seeing things.

The danger of not being sensitive to assumptions that need to be questioned is highlighted by Ram Charan and Jerry Useem in their analysis of failure at Cisco. Cisco, they claimed had developed a system that would enable them to predict the future. However, the future did not turn out as the system predicted. In coming to grips with why the future did not turn out as predicted, Cisco had to contend with the fact that it had not questioned key assumptions in developing its predicative system. As Charan and Useem maintain: "Cisco's managers, it turned out, never bothered to model what would happen if a key assumption–growth–disappeared from the equation. After all, the company had recorded more than 40 straight quarters of growth; why wouldn't the future bring more of the same?" (Charan and Useem)

Questioning of assumptions is not an elementary process. Assumptions do not just show themselves or present themselves for questioning. We need to be able to notice that we are making assumptions which, as we see in the case of Cisco, we are not always aware of. We are usually blind to the assumptions that we make. And because we are blind to them, we cannot just decide to question our assumptions. For by definition that which we are blind to is outside of the scope of what we can see. We cannot simply decide to see what we are blind to. We would not know where to begin. We need to be able to make that which we are blind to explicit for ourselves. How do we go about doing this? How would Cisco be able to sensitise itself to the fact that it is making assumptions? And how would it work with the assumptions once it had made them explicit? These are philosophical questions, questions that we need to develop a philosophical discipline to handle. Grove makes this point: "All businesses operate by some set of unstated rules and sometimes these rules change. ... Yet there is no flashing sign that heralds these rule changes. They creep on you ... without warning." (Grove, 1997, p. 20)

For Socrates the examination of experience requires what has come to be known as "Socratic humility." This is the humility of being attentive to what is taken for granted in our own opinions and perspectives – indeed it is the humility to treat our perspectives as opinions, as views open to doubt and not as knowledge that is beyond doubt. This allows us to not only examine the perspectives of others but to examine our own perspectives. The basis of Socratic humility was Socratic ignorance or Socrates' view that he knew nothing. Because he believed he knew nothing, he took less and less for granted and so was able to see and examine more and more. He never took his own or others way of framing experience for granted and so was able to examine the assumptions hidden in experience. The resolute acceptance of not knowing then is the basis of Socratic reflection.

We see this attitude in a number of leaders today. It is to be found in the humility of Nelson Mandela who is known to interrogate himself through his secretaries. As Andrea Brink writes: "The human side to Mandela's stumblings is revealed by an account one of his private secretaries gave of his recent visit to Scandinavia: it seems that every night, after retiring, he would summon his three secretaries to his bedroom where he would ask them, "Now tell me what I have done wrong today, because I don't want to make the same mistakes tomorrow."

It is precisely with being aware of the fact that we are not always aware of our assumptions that philosophy is concerned. The job of Socratic philosophy is to be sensitive to that which we are not aware of in our way of experiencing the world. By becoming aware of that which we are not aware of we are able to catch sight of the beliefs, worldviews, paradigms and assumptions in which we do make sense of experience. To understand ourselves as leaders and managers we need to understand the frameworks in which we carry out our day to day activities in the workplace. We need to understand our perspectives as managers and leaders not by reading and learning already established theories of leadership and management but by developing a way of examining our own experiences. Our experiences allow us to understand our own assumptions. Only by understanding them can we come to terms with blind spots in ourselves and create the opportunity for excellence in our professional practices.

In the corporate context another example of this form of questioning is to be found in the management style of Ricardo Semler. Having been brought up in a scientific management view of organisations, he experienced a personal crisis which led him to question the assumptions which regulated his company, Semco's activities. Like Welch he saw that the routines of organisational management practice had deprived Semco of its vitality and he sought to return the vitality to Semco by questioning all of the old practices and developing new practices: "One of my first acts at Semco was to throw out all the rules. All companies have procedural bibles. Some look like Encyclopedia Britannica. Who needs all those rules? They discourage flexibility and comfort the complacent. At Semco we stay away from formulas and try to keep our minds open ... All that new employees at Semco are given is a 20-page booklet we call 'The Survival Manual'. It has lots of cartoons but few words. The basic message: Use your common sense." (Semler, 1993, p. 3)

The challenge of questioning the status quo is a deeply emotional one. It is one that often means standing alone, outside the herd of common sense opinion, having the resilience to trust one's perspective even when others do not. It is a position shared with Anita Roddick who is always bumping up against and challenging conventions: "...years ago (1988) when I lectured at Harvard about social responsibility, it was like I had just walked off the bloody moon. Now I have hundreds of letters saying 'Tell us more about socially responsible companies'". (1996)

The process of constantly questioning the status quo prevents leaders from functioning on automatic and thus of taking the conventions of the organisation for granted. It allows them to be constantly attuned to the changing identity and culture of the organisation. It is in this context that Mort Meyerson sees the primary function of leadership as enabling an organisation to know itself. Like Semler he was reared in a culture of scientific management in which the leaders role was to make all the decisions, have all the knowledge and all the plans. However, like Semler, a crisis in his leadership experience propelled him into another, more "Socratic" view of leadership in which his role shifted to being a mirror in which the organisation could see itself: "The way to be a leader today is different. I no longer call the shots. I'm not the decision maker. So what is my job as a leader? The essence of leadership today is to make sure that the organization knows itself." (Meyerson, 1996)

Socratic humility is the commitment to experiencing our mistakes not as the source of shame but as an opportunity to learn more about our knowledge and skills practices. Andy Grove, CEO of Intel, demonstrates a Socratic humility in his resolute acceptance of, but refusal to take his vision for granted. Quoting Mark Twain he says "Put all of your eggs in one basket and watch that basket." It is the commitment to watching the basket that exemplifies the spirit of Socratic humility. Develop a vision. Be guided by it. But do not get lost in it. Watch your vision. Do not let it blind you.

Traditionally management education and training is not geared towards the development of Socratic humility. It is grounded in rational and objective knowledge practices in which to learn is to interrogate the "data" rather than the intuitive terms in which we experience our workplace. Management education and training is not geared towards a sensitive and attuned reading of experience. Yet both managers and leaders in practice are constantly bombarded by the need to interpret and make sense of experience. And to do this they rely on beliefs and assumptions inherited through their patterns of socialisation and which are often not explicit but deeply buried in them. As already pointed out, these patterns are also the source of prejudices that prevent constructive coping with the demands of leadership and management.

It is precisely with these hidden and taken for granted dimensions of belief that Socratic philosophy is concerned. The job of Socratic philosophy is to enable us to make sense of our experience by examining the beliefs, worldviews, paradigms and assumptions in which we do make sense of experience. To understand ourselves as leaders and managers we need to understand the frameworks in which we carry out our day to day activities in the workplace. We need to understand our perspectives as managers and leaders not by reading and learning already established theories of leadership and management but by developing a way of examining our own experiences. Our experiences allow us to understand our own assumptions. Only by understanding them can we come to terms with blind spots in ourselves and create the opportunity for excellence in our professional practices.

To enable an organisation to know itself and to examine our managerial assumptions is to take a step back from simply being absorbed in the day to day routine of the workplace. It is to engage in the activity of what Jan Carlzon, CEO of SAS calls helicopter thinking: "I am the president of a large airline, but I can neither fly a plane nor repair one – and no one at SAS expects me to. ... What is required is strategic thinking or 'helicopter thinking' – a talent for rising above the details to see the lay of the land. Thus, the new leader is a listener, a communicator, and educator – an emotionally expressive and inspiring person who can create the right atmosphere rather than make all the decisions himself." (Carlzon, 1987, p. 32)

There is a need to understand what Carlzon calls the "talent" for helicopter thinking. It is not something that just occurs but requires a self discipline. Helicopter thinking needs to be distinguished from scientific forms of thinking. In scientific forms of thinking, we tend to be concerned with observing and analysing objects out there in the world. It is not ourselves – our assumptions – but concrete objects that we are concerned with. In helicopter thinking we are concerned with the assumptions which underpin our own ways of doing things. We are taking perspective on what we ourselves are going through. We are lifting ourselves out of our preoccupation and reflecting on them. It is "self" rather than "other" reflection. As Douglas Mullen has said: "One feature peculiar to humans is the ability to detach ourselves from our lives and see ourselves as if we were 'just one of them.' For some of us the thought of this comes more often and stays longer. This type of person is described as 'reflective,' 'self-conscious,' 'neurotic,' 'ironic,' 'pensive,' 'deep', etc." (Douglas-Mullen, 1981, p. 11)

Helicopter thinking is the ability for reflective thinking rather than analytical thinking. It is not an analysis of data but a constant attunement to the conventions, culture or assumptions which are guiding the way in which we form judgments in the situation that we are in. This ability to distance ourselves from what we are involved in is not easy. It is much easier to reflect on other peoples' behaviour in terms of our own assumptions. We never see our own assumptions directly and immediately. We need to learn the discipline of stepping back. The practice of stepping back is quite clearly visible in the management practice of Koichi Nishimura of Solectron: "When you are leading a company, you have to figure out, conceptually, what you are trying to do. ... You continually have to ask: Are the assumptions I made still good? My job is to continually reassess the assumptions or the foundation that the company is built on." (Nishimura, 2000, p. 184).

Nishimura needs to assess his assumptions because he realises that he always leads a company in terms of a set of assumptions and that if he does not have an explicit understanding of his assumptions, he does not have an understanding of the framework in terms of which he is leading. He also goes on to say that as circumstances change, there is a need to reassess assumptions. For they change with changing circumstances: "Then the Internet came along. And I had to go back and ask myself, 'Are my assumptions still true?'" (Nishimura, 2000, p. 184) It is thus not the case that our assumptions are static. They change with changing circumstances and we need to be continually attuned to such change.

Thus it can be clearly seen that there is a philosophical process at work in some of the leading leaders of the corporate world today. However, the idea of "philosophy" that is central to management needs to be distinguished from the more scholarly views of philosophy. Managers and leaders are not philosophers in the traditional sense of the word. They are not concerned with the analysis of philosophical theories. Rather they are what I shall call philosophers-in-action. There is much in the way that leaders describe their activities and themselves that suggest that they are philosophers-in-action. Firstly, many of them tend to have "philosophies" or visions of how things are. Some, such as Welch, are explicit about calling them "philosophies." Even Al Dunlap speaks about his philosophy of leadership. These visions tend to be formed through their own experience and reflect their own voice rather than being mimicked or copied from another source. They tend to be independently minded, thinking for themselves. Very often their thinking emerges out of a questioning of conventional ways of doing things and opens up new or alternative ways of doing things. Unlike scholarly or academic philosophers, however, their philosophies are not expressed in the form of a treatise or written document but are expressed in the creation and sustaining of a way of life, a way of doing things. Furthermore their philosophies are not developed in the context of pure logic or abstracted rational thinking but as a response to the complexity of experience. As philosophers in action their thinking and their philosophies emerge out of the way in which they are involved in the world. It is through the risks that they have taken, the decisions that they have made, the battles that they have fought that their philosophy has developed. Often they do not even know their philosophies in advance of their activities in the world. Through their engagement in the world, their sense of the world develops.

Thus while philosophy as an academic and scholarly discipline has been more and more disconnected from the realities of everyday life, leaders in everyday life have been advocating and at least implicitly calling for the development of a philosophy that is responsive to the changes in everyday life. This is not only the case in a management context. It permeates all areas of everyday life. Our conventions of politics, sexuality, meaning, gender and race relations are changing and we need to be able to think outside of the caves or boxes which have historically informed our ways of acting. We are, and have for sometime, been in the process of rethinking the assumptions underlying male-female relationships, the nuclear family and sexual habits. As our old conventions break down, we are challenged to think about what we had previously taken for granted in new ways.

However, I do not wish to simply reject academic philosophy and idealise corporate leaders as philosophers. Today, the ancient art of philosophical questioning is being reinvented. Over the last 20 years the field of philosophical counselling has emerged throughout both the Eastern and Western world. Beginning in Germany in the early 80's it grew out of disillusionment with academic philosophy and the narrow focus on self in psychology. Against academic philosophy, it asserted that an understanding of our beliefs and assumptions cannot be gained in the ivory tower setting of a university classroom but only by challenging ourselves in our experiential settings. And against psychotherapy, it said that knowing thyself does not mean knowing only about one's psyche or personality but about the paradigms and worldviews that shapes our professional practices.

The perspectives of philosophical counselling have a role to play in bringing out in a clear and systematic way the role of philosophy in leadership. And corporate leaders are often philosophically naive. Indeed, as many commentators on the autobiographies of these leaders point out, the leaders' views are more often than not imbued with a spirit of egoism and "follow a structure that's as predictable as any James Bond film." In many cases these leaders are opinionated rather than thoughtful in a disciplined and wise way. Many of them have risen and then fallen quickly. As Bruce Feirestein has put it: "What do A. Dunlap, Bill Gates and Michael Eisner have in common? Nothing, save for their reversal in reputation after the books came out." (Feinstein, 2001, p. 128)

Yet there is no doubt that we need to be able to learn from the experience of these leaders. They are people who have led not only many of the world's most successful organisations but they have pioneered new forms of organisational being. Furthermore, they also create and reflect the consciousness of the times in which we live. They speak on behalf of an "age" or a "time" not only in corporate but in human history. Whether we like it or not, as world corporate leaders they define the cultural temper of the organisational world. Bruce Pasternack, senior vice president with Booz Allen Hamilton, has said that these leaders provide a vision of the world in which organisations make sense today. "Perhaps the most important leadership lesson to be learned from Welch (and from the likes of Roger Enrico of PepsiCo and Andy Grove of Intel) is that true leaders are not just teachers – they also have teachable points of view. That is, they help the leaders they mentor to see the world more clearly, to articulate vision and values simply and to motivate their own followers to confront reality and make tough decisions."(Pasternack, 2001, p. 77)

So, while leaders have philosophies, these philosophies are not always developed in a critical or methodological way. Some leaders are acutely aware of the process of reflecting on experience. The difficulty of developing a philosophy based on personal experiences is hinted at by Lou Gerstner who, in developing a philosophy based on his experience, says: "I've never been certain that I can abstract from my experiences a handful of lessons that others can apply to their own situation." (2002, p. 217)

As Jan Blits tells us, Socratic and existential philosophy is precisely that process which enables us to abstract from our experience. Good philosophy from Blits's perspective is not philosophy that begins and ends with abstractions but one which critically analyses experience in order to uncover the assumptions and principles which are informing the way in which that person experiences the world. Blits maintains that philosophical education as exemplified by Socrates begins not with abstractions but with peoples' concrete opinions. Socratic "inquiry begins not from theoretical constructions or scientific theories or definitions , but from commonly held opinions about things ... Our opinions about things are our only access to ... truth." (Blits, 1989, p. 293) By examining our experiences, we discover the assumptions that underpin our experiences.

On this account philosophy is a process of abstracting from personal experience principles or ideas that others can use to make sense of their own situations. In turn, we can use the views of others to examine our own experiences and the assumptions underlying them. Philosophy gives us a sense of the path that we are on when we are abstracting from experience and looking at the principles or assumptions underlying experience.

One of the methods that is currently used in philosophy to examine and abstract principles and assumptions from experience is known as "existential hermeneutic phenomenology." It is a method that has been elaborated by the philosopher Martin Heidegger. This method will be used in the book to enable us to abstract from the experience of leaders' assumptions and principles that can be used as a basis upon which to think about or own practices of leadership and management in new ways. This method will act as a mirror in which to see our own practices and experiences. The method of Heidegger allows us to examine in a disciplined way the views of leaders.

Examining the role of philosophical experiences in management through the lens of a discipline within philosophy will allow us to provide a systematic, and critical way of viewing the philosophies of leaders. It will provide a framework to look at the relationship between insight and blindness in their points of view, the relationship between the resolute will to question their experience and a smugness or self-righteousness in their self evaluation. Because their points of view as articulated in their biographies are neither sciences nor psychologies but philosophies, it would seem that the discipline of philosophy has a role to play in helping to bring out what is worthwhile in many of these autobiographies.

But there is a deeper level in which the leaders used in this chapter exemplify the philosophical process. All of them call into question the conventions of management that dominated the twentieth century. Jack Welch, Andrew Grove, Mort Meyerson and Lou Gerstner are recognised as leaders who stand at the cross roads between the old conceptions and habits of leadership and the emergence of new ways of leaders. All underwent a transition from the conventional, rational and scientific management style of leadership to one that acknowledges the vital role of "business feel" or what I shall call "existential attunement" in their leadership philosophies. With the exception of Welch, none of them expected to go through this kind of transition and had their breath taken away by having discovered the need to see organisational life and their role as leaders in organisations in new ways. All were excited at the discovery of a new way of seeing and being in organisations. All went through a period of the unknown in moving from the old habits to the new way of doing things. All grappled with the unknown in a resolute, "proactive" way which allowed for a creative emergence out of the unknown.

Furthermore, this transition was not just a transition in their technical skills as managers but was a transition that was experienced in the depth of their being. It was a personal or existential transformation, one that stopped them in their tracks, often gave rise to experiences of self-doubt, anxiety and depression. It was their feelings experienced in disruption that allowed them to think about their perspectives on leadership and organisations in new ways. As we shall see, this will have significant implications for management education.

None of them rejected the role of rationality in management but began to see rationality in a broader context. They learnt to situate rationality in the context of business feel or what I am calling existential attunement.

These leaders are models of how to embrace and emerge out of the twighlight zone between the collapse of old ways of doing things and the not-yet of new ways of organisational life. As such they are not only organisational leaders but teachers who can challenge us to develop our own skills of working effectively in the disruption of existing conventions. Indeed through an examination of their philosophical processes, a number of skills for working effectively in the experience of disruption of conventions will be outlined. Just to mention a few of them, these skills are the skills that enable leaders to turn the experience of doubt, uncertainty and confusion that occur at the moment of disruption into new possibilities both for themselves and for their organisations as a whole. Instead of being paralysed by doubt or defensive in the face of being threatened, these are all leaders who were able to create when the conventions that had given them and their organisations security were in doubt. The questions that I shall seek to answer is: what is it in them that allowed them to create in the face of uncertainty? And how can we learn from them?

Again the philosophy of Martin Heidegger will be used to open up these questions. But before delving into the philosophy of Heidegger, we need to see just why it is that philosophy rather than science is the tool that is needed to unpack the "philosophical experiences" of leaders. We also need to elaborate on the turn towards philosophy that is implicit in the perspective of scholars who theorise about management.

4
Unmasking Management Theoreticians

The turn to philosophical experience is reflected not only in the experiences of corporate leaders but in the theoretical literature on management and in the practices of educating managers. In both cases there is a turn towards a new "paradigm" for management. This view is widespread in management and is summarised in the work of Chris Davis who maintains that "Managers, CEO's and academics alike are thirsty for a new paradigm through which to interpret our rapidly evolving global culture. As the focus turns from tangibles, like widgets to intangibles, like quality and customer satisfaction, we are facing the foundation of a new culture; hyperconnectivity, new economic standards and measures, wholly new mediums for communicating, new interpretations of power, value and waste."

To turn to a new paradigm is to turn to a new way of making sense of experience. It is a concern with the assumptions in terms of which we read experience. The idea that scientists, academics, and CEOs are becoming philosophical when concerned with their paradigms emerges out of the philosophy of Thomas Kuhn. Thomas Kuhn in the development of his philosophy of science maintains that scientists are, for the most part, not concerned with being philosophical. Rather, they are concerned with getting on with their everyday activities as scientists. This involves issues such as puzzle solving, conducting experiments, observing and analysing reality. In these activities there is neither need nor room for philosophy. Philosophy, in this context would be a distraction which takes them away from their everyday activities. However, when scientists cannot take their habitual ways of doing things for granted, they tend to become philosophical. They tend to question the paradigms and assumptions underpinning them: "Scientists have not generally needed or wanted to be philosophers. Indeed, normal science usually holds creative philosophy at arms length, and probably for good reason. To the extent that normal research work can be conducted by using the paradigm as a model, rules and assumptions need not be made explicit. It is, I think, particularly in periods of crisis that scientists have turned to philosophical analysis as a device to unlock the riddles of their field." (Kuhn, 1970, p. 88)

Here it can be seen that the activity of questioning paradigms is not a scientific but a philosophical activity. This is because it involves the experience of questioning our fundamental assumptions – not objective reality but the terms in which we make sense of objective reality. It is also important to highlight that the experience of questioning our assumptions is not a psychological but a philosophical activity. An interesting way in which this point has recently been developed in popular management literature is to be found in Stephen Covey's *The Seven Habits of Effective People*. He distinguishes between what he calls the "Personality Ethic" and the "Character Ethic." He maintains that views of success in the twentieth century have for the most part been dominated by the Personality Ethic, the view that success is a "function of personality, of public image, of attitudes and behaviours, skills and techniques...." (Covey, 1989, p. 19)

In contrast to this, the Character Ethic asserts that success is underpinned by "basic principles of effective living." In turn these principles are rooted in a "paradigm." A paradigm, from his perspective, is a kind of mental map that allows us to see the world in a certain way. Just as we need a physical map of a new city to guide us, so we are always guided by mental maps. We cannot function without such maps. Furthermore, for the most part we tend to take our mental maps for granted. We use them without explicitly thinking about them. It is in times of change or in the moment of a paradigm switch that we become attuned to our mental maps or paradigms of doing things. It is in change that we think about our ways of seeing things. And thus it is in times of change that we tend to become philosophical.

Historically, management has been dominated by the personality ethic, by the view that our personality rather than our paradigm shapes the way we behave. While not denying that personality has an effect on our behaviour, there is more and more literature suggesting that we need to move towards an understanding of management paradigms. An example of such a move can be found in the work of Boleman and Deal's book *Reframing Organisations*. In their work, Boleman and Deal see the central task of managers as being able to reframe organisational behaviour by drawing on what they see as the four frames of organisational behaviour. They call the frames the structural, human resource, political and cultural frame. Each frame provides a manager with a different lens through which to understand organisations. Each lens is underpinned by a certain set of assumptions. In order to switch frames managers need to be familiar with the set of assumptions contained in the frames. These four frames define the paradigms in terms of which organisational experience is intelligible. Reframing is a philosophical activity because we are not examining the world as such but the terms or assumptions in which we make sense of the world. We are not concerned with this or that aspect of our experience but of the frameworks in which we make sense of experience. We are taking a step back from the everyday world and examining the terms in which we make sense of this world.

Here we can remind ourselves of the distinction between scientific analysis and philosophical reflection: whereas science – especially in its positivist forms – is concerned with the analysis of objects and data out there in the world, philosophy is concerned with reflecting on the assumptions that guide a scientist's observations and analysis of data in the world. It is concerned with reflecting on the frames in terms of which scientists view the world. To be concerned with the frames of scientists, managers, leaders, organisations is to enter into a philosophical activity.

From Boleman and Deal's perspective, reflection on the assumptions underlying our experience needs to be distinguished from rational deliberation about data: "Prevailing mythology depicts managers as rational men and women who plan, organise, co-ordinate and control ... What a reassuring picture of clarity and order this is! Unfortunately it is wrong. ... Led to believe that they should be rational and on top of it all, managers become confused and bewildered." (Boleman and Deal, 2003, p. 304). It is by accepting the experience of being confused and bewildered that managers can begin to develop a reflective relationship to their experience. Boleman and Deal say that it is when "someone's actions make no sense" that the opportunity for reflecting on our own and their frame of reference becomes possible. For when things make no sense, we are stopped in our track, feel perplexed and are then ready to reflect on underlying frames or assumptions. They call these moments of being unable to make sense, moments of "cluelessness". Such cluelessness, they maintain, is rife in management but more often than not avoided rather than accounted for.

Boleman and Deal see the need for managers to come to terms with cluelessness. In fact they see cluelessness as the basis of a paradigm shift. For when we lose sense of one way of doing things that we become open to a new way of doing things. Unfortunately Boleman and Deal do not develop an understanding of the process of moving from one frame of reference to another. They do say that it requires a process of "helicopter thinking or "thinking from the balcony" but they do not say what goes into this process of thinking. They say that it involves a combination of "analysis, intuition and artistry" but they do not describe the art-like process of such thinking. The central focus of this book is to describe the process of moving between frames or paradigms. This will be done by focusing on the experiences of corporate leaders at the coalface of change.

The turn away from rationality towards reflection on assumptions that guide experience is echoed in the literature on the relationship between leadership and management. Managers are seen to be rational, committed to order, control and planning whereas leaders are seen to be committed to developing visions in the face of the unknown and leading their followers through the unknown. Managers maintain the system whereas leaders are able to read situations and provide a vision in terms of which organisations can make sense of their experience. To make sense of experience is to provide a narrative framework in which to reflect on experience. The philosophical framework in which we situate the rationality of management is very different from that in which we situate the visionary qualities of leadership. The very language that is used to describe leadership and management is indicative of different frames or paradigms. When we think of the rationality of management we think of the disengaged scientist whose world is dominated by data and systems, whereas the visionary leader is situated in an artistic framework, a framework which is populated by people and experiences. Leaders are attuned to and can articulate the mood of an organisation.

The exclusive reliance on rationality in management is more and more being called into question by writers in the field of emotional intelligence. They claim that we need to understand the role of emotions in management. This point is reinforced by many managers. Andrew Grove of Intel makes the point that: "So, when your business gets into serious difficulties, in spite of the best attempts of business schools and management training courses to make you a rational analyser of data, objective analysis will take second seat to personal and emotional reactions almost every time." (Grove, 1997, p. 123)

Here we see that in times of disruption what is crucial for managers is not only their ability to deal with their moods but to understand that their moods are the basis of insight into their management practices. Indeed Grove sees worry, a non-rational mood, as being instrumental to his success as a manager: "I attribute Intel's ability to sustain success to being constantly on the alert for threats, either technological or competitive in nature. The word paranoia is meant to suggest that attitude, an attitude that constantly looks over the horizon for threats to your success." (Grove, 1997)

It should be mentioned that seeing the role of mood in his management style was somewhat of a revelation for Grove. For he had been habituated into a rationalist management style where management was seen as a disengaged, non-emotional and objective process. It was through his experience of crisis at Intel that he came to see that management was much more than a rational process and that it depended in many ways on emotions. In other words, it was a crisis in his conventional management style that allowed him to experience the limits of that management style and open himself up to new management styles. Somewhat sheepishly he had to discover that: "Businesspeople are not just managers; they are also human. They have emotions, and a lot of their emotions are tied up in the identity and well-being of their business." (Grove, 1997, p. 123)

Logically Grove's point is circular and thus trivial. For it is by definition true that managers are human beings. But in the context of a history of management education which has seen management as primarily an objective process and thus one in which the humanness of the manager plays no role, to realise that the human dimension is vital to his being as a manager is somewhat of a realisation. It changed his whole way of thinking about management – a change that we will consider in the chapter on Grove.

In a similar context, George Soros has seen his sensitive attunement to his moods as the basis for his success as a Fund Manager. He believes that his ability to worry in a reflective way was the basis for his success as a fund manager: "By and large I found managing a hedge fund extremely painful. I could never acknowledge my success, because that might stop me from worrying, but I had no trouble recognising my mistakes. Only when others pointed it out to me did I realize that there might be something unusual in my attitude towards my mistakes. It made so much sense to me that discovering an error in my thinking or in my position should be a source of joy rather than regret that I thought that it ought to make sense to others as well. But that is not the case. When I looked around, I found that most people go to great lengths to deny or cover up their mistakes." (Soros, 1998, p. 24)

Again the Socratic temperament can be seen: an appreciation of ignorance through the experience of a mood and the willingness not to cover up the ignorance but to turn it into an opportunity for refining his attunement to his practice. What is also interesting in the quotation from Soros is that so habituated was he to working through the emotion of worry that he was not explicitly aware of it. Only when he experienced that others did not work in this way, did he become aware of his own way of working, that is, in the experience of the disruption of his ways, he became attuned to his own way of working.

The role of mood is also central to the management style of Jack Welch who says that: "More often than not, business is smell, feel, and touch as much as or more than numbers. If we wait for the perfect answer, the world will pass us by." (Welch, 2001) Jack Welch, as we know, is anything but a "soft man" – he can and has been pretty "hard" at times, being for a long time called "Neutron Jack." How does someone who can be hard, identify the soft skills of "feeling" as underlying his leadership know how? At the very least this contradiction forces us to reconsider what we mean by the soft skills. It calls us to take seriously and understand the role of business "feel" in detail.

Emotion also has a central place in the philosophy of Lou Gerstner of IBM who came to believe that cultural transformation is "counterintuitive, centred around social cues and emotion rather than reason." (Gestner, 2002, p. 188) This was something of a revelation for Gerstner. Having been socialised into a view of management as an exclusively rational process, he came to see that emotions were central to cultural transformation

Historically managers have not been educated to appreciate the reflective dimensions that are opened up by emotions. They have not seen how emotions experienced in moments of disruption disclose the assumptions of a culture or set of conventions and open up the possibility for new way of doing things. Rather managers, trained in rationality, have been too busily focused on the data, the numbers, the quantities, that which can be analysed and verified. Yet, as we have seen some of the major icons in management have been suggesting that this is not enough, that managers need to develop the ability to reflect in the face of disruptions to their ways of doing things. They need, in the terms of this book, an appreciation of the process of philosophising.

The turn towards reflection is present in Peter Drucker's notion of the theory of the business. He claims that every business has an implicit theory of how the world guides it and forms the basis of the way in which it makes judgements. A manager's theory of the business allows him to see the world in the particular way that he does. It also precludes them from seeing things in other ways. This is dangerous. For in times of change, we need to be open to changing our theory of the business. For only by changing our theory of the business can we see things in new ways and thus are ready to respond and take charge of the way in which circumstances are moving. But because our theory of the business is for the most part implicit, we tend to take it for granted. We do not see how it is operating on us and shaping the way in which we see things. Only by an act of reflection do we come to see and question our theory of the business. Central to questioning our theory of the business is the act of what Drucker calls "abandoning" it: "Every three years, an organisation should challenge every product, every service, every policy, every distribution channel with the question, If we were not in it already, would we be going into it now?" (Drucker, 1998, p. 29)

Drucker believes that abandoning the theory of the business poses a constructive threat to the existence of the business because it forces the organisation to question its theory of the business: "By questioning accepted policies and routines, the organisation ... forces itself to test assumptions." (Drucker, 1998, p. 30) Testing assumptions allows an organisation's management to ensure that they are in tune with the rapidly changing nature of circumstances in which business is conducted. The danger with Drucker's approach to abandonment is that it seems to routinise the experience, that is, managers are expected to be able to do it every three or four years. It is as though Drucker believes that we can deliberately and rationally choose to abandon our perspective on things – as though we can deliberately disrupt ourselves. As we shall see during the course of this book, it is with a sense of shock that we find ourselves abandoned. It is with a shock that we find our habitual ways are not working for us. Questioning emerges out of this shock. We cannot intentionally abandon our perspective.

The process of abandoning a theory of the business presupposes a process of defamiliarisation or of estranging ourselves from the theory. Sometimes when we are so familiar with something, we do not see it anymore. When we experience it as strange, we start to see it and think about it again. For example, often when we are familiar with a place, we do not see its landmarks. Yet once we have spent time abroad or in another place, we lose our sense of familiarity with home in such a way that when we come back we see all those things about it that we were accustomed to taking for granted. So it is with our theory of the business. We are so familiar with it that it is only by abandoning it that we begin to see it again.

Interestingly, the process of making explicit through abandoning our theory also underpins re-engineering perspectives on organisations. Re-engineering is a process of questioning the traditional assumptions underpinning the process of work as a basis of opening up new ways of working. It believes that in order to work in new ways we need to be able to think about work in new ways, that is we need to change our assumptions about work. Specifically it is concerned with moving away from Taylorist and scientific management assumptions of work, assumptions in terms of which work is subject to ever increasing fragmentation. It believes in seeing work in process terms.

The process of moving from the old habitual ways of work and the assumptions underpinning them to a new way of working involves a process of abandoning our old assumptions. Reengineering, at its best, involves what Keith Grint calls a process of "defamiliarization – making the world strange as a device for scrutinising it. … This shifts the debate from prescription (and there is enough of this around at the moment) to estranged (re)description. There is no specified end product … but merely an examination of the present in the light of potential, and plural, alternatives." (Grint, 1995)

Both the process of questioning our assumptions and the process of defamiliarisation are central elements of the philosophical experience. They are also central to an understanding of capitalism. The process of questioning the habits and conventions of conducting commerce is not something sudden or new in capitalism. It, in fact, characterises the essence of capitalism. This is a perspective that underlies the work of the economist Joseph Schumpeter, who believed that capitalism is a system which is constantly transforming itself and in doing so transforms the habits of doing business. Writing in the 1930's he called this process creative destruction. Schumpeter maintained that the most dangerous and challenging form of competition comes not from existing products but from new products. This is because new products challenge the very existence of existing producers. As he puts it: "But in capitalist reality as distinguished from its textbook picture, it is not [price] competition which counts but the competition from the new commodity, the new technology, the new source of supply, the new type of organization …competition which … strikes not at the margins of the profits and the outputs of the existing firms but at their foundations and their very lives." (Schumpeter, 1955, p. 26)

It should be noted how Schumpeter is introducing an existential language into our understanding of capitalism, for the idea that competition strikes at the "lives" and "foundations" of producers is to enter the language of existential attunement. It creates an appreciation for the angst or anxiety that goes into business. Business here is not only the rational pursuit of pre-given ends but, when competition from the new commodity strikes, can be an experience in which producers' lives are experienced as being at stake.

Describing the process of creative destruction, Schumpeter says that it is a process of "of industrial mutation—if I may use that biological term—that incessantly revolutionizes the economic structure from within, incessantly destroying the old one, incessantly creating a new one." (Schumpeter, 1955) Schumpeter uses the imagery of a "gale" to describe the experience. The destruction of our old conventions opens up the possibility of seeing things in new ways but it also creates a fundamental uncertainty, one that penetrates to the very core of the producers, the organisation and the people in the organisation. This is because there is no way of knowing how and that we will come out of the "gale" of the valley of destruction.

Schumpeter's thinking on creative destruction is being used by a number of consultants and theorists today to describe the kinds of changes that are taking place in the free market. An illuminating way of using the work of Schumpeter is to be found in Foster and Kaplan's work on the relationship between corporations and the market place. They maintain that whereas organisations focus on efficient operations, the vitality of the market is underpinned by the generation of the new – the new product, the new way of doing things. The new disturbs operational requirements. Existing habits of operating cannot always account for the new product or way of doing things but is very often disturbed and made obsolete by the new. Whereas markets function in terms of the logic of creative destruction, organisations have historically operated in terms of a commitment to stability. They maintain that markets operate in terms of the dynamics of discontinuity in which the future cannot be expected to repeat the past but is always generating the new. Corporations, in contrast, have functioned in terms of the logic of continuity, building up their efficiencies on the assumption that the future will repeat the past. They argue that the need for control deaden organisations to the need for change – yet change is built into the very dynamism of the market place which unfolds by continually generating the new, that which cannot be reduced to the need for control. Organisations need to be able to adjust their mindsets to the dynamic nature of the market place.

One CEO who Foster and Kaplan point to as having done this is Jack Welch who, they claim was responsive to the patterns of creative destruction in the market place and was able to create in what they call the "apocalyptic" nature of the market place – again we see the existential theme popping up in the market place: "valley's of death," "gales" and now "apocalypses." This language does not belong to the rational language that has dominated understandings of the market place in the twentieth century yet writers like Foster and Kaplan see it as essential to our understanding of the logic of the market place. Foster and Kaplan maintain that the "distinction between the way in which corporations and markets function is not an artifact of our times or an outgrowth of the 'dot.com' generation. It has been smoldering for decades, like a fire in the wall, ready to erupt at any moment." (Foster and Kaplan, 2001, p. 10)

The general response, on the part of organisations to the dynamic nature of the market place has been, from the perspective of Foster and Kaplan, fear which has led to what they call "cultural lock-in." As the name suggests, it is the "inability to change the corporate culture even in the face of clear market threats" (Foster and Kaplan, 2001, p. 16) or to put it in the terms of this book, cultural lock-in, is the desire to cling to conventions or habits of doing things in the face of the disruptions of the market place. Cultural lock-in is a phenomenon that occurs when in the face of threats to an organisation's existence, the mindset in the organisation attempts to become more effective in the existing habits of doing things rather than embracing the need to change its way of doing things.

Foster and Kaplan, are concerned about the affects of cultural lock-in on an organisation's attunement to the changing environment in which they are situated: "As the corporation ages, the bureaucracy begins to settle in. Passions cool and are replaced by 'rational decision making,' often simply the codification of what has worked in the past." Foster and Kaplan maintain that we need processes of divergent thinking to cope with the experience of creative destruction: "Many divergent thinkers possess apparently opposing traits: They may be passionate and objective, or proud and humble; they may be both extroverted and introverted; in negotiations they may be flexible and unyielding, attentive and wondering." (Foster and Kaplan 2001, p. 19)

The challenge of this form of change for management is clearly described by Clayton Christenson who is sympathetic to managers who have spent a life time training in one way of doing things only to find that they can, in the face of "disruptive technologies" no longer trust their existing habits for doing things – the very habits that have brought them success in the past cannot be relied upon. Although he does not call it such, the experience of being unable to rely on the conventions and habits in terms of which we, as managers, have been socialised is an "existential crisis." In contrast to a technical problem, this is a crisis in which, because we cannot rely on our existing ways of doing things but have no new ways of doing things, we do not know where to turn – yet we have to continue. Such crises test our "spirit," passion or will. In contrast to this a technical crisis is one in which we need to refine or improve our existing techniques for doing things.

Existential crises can be described, as Albert Camus has done, in terms of the Greek myth of Sisyphus. Sisyphus was caught stealing fire from the gods. As punishment for stealing fire from the gods, Sisyphus was condemned to rolling a large and heavy rock up a mountain. Everytime he got near the top of the mountain, the rock rolled down and he had to begin the journey again. The relationship between management and the dynamic nature of the market place can be described in similar terms: as managers are refining and perfecting their habitual practices for doing things, as they are reaching the top of the mountain, so they are stripped naked and challenged to develop new habits and practices for doing things. The market place is too busy regenerating itself for there to be such a thing as a peak that is reached. Yet just as Sisyphus is becoming stronger through repeatedly climbing the mountain, so managers are becoming more flexible through the challenge of rethinking their ways of doing things. Although this is not the intention and we are not immediately aware of becoming stronger, it occurs as a result of the way in which we respond to change – for in the fire of the "apocalypse" of change we are coping with change rather than reflecting on how we are being transformed by the way in which we cope with change.

At the pulsating heart of the free market runs the logic of creative destruction. This is a logic in terms of which the new emerges out of the way in which we lose our bearings in the face of the disruption of the old. In order to become more attuned to the dynamic nature of capitalism, management needs to embrace "disruptive change" as an essential part of its self-understanding. This is why writers in management such as Christenson argue that managers need to prepare themselves for disruptive technologies, technologies which disrupt the habitual practices of managers and organisations and which demand of managers not improved permanence in a particular habit or practice of management but the ability to transform their conventions for doing things. The kind of thinking that goes into improving our existing habits and being able to transform our habits is very different. Improving our habits is an incremental process. It is a matter of applying ourselves to the task. Transforming our way of doing things requires the ability and willingness to step out of the security of our way of doing things, move into the unknown and allow the new to emerge in our practice. In improving our practice, we know exactly what we are doing. In transforming our practice, we do not know in advance of the journey, the road that we are taking. We need to be able to absorb the uncertainty of the unknown.

Fernando Flores and his colleagues have taken this form of questioning a step further. They maintain that the meaning of business has shifted. Business used to be seen as a rational activity aimed at the satisfaction of desires. They maintain business is now a form of disclosing new worlds. They point to entrepreneurs as examples to justify their position. Entrepreneurs do not just satisfy desires in new ways. They invent new worlds. Henry Ford's automobile, as Farson has said "has created not just cities but also their opposite, suburbs ... The existence of automobiles has changed our courtship patterns, our sexual practices, and especially our environment. It has also changed our identities." (Farson, 1997, p. 47)

Entrepreneurs like Ray Krock invent new worlds. Steve Jobs and Bill Gates have invented new worlds for us. Computers are not just means to an end. They enable us to experience the world in different ways and to become different people in the process. In order to adapt to the world that they are creating for us, we need to develop new mindsets. As Gates himself has said: "Entire professions and industries will fade. But new ones will flourish. ... We can't predict what the new job categories will be. ... It isn't easy to prepare for the next century because it's almost impossible to guess the secondary effects of even the changes we foresee, much less of those we can't." (Gates, 1996)

Businesses are not only means to an end. They shape our landscape. They give us our identities. Our consciousness is formed in and through them. They are ways of being and dwelling on the earth. Flores sees the process of inventing new worlds as an enduring feature of the industrial era. Ever since the development of the railroads, we have been on a roller coaster ride of innovation in business. This means that our frames for making sense of reality have also been undergoing continual shifts. We have been experiencing the world in different ways.

When seen from the "helicopter" perspective of Flores, business is about disclosing new worlds. Because entrepreneurs disclose new worlds, they become the model of business practice. As Flores puts it: "We are like Henry Ford's in the past. Henry Ford was not designing cars. Henry Ford was designing cities. He was designing economies. He was designing a form of life. We are doing that on a much bigger scale." (Flores, 1997)

To be at the cutting edge of business today is to be in the business of inventing and disclosing new worlds. To understand and attune ourselves to this process we need to question the rationalist assumptions of business in which business was simply seen as a means to an end. We need to move towards an understanding of the logic of disclosure which is an artistic logic. It involves the passion, commitment, wrestling with the unknown, and development of new visions that are characteristic of the artist.

But business is in question in other ways today. In the wake of corporate scandals such as Enron, the question of ethics is becoming more central in business. Yet the language of business is traditionally one in which concepts of ethics have no value. For the language of ethics is a qualitative language while that of business is quantitative. As George Soros has said that ethical concerns "are inferior to market values. They cannot be quantified – they cannot even be identified. They cannot be reduced to a common denominator, money." (Soros, 1998, p. 198)

The challenge concerns how to introduce the language of ethics which is a qualitative language into an area that has historically been dominated by an attunement to the quantitative. Basic assumptions need to be challenged and thought through in order for ethics and the market to enter a dialogue with each other. The same concern exists in relation to sustainability. Proponents of the sustainability thesis maintain that the very way in which business treats the environment is threatening the ecological integrity of the environment. In order to go beyond this, business has to rethink its assumptions about the environment. The environment is not only raw material waiting to be transformed into products. It is more than this; a dwelling place, a place in which we feel at home. Unless we want to see home as a kind of machine in which we live and which takes care of our living needs, we need to think through our "productionist" concept of the environment.

In terms of the issue of globalisation, modern corporate life has made possible the emergence of a boundaryless world but it has as yet offered no way in which people can live together in this boundaryless world. It has collapsed the boundaries but has put up no framework for interaction across culture. This is crucial for dealing with the "reign of terror" that is engulfing the world at present. It requires a thinking through of the assumptions about how people of different cultures, religions, nationalities and genders interact with each other. Business has thrown up the challenge but has yet provided no framework in which to work with it.

Philosophical experiences run like a rich vein of gold through the theory and practice of management. The experience of questioning the conventions and assumptions of management in the face of disruptive experiences permeates management literature. The ability to open up new possibilities and reframe the terms in which managers make sense of experience is a skill or attunement that is more urgently needed. The language that management theorists used to describe the practices of management in the context of change are suggestive of a philosophical approach. This includes the idea of "reframing" of "paradigms," "reflecting" through "estrangement" or "abandoning" of the "familiar."

The turn towards philosophy in management is in the process of being identified. There are a number of philosophers who practise in the tradition of management. Peter Koestenbaum is an example. Peter Drucker is someone who comes out of a philosophical tradition. The work of Robert Spillane in Australia is instrumental in this field. Fernando Flores has opened up the field of continental philosophy in management. In fact he quite explicitly says that "business thinking and practice would be understood as a branch of the humanities. When they are not, all of us lose." This is a position that is echoed by Brown who, as already mentioned employs people within the humanities to examine the social architecture of Xerox.

However, this does not mean that there is not much caution and resistance to speaking about philosophy in the context of management. James Champy, one of the leading writers on re-engineering believed that philosophy was a missing element in management literature. He wanted to write a book about it. However, he shied away from any reference to the term philosophy because, as Michael Finley has said, his "publisher painted a picture of the marketplace success of books with the word philosophy in the title." (Finley, 1995)

What's wrong with the word philosophy? How should we weigh up the relationship between the demands of the market place and doing justice to a lack within management? If the market rejects the word philosophy and management could benefit from an understanding of it, should it still be rejected? What has philosophy done to deserve a cold shoulder in the name of the marketplace? Or is it the case that t he marketplace is now ready for philosophy? These are questions that will be addressed in the next chapter.

5
From a Science to a Philosophy of Management

Whereas science operates under conditions of stability, philosophy operates under conditions of disruption. The way we think under conditions of stability is very different from the way we think under conditions of disruption. Under conditions of stability we look for regularities. Under conditions of instability, it is precisely the pattern of regularities that is disrupted. Science is based on a process of looking for regularities. Philosophy is an activity that occurs when we cannot expect regularities.

Traditionally management has been underpinned by a scientific methodology. Indeed, read almost any introductory text book on organisational behaviour and it will espouse the "scientific anchor" of organisational analysis. Yet, as I have suggested in the last chapter, there is a rich vein of philosophical experience that runs through management. Philosophical experiences are all those experiences in which we come to think about our own way of thinking about things – not about others ways of doing things but our own ways of doing things. Instead of simply doing things on automatic, in a philosophical experience we learn to stand back and detach ourselves from our activities so that we can examine the conventions and habits that inform our way of doing things. Science is also concerned with detachment but it is detachment from the other, from the object of observation, rather than from ourselves.

Science in management has always been based on a separation between the manager and the managed – the worker. The manager was seen as the thinker and the worker as the doer. The manager thought about the work of the worker while the worker simply did the work. He did not need to think about the work at all – that is, he did not need to reflect on his practice. This was done for him. All that he had to do was suspend his own mind, obey and perform. The absurdity of this position is now fundamentally in question today: effective and efficient workers need to own their own work processes. They need not simply do but think about their way of doing things. Thinking about their way of doing things contributes to the quality of their work.

The scientific process is always based upon a separation between the thinker (manager) and the subject matter of thought (worker). They are independent of each other – two different beings. Philosophical reflection occurs where we think not about other's ways of doing things but our own ways of doing things. The thinker is concerned with the assumptions, conventions, habits and culture of which he is a central part. In existential philosophical thought we take a step back from our own habits or conventions and critically examine them. We think about what we ourselves are involved in. We come to terms with the way in which our own assumptions, expectations, values and frames inform the way in which we work.

From the existential philosophical perspective, workers are not just blank slates on which management can imprint its instructions. Everything is filtered through the way of thinking of the worker. Philosophy is the activity of coming to understand our own way of filtering experience and the effect and influence it has on the way we work. This is the case for both workers and managers. Science – especially in its positivist forms – is not concerned with our own assumptions but with the nature of "objective reality." It is philosophy that is concerned with the nature of assumptions.

An interesting problem for scientific management is, if scientific management is the discipline through which managers understand the workers, who is it that understands and makes sense of the activity of managers? The danger is that we will have an infinite chain in which there are managers who understand the work of managers. Then there are managers who understand the work of managers who understand the managers ... ad infinitum! Or is it the case that managers simply understand themselves? From the philosophical perspective neither manager nor worker simply understand themselves. All need to be able to put their way of doing things into perspective. This is the task of philosophy. It is a task of understanding turning back on itself. It is a concept of philosophy which can be traced to the writings of Plato, almost 2500 years ago where he maintained that philosophy is what he called the activity of gaining a panoramic perspective by taking a step back from the immediacy of our everyday preoccupation and examine our conventions for doing things.

Insofar as management is concerned with gaining perspective on the practices of its own organisation, a department or even a team, it is a philosophical rather than scientific activity. Thus the concern is with what is known in management literature as "reframing," gaining a "helicopter" perspective, a perspective from the "balcony," or a "paradigm switch" – all of these are philosophical rather than scientific activities. They all presuppose a process of taking a step back detachment from our immediate concerns and developing an appreciation of the way in which our assumptions, beliefs, conventions or mindsets shape the way in which we get on with the job. They are all activities of taking a step back to gain a panoramic perspective of the whole in which we are situated.

However, that managers are and need to be philosophical in their attunement does not mean that philosophy has been made an explicit part of
management training and theorising. Indeed, there is very little writing on
management as a philosophical activity and on philosophy as a disciplinary framework in which to make sense of the activities as managers.
One of the reasons for this is that science has had such a stranglehold on
management. Anything that is not scientific is not seen as a legitimate
part of management. It is this stranglehold that needs to be broken for it
will liberate management to embrace non-scientific but nevertheless very
disciplined processes of thinking.

The scientific framework that has historically underpinned management
does not offer a framework for managing in the experience of disruption.
The scientific framework presupposes stability and routine. It is based on
the need to predict the future based on past patterns. It is concerned with
analysing already existing data or information. It is geared towards objects
or entities that already exist. It is concerned with what is out there in the
world rather than with gaining a "helicopter" perspective on our own
habits or conventions for doing things. It is concerned with what is quantitative rather than qualitative; with being objective rather than establishing
meaning.

As the philosopher David Hume has maintained, science is based on the
expectation that the future will repeat the past, that what we observed in
the past will hold for the future, that if we observed the sun rising yesterday, we can expect it to do so again tomorrow; that if we saw a match
"causing" a fire yesterday, we can expect it to do so again tomorrow. This
expectation underlies the scientists belief in prediction. We could not make
predictions about the future if we did not believe that the future repeats the
past. It is also the basis of the scientists' belief in induction. Induction is
the belief that we can make theoretical generalisations based on repeated
observations of the same events, that we can make assertive claims about
the relationship between the events of yesterday and tomorrow.

However, one of the dimensions of change in which we now find ourselves is that we can no longer expect the future to be like the past.
Exemplifying the spirit of this statement, Phil Knight of Nike has said: "My
biggest fear is that a few years from now I'll hold a grandkid on my knee
and she'll look up at me and ask, 'Grandpa, what did you do when you
were young?' I'll say, 'I started Nike.' And she'll say, 'Nike? What's that?'"
(Rubin, 1998)

What is implied in this quotation is that the future is so unlike the past that
Nike and Knite will be obsolete in ten years time. We are not at a moment in
business history in which we can expect the future to repeat the past. This is a
theme that permeates much management literature today. In fact Jack Welch
has warned us about getting away from a model of thinking that is based on
prediction: "Predicting what changes will take place is less important than

having a company that does not get paralysed by change. Who would have predicted SARS; 9/11, the Asian crisis ... A company needs to assume rapid change and be more prepared for intense global competition. But people like the status quo. It's comfortable doing what you know." (interview with Welch in *The Australian Wednesday*, June 18, 2003)

What is implied in Welch's quotation? Welch is telling us that the psychological contract between the future and the past has been broken. We can no longer expect the psychological certainty that comes with a stable relation between the past and the future. For above all else, the rhythm of the future repeating the past has given the human being a sense of security, a sense of familiarity, and a sense of trust in the way things work. Now Welch is telling us that we can no longer take for granted our expectation of the way in which things work. We can no longer take for granted that the way in which business is done today will hold for tomorrow.

The breakdown in the psychological contract, in which we can no longer expect the future to be like the past, means that we are living in the unknown. In the unknown we cannot plan for tomorrow based on expectations of today. There is no way of knowing, based on today, what tomorrow will look like. We cannot expect repetition in the unknown. Philosophy, as Ernst Gellner tells us, is that kind of thinking that occurs where we cannot assume a stable relation between the future and the past. For Gellner, philosophy is orientation in the chaos and confusion of the absence of regularity. It occurs where the habits of the past have been disrupted but no new conventions have been formed. There is no stable pattern underlying the past, present and future. Under conditions of disruption "Modern history is rather like a football cup in which only the first round was played as soccer, the second round is played as rugby, the third as ice-hockey, etc." (Gellner, 1964, p. 64)

The point is that there is no way of knowing what the next round will be played as because "by the time the next round has come, the identity of the game ... has changed." (Gellner, 1964, p. 65) So too in a business world dominated by disruption and the lack of stability – we do not know in advance what the next round will be played as. And we need to take into account that we do not know what the next round will be played as. To take into account that we do not know what the next round will be played as is, in terms of the quotation from Welch, to build the flexibility so as not to get paralysed by change. For in the unknown it is easy to get overwhelmed by a sense of uncertainty. This is not an experience of only neurotic people. Many CEOs including Jack Welch, Andrew Grove, Mort Meyerson and Ricardo Semler have experienced intense moments of uncertainty when caught in the breakdown of the psychological contract. Grove calls this an experience of the "valley of death" in which we have left the familiarity of one way of doing business but do not yet have a new way of doing business.

The Clue Train Manifesto describes the experience of having no routine or habit on which to rely as an existential moment: "It's characterized by uncertainty, the dissolving of the normal ways of settling uncertainties, the evaporation of the memory of what certainty was once like. In times like this, we all have an impulse to find something stable and cling to it, but then we'd miss the moment entirely." (Locke et al, 2000)

Existential uncertainty needs to be distinguished from what I shall call objective uncertainty. Objective uncertainty occurs where I am uncertain about something outside of myself. For example, I may be playing a poker game and am uncertain about my hand of cards in relation to my opponent's hand of cards. Existential uncertainty occurs where I lose all sense of the basis of what to expect from the future. In existential uncertainty I have no compass to guide me. I cannot trust my familiar or habitual ways of doing things and I do not have another, ready-made convention to guide me.

The experience of existential uncertainty permeates business under times of creative destruction where old business practices are being destroyed but the new is only beginning to emerge. We see this quite clearly in the dot.com era of doing business; where new businesses were formed overnight while other companies "built to last" crashed unexpectedly. Because there was no basis for stability, there were both intense "high's and low's" all of which came suddenly and without warning. The playing fields and our minds were constantly being switched from one to another way of doing things. In existential uncertainty we can no longer trust the habitual rules and practices for doing business. Our fundamentals are in question.

Where the future does not repeat the past we cannot trust systems, formula, methods – or even habits. We need to be able to develop our capacity for judgment. For it is in terms of the faculty of judgment that we respond to that which cannot be predicted or anticipated in advance. As Andy Grove says: "Even those who believe in a scientific approach to management will have to rely on instinct and personal judgment … When you're caught up in the turbulence of a [disruption], the sad fact is that instinct and judgment are all you've got to guide you through." (Grove, 1997 p. 35)

In times of disruption we cannot rely on a method or system for they are developed for times of stability. It is ourselves – our own capacity for judgment that emerges in times of disruption. Yet, it is important to note that we can no longer simply and uncritically trust our own judgment. For judgment is, in large part, based on experience and experience is based on the expectation that the future will repeat the past. To learn experientially means to learn based on past experience. To learn based on past experience means to assume that the future will be like the past. We can no longer simply trust past experience.

It is thus not judgment alone that is needed but what I shall call the capacity for existential detachment. This is the capacity to detach oneself from one's habitual, familiar or customary ways of doing things and open up the possibility of seeing things in new ways. An example of this process is given in the autobiography of Terry Anderson, held captive with three other hostages in Beirut in the early 1980's. He describes an incident in which he did not get on well with one of the other hostages. He assumed that the other hostages also did not get on well with this particular hostage, named David. But, for the most part, he did not have an opportunity to discuss the attitudes to David of the other hostages. One day, however, when David left the room to go to the bathroom, he took the opportunity to discuss David with the other hostages. He thought that they would share his view. Instead they began to reprimand him for the way he treated David: "You challenge David all of the time. You seem to want to top him, to prove something to him. It's like a pair of bulls trying to dominate the same herd." (Anderson, 1995, p. 10)

Terry was shocked at the response of his fellow hostages. He did not expect them to challenge his view of David but to agree with him. However, rather than becoming defensive – which would have been very easy – he began to examine and challenge his own perspective in the light of what his fellow hostages had said to him: "I've been sitting here thinking about all that. It's not a view of myself that I like – argumentative, bull-headed, trampling on other people. Especially in a situation like this. It's hard to accept, but I have to, since both Father Martin and Tom agree...." (Anderson, 1995, p. 10)

Here we see that through the gaze of his fellow hostages he was shocked into abandoning and challenging his habitual way of seeing things. The shock of the way others saw his encounter with David enabled him to detach himself from his own perspective, and see it rather than take it for granted. He had to face his own way of seeing David. Rather than refusing the challenge and becoming reactive, he questioned his way of seeing things. This is a difficult and anxiety provoking exercise because we are generally wedded to our own way of seeing things. It is the source of familiarity and thus security. It would have been quite easy for him to be, as Welch calls it, "paralyzed" by the challenge. Yet he was not. Even though he was unnerved and uncertain, he embraced it.

An example of this in the corporate context is the experience of Andrew Grove at Intel. Grove describes how he changed his way of thinking about Intel by seeing himself at Intel through the eyes of another CEO: "After this aimless wondering had been going on for almost a year, I was in my office with Intel's chairman and CEO, Gordon Moore, and we were discussing our quandary. Our mood was downbeat. I looked out the window at the ferris wheel of the Great America amusement park revolving in the distance, then I turned back to Gordon and I asked, "If we got kicked out and the board brought in a new CEO, what do you think he would do?" Gordon answered without hesitation, "He would get us out of memories." I stared at him, numb, then said, "why shouldn't you and I walk out the door, come back and do it ourselves?" (Grove, 1997, p. 89)

By seeing Intel through the gaze of another CEO, Grove broke free of his habitual way of seeing things. By seeing Intel in a new light, he was able to open up new possibilities for Intel. The activity of seeing things through the eyes of another allowed him to "abandon" and stand back from being caught in his habitual way of seeing things. Through the eyes of another, he disrupted and stood back from his own familiar ways of seeing things such that he could see his own familiar ways of seeing things.

Grove was able to put his own perspective into perspective; he was able to have a critical relationship to his own terms of judgment. This is not a scientific activity. For historically, science has not been concerned with putting our own perspective in perspective but with observing and analyzing the world external to the analyzer or subject. In this activity, science tends to take its own perspective for granted. It brackets or neutralises its own perspective rather than examining it. Grove in putting his own perspective into perspective is by his own admission shifting away from a scientific approach to management and into what I am calling a philosophical approach; an approach in which he challenges and reframes the assumptions that he had about Intel.

To do philosophy is to be able to examine one's own perspective in terms of the gaze of the other. For it is only through this gaze that we can come to see our own blind spots. We all have blind spots. And by definition we cannot see our own blind spots – otherwise they would not be blind spots. We require the ability to see ourselves through the way in which others see us to be able to see our own blind spots. Through the gaze of the other, we are able to distance ourselves from our own assumptions so that we can see them and question them and change them where necessary. We also see that it involves a process of dialogue, a process of seeing and allowing oneself to be seen from the perspective of the other. For Socrates dialogue, and not the development of a treaties, was the central practice of philosophy.

Both Grove and Anderson were able to embrace their uncertainty. Rather than being paralysed by their uncertainty, it became for both the motor in terms of which they questioned their habitual practices and began to see things in new ways. It would have been easy and much safer for Anderson to refuse to see himself in the way his fellow hostages saw him. He would not have had to risk losing his own perspective on himself. But it would also have made him more defensive and pushed him into a corner. Rather than being paralysed by their perspective on him, he embraced it and thus made it possible to entertain their perspective of him. Similarly, Grove did not remain fixed in his perspective on Intel. He was able to embrace the anxiety of a fundamental transformation for Intel. This prevented him from being paralysed by change.

It is crucial to appreciate that the process of detaching ourselves from our own perspective –as in the case of Anderson and Grove – does not occur automatically or by an act of reason or even of will. For again, we cannot use reason to see what we are blind to. For our reason is itself blind to what we are blind to. So we cannot decide to rationally see our blind spots. Furthermore, it is well known that reason can be used to defend rather than detach ourselves from a position. Instead of through reason, detachment occurs when we are disturbed or disrupted in our habitual ways of seeing and doing things. One such form of disturbance is the gaze of the other but it is not the only form of disturbance.

There are a number of other forms of existential detachment which underpin philosophical experiences – those experiences in which through questioning our assumptions we come to see things in new ways. Anita Roddick, for example speaks about the role of being an outsider in questioning the status quo and seeing things in new ways. She believes that entrepreneurs need to be "crazy" and obsessive. In a number of ways this is a view upheld by Jack Welch who also believes that to be a leader a person needs to be a little crazy. Ricardo Semler sees himself as a maverick and Andrew Grove sees himself as paranoid.

Of course the ways in which the abovementioned leaders use these terms cannot be taken in a clinically serious way: if we are clinically paranoid, we cannot see clearly. For we are projecting our own self hatred onto others. In a clinical sense we are seeing people hating us when in fact there is no objective basis for the claim. Yet these leaders are using the terms in precisely the opposite way. By the idea of paranoia, Grove wants to convey the idea of seeing clearly and of being highly attuned to his environment. However, he wishes to include the vigilance that is characteristic of the paranoid. For it is the vigilance that allows him or her to see possibilities where those who are not vigilant cannot.

By the notion of craziness both Welch and Roddick wish to convey the idea that they can see things which most people are blind to. The idea of craziness being a place of insight has been developed by a number of philosophers. Philosophically speaking, craziness, being an outsider, a maverick and paranoid are all processes of disrupting the "yoke of custom and convention." (Levinas, 1985, p. 49) To stand outside of the yoke of custom and convention is a kind of madness because we are no longer constrained and confined by common sense. Being outside of the boundaries of common sense is a kind of madness. For outside of the boundaries of common sense we have no established framework for making sense. Yet this is a madness of insight. It is a madness which allows us to see things in a way that we cannot when dominated by common sense. The outsider, the crazy person, the maverick and the paranoid can see clearly because they are detached from the common sense perspective. It is imperative also to understand that these leaders and entrepreneurs were highly attuned to what was surfacing in them in their craziness. They knew how to listen to themselves; to what was emerging in them.

Perspective through detachment; detachment through disruption – these are the central dynamics of the philosophical process. They are processes that work with the uncertainty of the unknown. In them existential uncertainty becomes, as we have seen in all the examples, a basis for philosophical questioning. Instead of leading to defensiveness or paralysis – as Welch calls it – in the face of change – the philosophical attitude allows the uncertainty to become an opportunity to envisage things in new ways.

In so far as both the theorising about management and the practice of management are calling for a new perspective, this philosophical process is central to management. It is a process that is crucial for times of disruption; times in which we cannot expect the future to repeat the past. In such times we cannot rely on a scientific view of management which is based on the observation of repeated regularities. Rather we need to develop our own practices of philosophical attunement. This does not mean that we develop our own philosophies. Rather it means that we learn how to gain perspective through detaching ourselves from the immediacy of experience. It is vital in all those instances where change disrupts our way of doing things. In order to avoid being paralysed by change, we need to be able to transform the uncertainty experienced in change into opportunities for detachment; opportunities which allow us to envisage and implement new possibilities; new futures.

We need to be able to change from simply trying to change circumstances to fit our mindset to developing a mindset that is itself changeable and thus does not, as Welch calls it, get paralysed by change. Managers need not only to think about their doing but they also need to think about their way of thinking about their doing. For a number of reasons, this is not easy or elementary. Firstly, it involves taking a step back from simply doing to reflecting on the mindset in which our doing takes place. As is well known, managers are especially resistant to this process. For anything that is not concerned with "doing" is seen as irrelevant and unpragmatic by mangers. However the commitment to doing creates a set of problems which require reflection. Doing provides no guidelines by which to monitor itself. It leads to activity for its own sake.

Yet, because of the violation of the psychological contract between past and future, managers cannot simply take their way of thinking for granted. They may very well not have the appropriate mindset in which to make judgments – and they may be blind to this. They may believe that, in terms of their habitual mindset, they are making sound managerial decisions, only later to find that the mindset in terms of which the decisions were being made is itself questionable. If, as this work is suggesting, change requires managers to change not only the objective circumstances but the mindset in which they view circumstances, reflection becomes crucial to managers. This is a point of view that is echoed in so many management texts today.

Philosophical detachment is vital to empowering managers in the face of the uncertainty of change. As Welch suggests, one of the dominant responses to uncertainty is a sense of emotional paralysis. Uncertainty undermines the spontaneity of our actions. It affects our situational attunement, our ability to pick out opportunities and possibilities. It blinds us to new opportunities. We need to be able to "manage" the uncertainty that is experienced in the disruption of the psychological contract between past and future. We cannot assume that we can automatically do it. We need to develop the art of managing the disruption of the psychological contract.

Philosophy begins where we recognise the need to have a detached relationship to our own experience. Because, in moments of disruption, the psychological contract between past and future has been disrupted, we should not rest in our habitual patterns of judgment – we will be left behind if we do. We need to be able to challenge our own ways of making judgments. This is crucial so that we do not take our views of reality for granted but can develop the flexibility to change with the way in which the business environment is changing.

Indeed, many corporate leaders who have simply trusted their judgment have found themselves perplexed and confused when in the position of evaluating new situations in the light of past expectations. This was generally the case in the years of the IT boom where CEO's made predictions about the future based on the past without seeing how information technology was changing the way in which we did things. In many of these cases, they have struggled to fit the new events into their old expectations. The more they have done this, the more they have disempowered themselves – and quite frankly, the more depressed they have become. Only when they begin to realise that they cannot evaluate new situations based on past expectations do they begin to see hope and new possibilities in their business environment. This hope comes from being willing to throw their habitual ways of seeing things into question, thereby opening up new ways of seeing things. The process of being able to do this is a process of existential detachment which underpins philosophical experiences.

6
Leading Managers out of Plato's Cave

It is now time to turn to an exposition of philosophy itself. All along I have been describing philosophical experiences without situating them in terms of a tradition of philosophy. Indeed, I have not wanted to write theoretically about philosophy but to demonstrate its place in the context of practice; to say that philosophy is not just an abstract activity but, in fact, that it is a practical activity and that it becomes practical in times of disruption. It is very practical in times of change where the habits, conventions and assumptions that had been the bedrock of our way of doing things can no longer be taken for granted but we do not yet have the security and focus of a new way of doing things. In such experiences we are jolted, shaken or shocked out of the complacency of taking our conventions for granted. The emotional disruption is experienced in such a way that we cannot simply get on with the job. We are too disturbed or distracted to get on with the job. Whether we like it or not, our attunement shifts from a preoccupation with getting on with the job to the perplexity, confusion and questioning of our habits and practices of doing things. This is not always a pleasant experience. It can be very frustrating, full of anxiety, uncertainty and self-doubt. We have called this an experience of "existential detachment." We become philosophical when we are detached from simply being able to get on with the job. However, such existential detachment is not an end in itself but the condition of opening up new ways of seeing and being. If we follow its path, it does allow for new and exciting possibilities to be opened.

Philosophy is a process for creating new visions, possibilities and ways of doing things by working through the disruptions to the existing conventions. Through the disruption of existing conventions we are detached from our everyday taken for granted habits. This detachment allows us to imagine and act on other possible ways of doing things. This is a definition that runs through the entire history of philosophy, both Western and Eastern! It also cuts across gender boundaries, and can be found in both female and male philosophers.

Yet by and large this definition is not explicit in modern philosophy. Indeed, if anything modern western philosophy has turned away from the idea of philosophy as an experience of existential detachment. Rather the tradition that has dominated philosophy has been characterised by what Ran Lahav calls the cognitive attitude. (1992, p. 34) This is an attitude in which logical analysis of theoretical propositions has been the driving force of philosophy. This tradition is known as the analytic tradition in philosophy. In this tradition only that which is rational is real and only that which can be subjected to rational analysis is deemed worthy of philosophical attention. Anything that falls outside of the scope of the rational is seen as not being philosophically significant. This means, for example, that emotions, experiences, and more broadly speaking the crises in living that are experienced by people are not seen as philosophically significant. In fact questions of the meaning of existence, questions in which people are searching for purpose and meaning in their lives are seen as too personal for analytic philosophy. Or putting it another way, the question of meaning is a meaningless question from an analytic perspective. It is just not rational enough.

Ironically, it was these kinds of questions that initially inspired the ancients to become philosophers. They were consumed by a sense of wonder about the meaning of existence. Plato tells us that philosophy began with a sense of wonder. The danger of excluding questions of the meaning of existence from philosophy is that such questions do not disappear but are taken up in the context of cults, in New Age movements, and in fads. That they are deemed meaningless by philosophy does not mean they disappear. All it means is that people seek to find other avenues to work in these areas – avenues which are often, but not always, not underpinned by a strong history and disciplinary framework. Philosophy has a long and deep history and it is a tragedy that philosophy excludes itself from an area that has historically been of central concern to it. In this context it is time that philosophy begins to address its own limitations, begins to open itself up to questions that were once part of its discipline and provide a framework within which people, who are struggling with questions of the meaning of existence or problems in living, have a forum to express their questions. This would provide philosophy with a much needed link to the society and community in which it is situated. For one of the effects of defining philosophy in terms of the rational analysis of propositions is that it has led to the seclusion of philosophy – to an ivory tower image of philosophy in which philosophy detached itself from everyday life and was seen by everyday life as irrelevant and insignificant. Indeed the very existence of philosophy is in question: what value can a discipline that disengages itself from everyday life have for the community and society in which it is situated? Philosophy cannot simply dismiss this question as a question asked by uneducated people but needs to tackle it head on. Philosophy needs to find its place in everyday life.

In contrast to the analytic image of philosophy, I want to recover a view of philosophy which is all about making sense of our lived experiences. Instead of being concerned with propositions or sentences, existential philosophy is concerned with how we make sense of the way in which we experience our world. The tradition which is concerned with understanding lived experience is known in philosophy as the existential hermeneutic and phenomenological dimension of philosophy. It culminates in the work of the German philosopher Martin Heidegger but is certainly not limited to his writing. It includes the whole range of existential philosophers: Jean Paul Sartre, Martin Buber, Frederic Nietzsche and Soren Kierkegaard are examples. It includes phenomenological philosophers who are not existential. Edmund Husserl is an example. And it includes a whole range of sociologists and psychologists who have called themselves existential psychologists. This includes Viktor Frankl, Rollo May, Mernard Boss and Ludwig Binswinger.

What distinguishes existential from analytic philosophy is its emphasis on experience and detachment from experience as the basis for philosophy. Existentialism is very concerned to embed thought within the context of experience. We do not first come to think about the world and then experience it. Rather we begin with experience and only then move on to thought. We do not acquire our culture through thinking about it but by experiencing it. For example, we acquire the terms "mummy" and "daddy" not by detached thought about the world but through experience. Even in adult life many of our most important understandings are formed through experience rather than thought. For example, we learn to use an instrument not by thinking about it but by using it; that is, by experiencing it.

Thought occurs for the existentialists at a particular moment in our experience. What is important for the existential philosopher is that we become philosophical in the moment of detachment through disruption. It is very important to note that we become philosophical rather than just think philosophical thoughts. Philosophy, from the existential perspective, consumes our whole being. It is not just a cognitive process. It is a process in which our whole mode of attunement shifts from simply being involved in something to a reflective relationship to what we are involved in. For when we experience a disruption it is our whole being that experiences it. And so philosophy is both a cognitive and an emotional process. Indeed the terms used by existentialists to describe the disruptions are highly emotional: nausea, anxiety, a sense of the absurd, estrangement from our habitual ways of doing things, self-doubt and uncertainty are some of the terms that existentialists use to describe the moment of detachment. Although existential philosophers have used "negative" emotions to describe the moment of detachment, this is not always the case in the history of philosophy. For Plato philosophy began with a sense of wonder. Others have pointed out the role of love in philosophical detachment. For lovers are said to be detached from the everyday way of doing things in such a way that they may begin to wonder at the marvel of existence.

Although existential philosophers share a commitment to detachment from experience as the basis of philosophical attunement, they do not share much else. Indeed, they see the outcome of detachment as quite different. For Sartre, detachment leads to a realisation that existence is meaningless and superfluous. Kierkegaard maintains that through detachment we can develop a unique and passionate relation to God. This is a position that is shared by Martin Buber. Frederic Nietzsche and Martin Heidegger offer us different possibilities. For Nietzsche the experience of detachment becomes the occasion for what he calls a "re-evaluation of all values." Nietzsche believes that our values are for the most part implicit in our experience. They guide us without us being explicitly attuned to the way in which they guide us. It is in an act of detachment through disruption that we come to see the values that guide us, that we are able to assess the values that have guided us and that we can begin to create or construct new values that are more appropriate for the disruptive world in which we live. This is a position that is shared by Heidegger. Heidegger believed that the conventions and habits which guide us are for the most part implicit in our experience. We acquire them and are guided by them in a way that we are not explicitly aware of. In the moment of detachment through disruption, they become explicit themes of examination and their critique is the basis for creating our lives in new ways.

In what follows, I will develop Martin Heidegger's understanding of the philosophical process. However, I will do this in a most unusual way. Because Heidegger is recognised as a philosopher who is difficult to understand I want to build a bridge to the philosophy of Martin Heidegger. I will build this bridge in three stages. Firstly, I will develop an idea that is central to the work of a marketing expert. The marketing expert is Jean Marie Dru who developed a model of what he called convention-disruption-vision as the basis upon which to help companies reframe their products and brands. This is a model that allows us to situate the existential experience of detachment. Secondly, I will situate Dru's work in the context of the philosophy of Plato. This is because Plato provides the first metaphor for the process of philosophical detachment. Indeed Plato was the first thinker who taught us to think outside of the box – or as he called it, the cave. Just as we believe that creative thinking begins when we learn to think outside of our boxes, so Plato outlined the process of leaving our boxes not only to think outside of them but to see that we are "boxed in" in the first place.

I will then situate the work of Plato in the context of Heidegger. This will take place in the next chapter. It may seem strange to put a marketing expert and two philosophers in the same category – especially after the conclusion of the last chapter in which it was stated that it was due to the advice of his marketing manager that Champy decided not to develop his work on the philosophy of management. Yet it is precisely to show that philosophy is relevant in the marketplace that I use a text from marketing to frame the concept of a philosophical process. For what I will show is that implicit in the marketing methodology of Dru is a philosophical process. Furthermore, Dru's concept of what I have called the philosophical process makes philosophy both accessible and allows its value in the market place to stand out.

I should also like to make clear that this is only a sketch. The history of philosophy is full of different perspectives, each of which are detailed in a scholarly and disciplined way. There will be no details in my sketch. My hope is to create the sense that the tradition of philosophy has something to contribute towards the understanding of management. If other chains of association of ideas should be triggered off by the sketch, the details can be taken up by others in a more disciplined way.

Dru does not call his process a philosophical one. Rather, he sees it as a disruptive technology which is compromised by three elements: convention, disruption and vision (hereafter called the CDV model). It is a technology that he uses to reframe brands and products. He claimed that if we wish to change the way we and consumers think about our products and brands we need to change the conventions in terms of which the community experience the brand and product. We cannot change their way of thinking in terms of existing conventions – all we can do is refine and improve our image in this way. He maintains that for the most part our perceptions and experiences in the world are regulated by conventions which we do not think about us as such. For example, we use knives and forks without thinking about them as being conventions. We eat! We do not think about our practices for eating. Indeed, if we stopped to think about our practices of eating this would get in the way of our eating: "Although conventions are everywhere, they are generally hard to see. These are things that we don't even notice because they are so familiar. ... Depending on the case, we will talk about unquestioned assumptions, good old common sense, or the current rules of the game." (Dru, 1996, p. 56)

However, our conventions shape and limit the way in which we see and experience. If we want to change our way of seeing and experiencing, we often need to disrupt our existing assumptions: "All at once, we question the way we have done things in the past. We discover that our way of thinking has been conditioned by biases [and] adherence to outmoded frameworks." (Dru, 1996, p. 57)

By exposing our biases we open up the possibility of seeing things in new ways. The new vision emerges out of the way in which we work with the disruption of existing conventions: "Disruption is about developing new hypotheses and unexpected ideas ... a quest for angles of attack that have never been used before. ... It provides a glimpse of what does not yet exist." Dru maintains that it was through a disruption of their existing conventions that IBM was able to move from being seen "only as a mainframe computer manufacturer; instead, it [became] ... the provider of solutions for a small planet." In his work he shows how a number of companies were able to reinvent their brand through the process of disruption. (Dru, 1996, p. 59)

This simple model is also a model of the history of original thinking in philosophy. Socrates' way of thinking, for example, emerged out of the disruption in the conventions of ancient Athenian society. In the face of this disruption Athens moved from being a military empire to being the home of scholarship. Descartes' philosophy of rationality emerged out of the disruption of the conventions of the catholic conventions of his heritage. He was caught between a commitment to the Church and an excitement at the emerging possibilities of new science. It was out of this contradiction that his thinking emerged, a thinking that has formed the basis for the western concept of rationality. And when we turn to the broad sphere of existentialism and postmodernism, we see quite clearly how disruption of conventions formed the basis for new visions of human beings and their destiny. In Nietzsche, for example, it was the death of God that formed the basis for a new view of the human being. In Kierkegaard it was the disruption of the conventions of Christianity which formed the basis for a re-enchantment of Christianity.

The theme of this book is the way in which this model underpins the practices of managers who need to cope with the disruption of existing conventions. We have already had a glimpse of this in a number of ways. We have seen it, for example, in the case of Andrew Grove who was CEO of Intel, how he took Intel through a fundamental disruption of its way of doing business and finding a new way of doing things on the other side of this disruption. We will see it in the case of Mort Meyerson, a leader at Ross Perot systems who, through a disruption in his professional practice as a leader was challenged to develop a new vision and practice of what it means to be a leader. We will see it in the way in which Welch transformed GE; the way in which Semler transformed Semco and the way in which Gerstner transformed IBM.

But before examining the corporate context in detail, it needs to be shown that philosophers themselves would buy into this model. How do philosophers conceptualise this process of CDV?

The origins of this process can be found in the writing of Plato. What Dru calls thinking in terms of convention is articulated as thinking in a cave by Plato. He asks us to imagine a group of people chained to the floor of a cave. They are facing the back wall of the cave. Because they are chained, they cannot turn around and see the entrance to the cave. There are a number of people walking past the entrance to the cave. The light of the cave is projecting an image of these figures on to the wall of the cave. The people imprisoned in the cave can see only the images projected on to the wall. Because this is all they can see, they take the image to be the real. They do not see that it is just an image. It is only when, through being unchained, they are able to turn around and take a step back from the cave that they can see that what they had assumed to be reality is nothing but an image of reality.

The experience of distinguishing between the image and the reality is initially a jarring experience for the unchained prisoners. The stability of their familiar world is thrown into question. They did not expect to experience the world in another way, a way that is initially strange for them. They are initially overwhelmed by this way and need time to adjust to their insight. As they adjust to their insight they are able to leave the safe but imaginary security of the cave and move out of the cave where they are able to see dimensions of life that they never even imagined existed. There are various dimensions to the experience of being unchained and led out of the cave. The first observation, as has been said, is the ability to distinguish between the image of people projected on to the wall of the cave and the actual physical people at the entrance to the cave.

The next insight is the ability to see that what people in the cave took for the whole of reality is that they were in a cave. Whilst in a cave they did not see that they were in a cave. They thought that they were in reality as a whole. It is only in stepping out of the cave that they see that they were in a cave. For here they are able to see that the cave is situated in a broader environment of other caves, mountains, valleys, the sea etc. So it is with our conventions: When we take our conventions for granted, we do not even know that they are conventions. We tend to think that they simply describe the way things are done: eating with a knife and fork in Western culture, with chopsticks in the East and with hands in Africa. When, however, we enter the broader environment, we see that there are other ways of doing things. We can see that our way of doing things are only conventions or habits and not the natural way of doing things – much like the Scandinavian and North African strangers who, as we saw in chapter one, discovered their own habits of social distancing by meeting each other. We begin, in Plato's terms to make a distinction between taking the cave for granted and seeing that we take the cave for granted.

Again, the experience of the distinction between taking the cave for granted and seeing that we live in a cave is a jarring experience. It is not expected and so jars the way that we are accustomed to seeing the world. But as we adjust to the new way of seeing our world, we are placed in a position of questioning our cave and conventions. We can now begin to see our existence in a new light. The third dimension for Plato is the ability to see the light in terms of which we can see our environment. And finally from a Platonic perspective we are able to see the sun which makes light possible. Seeing the sun is like seeing the source of vision which means, not that we have a vision, but that we see how visions are made possible.

However, I am not going to detail the latter dimensions of Plato's theory of vision. What is important from the perspective of this book is that Plato offers a theory of the way in which disruption of our cave-like-conventions opens up the possibility for seeing our world and ourselves in new ways. He also enables us to see how whilst absorbed in one cave, we cannot even see that there is an outside of the cave – let alone another cave. Thus whilst we are absorbed in one set of conventions, we cannot see that there is another set of conventions and another way of doing things. In the corporate arena this is exemplified in the case of Intel: whilst it was caught in the cave of microchip technology it could not see the cave of microprocessing techno- logy. It could not see that there was another way of doing things. Instead of questioning its conventional, cave like ways of doing things, it tried everything within the cave of microchip technology: "We fought hard. We improved our quality and brought costs down but the Japanese producers fought back." But as the Japanese were successful in fighting back, Intel became more and more despondent. It was only when it was able to un- chain itself from the cave of microchip technology, that it was able to open up the possibility of another way of doing things. However, because of the familiarity and security of the cave, there was initially much resistance to leaving the cave of microchip technology. It was only when Intel could embrace the shock of seeing the end of their habitual ways of doing things and the emergence of a new way that they were able to move towards a microprocessing framework.

What we can see for Plato is that we cannot simply think outside of our box. Out of the box thinking requires an unchaining of our embededness in the box, it involves the shock of having our expectations of reality shat- tered, the shock of the blinding light when we are not yet accustomed to seeing reality in new ways and eventually the ability to see our own exist- ence in new ways and to question our conventional ways of seeing things based on our new perspective. In turn this allows for a new vision of the way things are.

The process of moving out of the cave is a process of being "led out" of the cave. Plato identifies the act of being led out of the cave with the process of being educated. The identification of being led out of the cave and education can easily be seen when we realise that the Latin word for education means to "lead out." The identification of leading and education has important implications for modern theories of leadership. For some of these theories see leaders as people who lead others from one set of con- ventions, through the disruption of these conventions, into the unknown and through to a new way of seeing things.

The process of moving out of the cave can be seen as a process of gaining a "helicopter perspective" on our way of doing things. For we are con- tinually moving from being absorbed in our particular cave to gaining a wider and wider perspective of the cave and the world that we are in. We move from not even seeing that we are in a cave, to seeing that we are in a cave, to seeing the environment that the cave is in, to seeing that the environment is part of the world, to seeing that the world is, in Plato's terms, an imperfect finite representation of an infinite, perfect and universal world. Each time we are gaining more of a "helicopter" perspective on the world.

In philosophical terms, the move from being embedded in a cave to reflecting on the cave that we are embedded in, is called a move from the particular to the universal. We are moving from embedded and particular ways of seeing things to universal ways of seeing things. Sometimes this is also called a move from the "view from somewhere" to the "view from no where." (Nagel, 1989) Whilst we are in the cave we are located in a very particular place. We are somewhere. However, as we leave the cave and ascend to the universal dimension, we are no where in particular. When we are in a particular cave or place, we cannot see the whole. As we leave the cave, we get a greater sense of the whole.

From this perspective, leadership is not so much about having a strong point of view but a well developed point from which to view. The difference needs to be made clear. To have a point from which to view in contrast to having a point of view is to have a point from which to have a panoramic perspective in terms of which the "layout of the land," the horizon can be seen. To have a point of view does not necessarily mean to be able to see the layout of the land. An example of the difference between a point from which to view and a point of view can be found in Jack Welch's notion of vision. He believes that in a complex organisation in a changing world, a CEO cannot define the details of the strategy of an organisation. Indeed he does not want to do this, seeing strategy not as a lengthy action plan. Rather for him strategy becomes what he calls a "central idea" that gives direction to GE and which takes on concrete form as it emerges "through continually changing circumstances." (Welch, 2001, p. 448) The way in which it emerges through changing circumstances depends on how people within GE respond to and interpret it. What the idea does is provide the horizon in terms of which GE does business. It provides a framework in which people can express themselves in their work. It provides a point from which to view without supplying a detailed point of view. The particular point of view that people within GE take from the idea depends on their particular situation. Having a point of view can make one blind to other possibilities whereas to have a point from which to view allows one to open up to other perspectives. The latter provides a framework in which people can act and interact.

The process of leaving the cave and moving from the particular to the universal is called dialectics by Plato. Dialectics is thus a process of stepping back from being involved in the cave to examining the cave that we are involved in to examining the environment in which the cave is situated to examining the world in which the environment is situated. It is the process of moving from the view from "somewhere to the view from no where". It is the process of gaining a helicopter perspective. For we cannot automatically turn on a helicopter perspective. Just as we need to fly into the sky in order to get a physical helicopter ride so we need to detach ourselves from the cave in order to gain perspective on the cave and its environment. The process of detaching ourselves is known as dialectics. The activity of dialectics needs to be distinguished from scientific activity: scientists are concerned with analysing the world in terms of conventions. Generally, scientists are not involved in questioning the assumptions in terms of which they conduct their scientific activity. They get on with the task of analysing and examining the world. Dialectics is that process of examining the conventions in terms of which scientists analyse the world. It involves taking a step back from analysing the world and examining the terms in which the analysis of the world is conducted.

To put it in contemporary management terms, dialectics is the activity of examining the "frames" or "paradigms" or "mindsets" in terms of which managers operate. The examination of these frames requires a willingness and ability to step back from engagement in the world and questioning of the frames in terms of which managers operate. The condition, in Platonic terms, for this activity is an experience of being unchained from the habitual or taken for granted conventions or habits for doing things. When managers can no longer rely on their common sense ways of doing things, they are unchained in such a way that they are thrown into the dialectical activity of questioning their assumptions and conventions.

The same process occurs in organisational culture. The process of being concerned with our organisational culture is, from the Platonic perspective, a dialectical activity in which we come to detach ourselves from the everyday routines of the organisation, take a step back and examine the terms in which the culture makes sense. This is because culture is not something visible in the world but the background in terms of which we make sense of the world.

The detachment that occurs in the philosophical process of dialectics is quite different from scientific forms of detachment. The scientist distances him or herself from the object of study. The observer and observed are two separate and independent entities. The philosophical process of detachment is not a detachment from some object other than ourselves. It is a detachment from what we are ourselves involved in. It is a detachment and examination of our own way of doing things. We see our own way of doing things from a distance. This is infinitely more difficult. For, generally, we are so close to our own way of doing things. It is us. To get distance from ourselves is not easy. It requires, as Drucker said in the last chapter, an act of abandoning our own perspective in order to get a critical perspective on it; an act of estranging ourselves from our own way of doing things makes it possible to see our own way of doing things. We saw this experience many times in the last two chapters: in the experience of Gregg who in the context of the different ways of another culture, came to see his own attitude towards pregnant women in the workplace; in the case of Mandela who in the experience of a strange sensation came to see his own biases and, in the case of the meeting of Scandinavians and North Africans who came to see their own patterns of social distancing.

Plato calls the act of abandoning our own perspectives "aporia." The experience of aporia is one in which we lose our way, our path. It is in the experience of losing our way on the path that we come to see the path that we were on. The aporia is the condition of philosophical detachment and objectivity. The difficulty involved in detaching ourselves from what we are involved in is exemplified in Grove's experience at a changing Intel. In the midst of an organisational crisis, we tend to panic, hold on to the past and deny the changing nature of the business environment. We become very emotional. He says that "in spite of the best attempts of business schools and management training courses to make you a rational analyzer of data, objective analysis will take second seat to personal and emotional reactions almost everytime." (Grove, 1997, pp. 123–124)

Yet there is a danger of getting lost in an emotional response to the situation. For when we are overwhelmed by emotions of being threatened, we may panic and react blindly. What we need to develop is a sense of distance from what we ourselves are involved in. We need to take a "helicopter perspective" on our own involvements. Yet this is a difficult task: how do we develop a helicopter perspective on our situation when we ourselves feel threatened or overwhelmed by emotion? As Grove says: "If existing management want to keep their jobs when the basics of the business are undergoing profound change, they must adopt an outsider's intellectual objectivity ... unfettered by an emotional attachment to the past." (Grove, 1997, p. 93)

We need to be able to detach ourselves while feeling threatened. This detachment from our attachments or involvements is very different from scientific detachment which is a distance from something outside of us. Gaining a sense of distance from what we are involved in is not elementary – especially under conditions in which we feel threatened. In such situations we want to put our head down and fight – as was the case with Grove at Intel. Initially when they felt threatened by Japanese competition, they thought the best way to deal with it would be to fight the competition. Unsuccessfully they tried to do this. It was only much later that Grove was able to stand back from the immediacy of the feeling of being threatened and gain perspective on what Intel was going through.

What is important to note is the process through which Grove was able to detach himself from his attachments. It was, as described in the previous chapter (p. 50), by seeing Intel through the eyes of another CEO that he was able to detach himself. Seeing Intel through the eyes of another enabled him to stand back from his own perspective, put his own perspective into broader perspective and open up a new way of seeing Intel. Detachment from his own vision was achieved through the "gaze of another." This form of existential or philosophical detachment is very different from those practices of detachment in which we say bring in an outsider who has no emotional involvement in the organisation. The latter would be objective or detached in the scientific sense of the word, in that way of having no involvement. But because of this, they would not have the know how or feeling for the organisation.

Another example of the philosophical form of detachment is to be found in the leadership practice of Nelson Mandela: no matter how much he was threatened and humiliated by the apartheid authorities, he was always able to maintain a sense of detachment from what he was involved in. He never reacted to his enemies but was always able to put their hatred and fear of him into wider perspective. Very rarely did he lose his temper. He was detached while being engaged.

Plato calls the discipline involved in standing back from one's own involvements wisdom. For Plato, a condition of wisdom is being able to care for the whole. For Plato the major stumbling blocks to caring for the whole are fear and pleasure. For in both we lose the panoramic perspective and become focused on ourselves. As we saw, this was the case with Intel initially. Reacting out of fear, it tried to take on the Japanese competition. In order to gain a helicopter perspective we need to know how to put fear and pleasure in their place. Rather than being bewitched or seduced by them, we need to be able to transcend them in ourselves. In the case of Grove this occurred through seeing his own position through the gaze of an imagined but new CEO. Developing the attunement of wisdom is not easy but requires a well developed sense of emotional discipline. And, indeed, this training is an essential aspect of the education of what Plato calls the Philosopher King.

What has this got to do with management? If management is concerned with what Boleman and Deal call the "four frames," if management is concerned with reframing, with reflection, with getting a helicopter perspective, it has everything to do with management. To the extent that management is concerned with reflecting on its own assumptions, it needs a philosophical rather than a scientific underpinning. For reflection on the frames, paradigms, assumptions, theory of the business and conventions is essentially a philosophical activity. To fail to place these management concerns in a philosophical framework is to make what Gilbert Ryle calls a category mistake, a mistake in which we place something in the wrong category and remain confused because we do not have the appropriate lens in which to understand our activity. Just because scientific concepts of knowledge are the socially and politically correct forms of knowledge does not mean that we must force management concerns to fit within this framework.

Finally, it is worth re-iterating the differences between existential philosophical detachment and scientific detachment. Scientific detachment is a detachment from an object outside of itself. In scientific detachment we maintain a dispassionate attitude towards the other. We remain neutral observers of the other. In philosophical detachment, we are required to detach ourselves from what we are already committed to and involved in. We need to be dispassionate towards our own passions. We need to be steadfast in our own uncertainty. We need to be able to stand back from our own way of doing things, to maintain a reflective relationship to what is most vital in our own lives. We cannot separate ourselves from ourselves, our conventions or ways of doing things in the same way as we can separate ourselves from objects or others that are independent of us.

The movement from a scientific account of management to a philosophical account of leadership is a movement from the notion of a manager as a detached scientist to a leader who is able to detach himself from his and his organisation's own conventions and habits. This process of detachment is crucial for putting things in perspective. It is a philosophical process because it involves the activity of standing back from our everyday activities and examining the horizon or assumptions in terms of which we make sense of our everyday activities. As we have seen Plato calls this process of standing back "dialectics." Dialectics is aimed not so much at understanding the observable world but the assumptions or frames in terms of which we make sense of the observable world.

The notion of philosophical detachment is central to most wisdom traditions of thought. It is central to Buddhism which teaches us an ability to be observers of our own action through meditative processes that allow who we are to emerge. It is also central to the practice of psychoanalysis in which the analyst encourages and enables the patient to listen to their own voice by maintaining what is called an "evenly hovering focus of attention" that fixes itself on nothing in particular thus allowing what is silent in the self to express itself. But it is in the context of the philosophy of Martin Heidegger that philosophical detachment has been most clearly and systematically articulated in the modern Western tradition.

7
Strange Bedfellows: Jack Welch and Martin Heidegger

It is now time to turn to the philosophy of Martin Heidegger. His philosophy is central to an understanding of the philosophical experience. But his philosophy is notoriously difficult to grasp. Because it is difficult to grasp, I shall develop it through examining the experience of Jack Welch in becoming CEO of General Electric. Jack Welch is still thought of as one of the most fascinating CEO's of the last 50 years. Part of the fascination with Welch is that he was able, in the early 1980's to anticipate, rather than simply respond, to the changes that would come about as a result of globalisation and changes in technology.

Jack Welch may be described as an entrepreneurial leader. He is a leader who not only saw things well ahead of time but was able to act on his way of seeing things. On many occasions his call for transformation of GE has taken conventional business wisdom by surprise. This was particularly the case when he became CEO of GE in the early 1980's. Conventional wisdom was that GE was a stable company developing in a steady way. From this perspective GE was not in need of change. Yet Welch pushed for fundamental transformation of GE. His push was met by shock and astonishment. As one commentator puts it: "When Welch took over at GE, most observers thought he was lucky, stepping into such a successful, well-managed, respected, historic company ... The media, GE's workers, and many others were dumbfounded when Welch urgently demanded change before it was too late." (Lowe, 1998)

Conventional business wisdom could not see what Welch had seen. Welch understood the perspective of those who were dumfounded with his call for change: "There was no stage set for us. We looked too good, too strong, too profitable, to be restructuring." (Welch, 2001, p. 125) Yet this did not stop Welch from committing himself and the resources of GE to a transformation, a transformation whose terms had not yet become clear to even Welch himself. As he says: "I did know what I wanted the company to "feel" like. I wasn't calling it culture in those days, but that's what it was." (Welch, 2001, p. 92)

Welch saw and experienced GE in a way that nobody else did. He could see that as strong and powerful as GE looked, if it continued in its same path it would be heading for disaster. Before anyone else "Welch realized that the business world faced cataclysmic changes in its new global, high-technology environment. He also knew GE wasn't ready for it. ... Today, however, after nearly two decades of relentless turmoil, GE remains leader of the pack." (Lowe, 1998)

Although today, these comments may sound trite, in the early 80's no one else could see this. What is it that allowed Jack Welch to see that GE was heading on a collision course to disaster? And what is it that enabled Welch to see an alternative course for GE? For to foresee disaster is one thing. Many people become resigned in the face of impending disaster. They do not see new possibilities, possibilities for re-generation. Welch saw new possibilities beyond the immediate horizon. He was excited and captivated by what he saw. To be sure, the language in which to express these new possibilities was not clear at the outset even to him. The framework in which he would express the transformation of GE developed as GE developed. He did not have an advanced "blue print" but as already indicated a "feel" of what he wanted GE to look like.

Furthermore, even though he did not have a blue print for the new GE, he was able to act on his "feeling" for the new GE, commit his energy and the resources of GE to a transformation that he was not able to express in objectively verifiable terms. In addition, he did not get support from the conventional business environment who, in his words, tended to think that he was "crazy." What did it take for Welch to act on his foresight when those around him, doubted him and thought that he was "crazy"? And how do we distinguish the gift of foresight from down-right foolishness? For it could have been the case that Jack Welch was simply "building castles in the sky." History as we know is littered with false prophets, with visionaries who build grand dreams.

But Jack Welch's entrepreneurialism is not limited only to GE. He was part of a transformation in the very way in which business thought about itself. The movement from scientific management to values based organisations is one that received much inspiration from Welch. The turn from "management" to "leadership" in organisations has been a strong rallying cry of Welch. Again, these concerns are now common sense. But at the time, Jack Welch spoke in a language that was unintelligible in the context of the conventional business wisdom of the day. In the early 80's there was no talk of the "soft skills" of business. There was no talk of a "values" based organisation. There was room only for hard headed rational quantification of data. Welch challenged this. He spoke in the language of the "soft skills." As he himself says, people could not understand what he was saying. They could not see what his talk about values had to do with the realities of business. They thought that he was "nuts," that he would not last very long as CEO of GE. Yet instead of Welch being drowned out by the authoritative voice of conventional business wisdom, he was able to get conventional business wisdom to question its own assumptions about what it means to do business in an organisational context.

How then do we begin to speak about foresight in a meaningful way? This is a question that the philosophy of Martin Heidegger will enable us to answer. For Heidegger's philosophy focuses on those forms of knowledge or knowing that do not emerge out of rational or scientific deliberation but out of the way in which we are involved in the world. As we develop a feeling for a new environment, we develop an insight into that environment. This insight is not communicable in a purely objective or cognitive way. That insight becomes the basis upon which to see the environment in a new way. This is a theme that I will develop by looking at the experience of Welch through the lens of Heidegger's philosophy and using the experience of Welch to give a vitality to the philosophy of Heidegger.

But we may well ask: what has a philosopher who lived in the solitude of a German forest in the early parts of the twentieth century got to do with a highly engaged, "up-front" and active corporate CEO who dominated thinking about organisations in the last part of the twentieth century and is a role model into the first decade of the twenty first century? They share a similar understanding of the process of disclosure through disruption. What I shall show is that Welch practiced what Heidegger preached. Heidegger offers a framework in which to understand the novelty of Welch as a CEO. He will throw light on the Jack Welch way of thinking about and doing business in the context of change.

As we have already observed, Welch claims it was the fact of having a philosophy as a leader rather than a set of techniques as a manager that gave him his insight into GE and organisational life. However, he does not tell us in a direct and explicit way what he means by a philosophy or the significance of philosophy in leadership. Nevertheless there are a number of clues in his autobiography of what he means by a philosophy and of the way in which a philosophy of leadership can be distinguished from the techniques of managers. Taking these clues as my starting point, I shall construct both the philosophy of Welch, the significance of philosophy for leadership and the philosophical process involved in the development of Welch's philosophy. For as we shall see there are not only different philosophies but there are different philosophical processes.

In his autobiography, *Jack* he does give us clues to what would be involved in his philosophy. It involves what I shall call an "ethics of authenticity" or what he calls the willingness to fight "superficial congeniality" and "face reality." Jack Welch fights complacency. He objects to routine for routines sake. He hates going through the motions of something. His autobiography is littered with incidences showing how frustration with the complacent acceptance of routine at GE led him to begin to develop a vision of a new way of doing things at GE. This is worth emphasising: his vision for GE did not grow out of a scientific rationality. It grew out of a deep sense of frustration with the unresponsiveness of GE to innovation. Just as many other visionaries through the centuries, he was able to turn his frustration into a vision. His frustration gave him an emotional detachment from GE that allowed him to see it in a way that others were not able to. It is important to point out that Welch was detached from GE whilst still being inside GE. He did not have the disengaged detachment of an outsider but the concerned detachment of an insider. Rather than being a neutral and objective outsider, he was a frustrated insider. His frustration was the passion that drove him to re-invent GE.

It is at this point that I would like to turn to the philosophy of Martin Heidegger. For the concern with authenticity, the frustration with going through the motions of things and the way in which emotional detachment from the inside becomes an occasion to see or disclose GE in a new way are central to the philosophy of Martin Heidegger. Both Heidegger and Welch share a frustration with the way in which rituals, traditions and conventions deprive ways of life of their vitality. Welch was frustrated with the way in which the practices of organisational life at GE and in general had been reduced to rituals and routines which blinded them to the reality of life outside of the corporations. As Welch expresses it: "An awful lot of ritual goes on in companies. A lot of what I call 'selling hats to each other,' They come in with big thick boots, make presentations to each other; no customers know you're making it, the market doesn't know you've tied yourself up in a room preparing charts for weeks; so I constantly say, 'don't sell hats to each other,' go out and do business." (Lowe, 2001, p. 20)

Heidegger was frustrated with the way in which modern philosophers have forgotten how to "really" ask philosophical questions. Instead of being fascinated with the fact of human existence, philosophy had become, from Heidegger's perspective, inward focused, focused on its own scholarly texts and traditions. It had forgotten the sense of wonder and amazement in finding out that we exist. Describing this sense of wonder in the context of children, Terry Eagleton has said: "Children make the best [philosophers], since they have not yet been educated into accepting our routine social practices as '**natural**', and so insist on posing to those practices the most embarrassingly general and fundamental questions, regarding them with a wondering estrangement which we adults have long forgotten. Since they do not grasp our social practices as

inevitable, they do not see why we might not do things differently."
(Eagleton, 1990)

From Heidegger's perspective, academic philosophers have lost that sense
of "wondering estrangement" that inspires us to be fascinated with our
own existence and conventions for doing things. Instead it has become
a heavy and stodgy analysis of the texts of previous philosophers.
Philosophers have become cut off from everyday life – the very context in
which philosophy emerged at the time of Socrates. Socrates engaged in
philosophical activity within the market place – not by detaching himself
from it. Heidegger wants to return philosophy to its context in everyday
life.

Both Welch and Heidegger see the inward focus of organisations and
philosophers as dangerous because it blinds those in its grips to the
changing reality outside of them. In the organisational context of Welch
this means a blindness to the changing business environment and thus
the danger of not preparing for change and "seizing the day." In the
context of Heidegger the danger is that we are lulled into a "comfort
zone" in which philosophers are cut off from everyday life.

Both Heidegger and Welch see the need to re-vitalise and re-enchant
organisational life and philosophy. As Welch puts it: "My objective was to
put a small-company **spirit** in a big company body, to build an organization out of an old-line industrial company that would be more high
spirited, more adaptable and more agile than companies that are one
fiftieth our size. I said then that I wanted to create a company 'where
people dare to try new things – where people feel assured in knowing that
only the limits of their creativity and drive, their own standards of personal
excellence, will be the ceiling on how far and how fast they move." (Welch,
2001, p. xv)

Spirit here does not have a religious connotation. It means putting life
back into something that was running on automatic. It means putting
the "feel" back into "business." In Heidegger's terms business feel, "life"
and "spirit" will be read as "mood" or "attunement." Just like Welch,
he believes that philosophy has lost its "feel". He wants to express the
spirit or mood of philosophy rather than just the technical activity
of philosophy. For Heidegger, this means expressing the moods of wonder, anxiety and uncertainty in which philosophical questions were
originally posed. We become philosophical when we experience the
strangeness of our existence. In this book countless examples of the
sense of strangeness that underpins philosophy have been given. It is
this rather than technical reason that forms the basis for the revitalisa-
tion of philosophy.

Both Heidegger and Welch share a common understanding of the
process for re-enchanting organisational and everyday life. It is not a

process of rational discussion but in Welch's words a process of drilling down, "to get beyond the blinders and into the thinking that went into them. I needed to see the business leaders' body language and the passion they poured into their arguments. ... There were too many passive reviews." (Welch, 2001, p. 94)

Welch is telling us that he wanted to see how people thought in the context of their bodies – not in a disembodied and disengaged way, as is the habit of forms of analytic and theoretical forms of reasoning that divorce thinking from the context in which they occur. Welch wanted to see their convictions, their commitments, their way of thinking through – not only reason that was abstracted from the situation. Drilling down requires a blend of passion and reason – not just disengaged and rational analysis but embodied thinking.

In Heidegger the process of drilling down is known as a process of "destruction." Destruction is a process that allows us to examine reason in the context of the situation in which it occurs. Just as Welch wanted to see thinking in the context of the body language, so Heidegger says that thinking needs to be situated in the context of the body that thinks. Heidegger, like Welch, carries this further by saying that thinking occurs in the context of a mood or passion and that we need to understand not only the reasoning but the passion or mood in terms of which reasoning is situated – just as Welch is saying that he wanted to see the passion behind the thinking of his managers. Without the mood, reasoning loses its passion. It is abstracted from its context, becomes disengaged. It has a different vitality.

For both Heidegger and Welch, destruction is a process of removing the "blinders" – as Welch calls it in the above quotation – that veil the way in which we do things. They are processes which enable us to step out of the "cave" of conventions. From both Heidegger's and Welch's perspectives, destruction or drilling down is vital in those contexts in which we have become complacent in our habits or routines. Destruction and drilling down are processes that shake us out of the complacency of habit and convention and re-enchant our world. They enable us to take a "fresh" perspective on the situation that we are in. Destruction in Heidegger and "drilling down" in Welch thus plays the same role that disruption plays in Dru's convention-disruption-vision model. It allows us to see the conventions which shape our everyday activities but which we are blind to in the doing of our everyday activities.

Philosophical thought, for Heidegger occurs in moments of disruption. Indeed this is a perspective that is shared by Welch. He believed that the disruption of the stayed habits and conventions of GE was crucial to establishing a new vision for and way of doing things at GE. He saw himself as the catalyst of the disruption of the old conventions as the basis for the emergence of the new ways of doing things.

Both the organisational practice of Jack Welch and the philosophy of Martin Heidegger can be articulated in terms of the convention-disruption-vision model of philosophical experience. It is in this sense that Welch is a philosopher. For as we have said the process by which we become attuned to our conventions in the face of the disruption of our habitual ways of doing things is a philosophical process. In general terms, what Welch means by having a philosophy is now clear. The process of challenging GE to question its taken for granted conventions and assumptions through a process of drilling down is a philosophical process. The experience of opening new possibilities by challenging existing conventions is an essential part of this process.

Both Heidegger's and Welch's framework can also be situated in the context of the entrepreneurial philosophy of Joseph Schumpeter who developed the concept of creative destruction to explain the role of competition in capitalism. In chapter 4 we saw how Foster and Kaplan situated Welch's leadership style in the context of Schumpeter's writing. There we said that Foster and Kaplan see Jack Welch as a leader who was responsive to the patterns of creative destruction in the market place and was able to create in what they call the "apocalyptic" nature of the market place. Like Schumpeter, Martin Heidegger quite explicitly calls his philosophy one of destruction. Like Schumpeter destruction, for Heidegger, is not an end in itself but is about re-enchanting being. It is focused on uncovering a vitality in experience that is lost when life is reduced to the repetition of ritual. Referring to his hero-poet, Heidegger maintains that where the danger is , so the saving power grows, that is, where the destruction is, so the possibilities for creativity grow.

It would be interesting to situate Nietzsche's call for a re-evaluation of all values in the context of Welch, Schumpeter and Heidegger. For it is also a form of creative destruction. It is hard not to think of Nietzsche in the face of the constant generation of the new; the valley of death and the apocalyptic nature of capitalism. For it is one thing to celebrate the new but who or what is it that is driving the dynamism and fascination with the new in the market place? Is it we who are driving it or are we driven by it? Nietzsche was the philosopher who proclaimed the "death of God." This means not only the death of God but the death of any foundation upon which we can rely. Because, in the wake of the death of God, society has no foundation upon which it can rely, there is no stability or sense of continuity in society. There is nothing to hold onto. Everything is changing. Everything is new. The "new" seems to have become the "new" god – forever driving us to change and reinvent ourselves. Yet what is the value of the new? Should we assume that it is valuable in and of itself? Until we raise the question of the new in this way, we will be driven by it rather than drivers of it.

However, the significance of Nietzsche in the context of the logic of destruction is for another time. I would like to continue exploring the relationship between Heidegger and Welch.

8
How Touchy Feely is Jack Welch?

I

Under the spell of scientific views of management, business has tended to think of itself as an objective and rational process based on the analysis of data. Welch, however, disputes this: "I hope you understand that business is a series of trial-and-error. It's not a great science. It's just moving the ball forward, and nobody has any great formula."

Underlying the process of being able to move "the ball forward" is, from Welch's perspective a feeling for business – or what I shall call "business feel." Highlighting the significance of business feel in the context of his philosophy, he says:" More often than not, business is smell, feel, and touch as much as or more than numbers. If we wait for the perfect answer, the world will pass us by." (Welch, 2001, p. 18) Often Welch's guide in developing the culture of GE was not a rational plan but what he calls a "feel" for what he wanted GE to look like. In his early days of reconstructing GE, he says that he had no blue print for what he wanted GE to look like but only a feel: "I did know what I wanted the company to "feel" like. I wasn't calling it culture in those days, but that's what it was." (Welch, 2001, p. 92)

These are not once off comments but can be clearly seen in his reflections on his views of organisations. At times, he speaks of his desire to establish the mood of a "family feel" for GE. He also speaks about the "feeling of thinking" that is required for organisational transformation. He speaks about the importance of the "spirit" of GE and the role that the absence of "spirit" plays in the degeneration of GE. Another of Welch's favored notions is the idea of "passion" which he contrasts with the cold and rigid language of a bureaucracy. He is always highly attuned to the mood of the environment in which he is in. Even when he becomes vice president of GE, he is attuned to the atmosphere at corporate headquarters, an atmosphere that he finds cold and distant.

Welch is also always aware of the effects of the mood of the organisation on activity within the organisation. He believes that the mood affects the quality of work; that the disengaged atmosphere of a bureaucracy creates an atmosphere in which people are not committed to and involved in their work but go through the motions of working. This has devastating affects on the organisation. Welch believes that a sense of passion is vital for achieving excellence at work; that only as people are passionate about their work do they care for and become involved in their work. The over regulation of bureaucratic thinking had deprived work of its passion and thus taken out the element of care for the work. It had created a mood of indifference.

Welch contrasts knowledge based on business feel with knowledge gained from objective data. While the latter has its uses, it is not the only form of knowledge but is limited and in fact has too strong a hold on corporate life: "Head quarters loved data, and it took years to stop the financial people from overanalysing it." (Welch, 2001, p. 135) Of course there is a reason why headquarters would like data. It is objective, measurable, verifiable and quantifiable. Business feel, on the other hand, cannot be represented in neat little boxes. It belongs to the "soft" skills rather than in the realm of the hard skills. Be this as it may, from Welch's perspective, a leader who does not have an appreciation or feel for the business, deprives the business of its passion and vitality: "No matter what we put in our books – and we put everything in them – it's not simply the binders that count. What counts is the passion and intensity everyone brings to the table." There is a certain dimension of attunement that objective knowledge does not make accessible but for which one needs a feeling. Welch illustrates this in his awareness of the limits of a resume: "A resume did not tell me much about the inner hunger. I had to feel it." (Welch, 2001, p. 54)

The danger with defining business in only objective and quantifiable terms is not only a loss of passion but also a loss of attunement to the environment both within the organisation and in which the organisation is situated. For it is in terms of our feel for the environment that we read and make sense of the environments. It is in terms of our feel that we scan and are attentive to the environment. While Welch does not articulate the notion of business feel in terms of worry or anxiety (as we have seen others such as George Soros and Andrew Grove do), frustration becomes the central emotion for him. Frustration with the traditional ways of doing things at GE both alerted him to the need for a transformation in the business practices of GE, motivated him to change GE and inspired him to change GE in the face of tremendous opposition and doubt. His experience of frustration with GE prevented him from taking the practices of GE for granted and gave him insight into GE. It enabled him to "care" for GE.

Patricia Benner in her work on Heidegger and nursing has a very illuminating way of expressing the relationship between feel and technique. She uses the example of good parenting and maintains that while techniques can be useful for good parenting, technique without a sense of caring for the children is no good. She maintains that we need to care for the children in order to use the techniques effectively. For if we do not care for the children we will not even notice what needs to get done. Expressing this in her words she says: "Parenting techniques do not work unless a basic level of attachment and caring exists. In fact, parenting techniques are not even useful or possible unless the parent is engaged in the parenting situation through caring. But for those already involved in caring for and about particular children with particular concerns, some techniques will show up as more desirable and workable than others." (Benner and Wrubel, 1989, p. 4)

Welch is saying something similar in the context of business feel. Unless we are attuned to the environment in which we are working the techniques, the numbers, the rationality are of no use. We need to be able to care in order to notice things in our environment. And in order to be successful in business we need to be able to notice things. On a number of occasions he highlights the importance of caring. For example he says that as a leader "You've got to be able to energize people. You've got to care about them; they have to believe that you care about them."

It is care which keeps us alert, enables us to notice possibilities. This is why Ricardo Semler of Semco can say: "We are thrilled that our workers are self-governing and self-managing. It means they **care** about their jobs and about their company, and that's good for all of us." (Semler, 1993) The same point can be made in terms of management techniques: unless we care for the context in which we are working, no amount of management techniques will help – because we cannot even notice what needs to be noticed. When the techniques are situated in the context of care, they become embodied and responsive to the particularities of the situation. Welch was highly critical of those dimensions of scientific management which reduced the training and practices of managers to techniques.

It is interesting to see the "hard" man of business talking about the "soft" skills of business. For, as we know talk about feel in business is identified as a "soft skill." Jack Welch, as we know, is anything but a "soft man" – he can and has been pretty "hard" at times, being for a long time called "Neutron Jack" for laying off thousands of employees. How does someone who can be hard, identify the soft skills as underlying his leadership know how? At the very least this contradiction forces us to reconsider what we mean by the soft skills. It calls us to take seriously and understand the role of business "feel" in detail. In the business context, the criterion in terms of which soft in contrast to hard is defined is the notion of quantification. What is quantifiable is "hard." What is not quantifiable is soft. "Hard" has nothing to do with strength of character. (In fact it obliterates all talk of strength of character because the idea of strength of character is not quantifiable, and thus is in fact not discussable in a meaningful way). Yet there is no doubt that being hard or being tough are emotions and thus part of the soft skills of business. So to say that Welch was hard in the soft skills is no contradiction, for being emotionally tough – or even ruthless – is still emotional, that is, part of the soft skills.

Caring as we in the "West" are accustomed to think of it, is something "feminine," and along with that "weak." It is, along with the feminine, degraded. Yet what we are seeing in Welch is that caring is vital for a sense of business feel and attunement. In fact, it is neither "soft" nor "hard" in the sense of the word. Firing people, being called Neutron Jack are not soft. The significance of caring, business feel, being attuned to the situation is that they are all vital for making discerning judgments in a situation. They allow us to notice things in the environment – new possibilities for example – and respond as we notice. Sometimes we need to respond in a gentle way and sometimes we need to respond with fierce resolve and determination – or to use a phrase of Welch, we need to be able to know when to "hug" and when to "kick." (Welch, 2001, p. 30) Only if we care are we able to make such judgments. Caring is thus neither simply being kind to others nor being hard on others. It is the process of being attuned or attentive to the situation.

The contrary of caring today is not being "hard" but being indifferent. The state of indifference is one of being emotionally distanced and disengaged from the work that one is involved in. It is a state in which one is attuned in a mechanical and routine like way to the task at hand. The experience of indifference and the relationship between care and indifference are well brought out in the following description of a teacher in a classroom. "There has been much debate about what teachers should and shouldn't be doing, and implicit in it is the suggestion that they should be in tune with the children, listening to them, and caring about their needs. Yet the way to survive in the present school situation is the reverse. Many teachers build great walls of defence around themselves, teaching subjects in a cold and formal way, year after year, and distancing themselves from the children. They 'survive.'" (Woods, 1989, p. 94)

The same could be said of management, that is, that the way to survive is through not caring, but by managing in a way that is cold, formal and disengaged. In fact this is what Welch says he cannot stand in management: "I simply dislike the traits that have come to be associated with 'managing' – controlling, stifling people, keeping them in the dark, wasting their time on trivia and reports. Breathing down their necks. ... The word manager has too often come to be synonymous with control – cold, uncaring, button-down, passionless. I never associate the word passion with the word manager, and I've never seen a leader without it." (Lowe, 2001, p. 30)

From Welch's perspective the difference between leaders and managers is a difference between management as cold and disengaged whereas leaders, in spite of obstacles in their environment, are attuned and caring. They bring out in people and their environment the potential and possibilities which are not immediately obvious. Managers, because they are disengaged and emotionally distanced are not present in an environment in such a way that they can pick up on possibilities. They cannot, from Welch's perspective, nurture self-confidence in people. They are far too attuned to the data; they operate on a disengaged rational dimension rather than in terms of the business feel needed to notice possibilities and opportunities in an environment. The GE that Welch had grown up in promoted an attitude of indifference: "The bigger the business, the less engaged people seemed to be. From the forklift drivers in a factory to the engineers packed in cubicles, too many people were just going through the motions." (Welch, 2001, p. 99)

For Welch caring is to be contrasted with a disengaged and disembodied rationalist and scientific approach to management which is concerned only with the data, the numbers and not with the "feel" behind the numbers. Throughout Welch's stay at GE, he always fought the tendency of GE staff to move into a disengaged position in which their concern was primarily with the data and not with an attunement to the situation of their business. In contrast to a disengaged rationality, Welch wanted a mood of what he calls "family feel" to permeate GE.

Thus we begin to appreciate the limits of a disengaged rational approach to business. No matter how rational we are – rationality alone will not enable us to be attuned to the environment in which we are situated. We have all heard of the absent minded professor who in his study is highly rational but is absent – or not attuned to the environment in which he or she is situated. To make sense of attunement, we need to go beyond the idea of business as rationally understood. We need to embrace the notions of attunement, of caring and of business feel.

It should be noted that this does not in anyway mean a rejection of rationality as such. It means that rationality cannot be the underlying construct through which to make sense of organisational activity and business life in general. Rationality needs to be situated in the context of a concerned attunement, in the context of business feel – just as technique does. It is one amongst a number of ways of being attuned. It is valuable under certain conditions but not under others.

A theme that will be picked up on a subsequent chapter but is worth mentioning at this point is that education and training for business has focused almost exclusively on the quantifiable dimensions of business and not the "business feel" or caring attunement underpinning business. This needs to shift.

II

The theme of "feel" is central to the philosophy of Martin Heidegger. Just like Welch, he allows us to distinguish between two different types of knowledge, what I shall call "cognitive knowledge" and "pragmatic know-ledge" or, in the context of Welch business feel. Just as in the case of Welch, cognitive knowledge is based on the analysis of data. It breaks the object into its smallest parts. It is objective, rational and theoretical. It implies the detachment of a scientist, looking at and observing the world from a distance.

Pragmatic knowledge, on the other hand, implies an involvement in the world. It is the feeling for something that we gain by being involved in it – the feeling that we gain for a hammer by using it; the feeling for riding a bicycle that we gain by riding it. From Heidegger's perspective we gain a sense of familiarity with something by using it. The more we use something the more familiar we become with it. The idea of a feeling for something is thus grounded for Heidegger in a sense of familiarity with that thing. Our feeling for the business thus emerges out of our sense of familiarity with the business. Although not in the area of business, an interesting example of the significance of a "feeling for" something is the perspective of a German tank commander in the second world war, Erwin Rommel. He believed that his success as a commander depended not so much on his cognitive knowledge but on what he called fingerspitzengefuhl" which is described as "a sort of sixth sense, an intuition in his fingers." (Passagen) He needed to feel his enemy with his fingers. Only as he was able to feel his enemy with his fingers did he get a sense of the enemy. And only through getting a sense of his enemy was he able to strategise: "Rommel led his forces from the front, observing the battle from his Storch aircraft, which with his "Fingerspitzengefuhl" a feel in his fingertips for the ebb and flow of battle, made it possible to direct quick thrusts into the belly of the British, leaving open flanks and relying on speed and shock to freeze his enemy while he cut into its flanks." (World of Strategy, 2003)

Central to Rommel's military feel was an appreciation of the limits of a disengaged cognitive attitude to warfare. As one commentator put it: "'No admiral ever won a naval battle from a shore base,' he said, fond as he was of comparing desert combat to warfare at sea. His split second ingenuity under fire often violated textbook principles of military tactics and threw his enemy into confusion. He was a master of the unexpected, with a gift for improvisation."

In Heidegger's terms, it was the sense of familiarity that he gained by feeling the enemy that formed the basis of his "military feel." It was the basis of his military strategising. It should be noted that this notion of "feeling" does not imply anything "soft." In a military situation we cannot afford to be soft. His military feel rather than being "mushy" was the basis of his attunement, his attentiveness to the situation. Without such atten-tiveness or attunement he would not be able to notice possibilities and opportunities in his environment. It is feel that forms the basis of atten-tiveness and attentiveness is vital to noticing the winds of change.

Heidegger takes his argument a step further and claims that not only is pragmatic knowledge different from cognitive knowledge but pragmatic knowledge cannot be expressed and evaluated in cognitive terms. The "feeling" for something cannot be analysed – broken down into smaller parts. It is not reducible to anything else. He believed that we cannot capture the feeling of familiarity that comes from using something in abstract and quantifiable terms. We cannot express the feeling for using a hammer in quantifiable terms. We cannot express the feeling for playing a guitar in quantifiable terms. To be sure, we can define a hammer or guitar in quantifiable terms. We can analyse the "hammer" or the "guitar." We can form in cognitive terms an appreciation of the properties of a guitar or hammer but the feeling of familiarity is not something that can be analysed or broken down into parts. It is an irreducible whole.

Continuing his argument, Heidegger maintains that no amount of cognitive knowledge can convey the feeling for something that is attained by using that thing. We need to use a thing to develop a feeling for it. The feeling for something cannot be conveyed to us through a cognitive explanation. We cannot convey the feeling for a hammer through language. There are thus certain kinds of knowledge that cannot be learnt cognitively. Anything that has to do with using something or being involved with something cannot be gained cognitively. We cannot convey the sense or familiarity that is gained by being involved in something in a cognitive way.

This same argument applies to our relationship to other people. The sense of familiarity that we get by being involved with other people is different from a knowledge that is gained by simply thinking about other people. The more familiar we become with them, the more we develop a "feel for" them or a sense of them. We become attuned to others through our involvement with them.

Heidegger then asks us to take a step back and examine the importance of the idea of "being familiar" with something. What does it mean to be familiar with something? For Heidegger when we are familiar with something we know our way about; we have "know how," we are in charge. We can make sense of our world. We can read situations in which we find ourselves. He expresses this by saying that through familiarity we establish a sense of being at home in the world. "Home" for Heidegger is not primarily a physical structure. It is the sense of knowing our way about. It is being able to read and make sense of the world. More than this, it is the feeling of being able to make sense of ourselves. This is because, for Heidegger, our sense of who we are as people emerges through the way in which we are involved in the world. When we use things we do not only get a sense of familiarity with the thing being used but a sense of who we are emerges from our using things. For example, when, as a craftsman, we use a hammer not only do we get a feeling for the hammer but the hammer begins to shape our hand as well. Our hands become lined by extensive use of the hammer. When we play the guitar not only do we get a sense of the guitar but our fingers are themselves transformed by our playing the guitar.

Taking this point a step further our identities are formed by the way in which we use things and are involved in the world. Bob Joss has exemplified this point in the context of leadership when he says that we become a leader through the ways in which we are involved in the world: "It is not for leaders to define themselves. Therefore, if you actively set out to be a leader, you will probably fail because you will be too self-focused. Leaders set out to accomplish some task or goal, and it is through the successive experiences of trying to achieve those tasks that leaders are made." (Joss, 2000)

A person's identity as a leader emerges through the way in which they are involved in the world. For example, as much as Jack Welch transformed GE, Welch's identity was formed by his involvement in GE. "Jack Welch," the "turn-around" artist of GE did not exist before he transformed GE. His identity as "Neutron Jack" emerged out of the way in which he was involved in GE. Even Jack Welch's philosophy emerged out of his involvement with GE. His philosophy emerged as a way of coming to terms with his frustration at GE. He did not have a philosophy which he then applied to GE. It came out of his involvement in GE – or what he calls his "journey" in GE.

For Heidegger there is no identity outside of a person's involvement in the world. It is how I am involved in the world that shapes who I am. This is true not only for Jack Welch but for all our identities; whether I am a businessperson, a professional, a tradesman or husband or father – in each case my identity emerges out of the sense or feeling that I develop for being involved in these activities. As I engage in the activities of being a teacher I develop a sense of what it means to be a teacher. As I develop this sense, my identity as a teacher is formed.

Heidegger takes this a step further and claims that it is not only our identities that are established through our involvements but our world is created in this way. This point is made most explicitly by TS Elliot who says that culture is formed through the way in which we are involved in the world: "Culture is the one thing that we cannot deliberately aim at. It is the product of a variety of more or less harmonious activities, each pursued for its own sake: the artist must concentrate upon his canvas, the poet upon his typewriter, the civil servant upon the just settlement of particular problems as they present themselves upon his desk, each according to the situation in which he finds himself." (Elliot, 1970, p. 62)

In the above quotation, Elliot allows us to see that culture is formed through the way people are involved in their tasks. It is formed almost as a by-product of their involvements in their tasks. Henry Ford is often cited as an example of someone who created a culture through a way of being involved in the world. As Fernando Flores has expressed it: "Henry Ford was not designing cars. Henry Ford was designing cities. He was designing economies. He was designing a form of life." Of course he was not intentionally designing cities – far from it but through the form of involvements that the mass production of cars gave rise to, a whole world was created. As Richard Farson has put it: "The automobile has created not just modern cities but also their opposite, namely suburbs. ... The existence of automobiles has changed our courtship patterns, our sexual practices and especially our environment." (Flores, 1997)

From Heidegger's perspective the sense or feeling for a culture cannot be gained simply by thinking about it but requires the familiarity that comes from involvement. The more familiar we are with a culture, the more of the nuances we can see and feel in the culture. The same point would apply to an understanding of the notion of "corporate culture." It is by being involved in an organisation's culture that we develop a familiarity with it and thus a feeling for it. The more familiar we become with a culture, the more we can see in it. No amount of thinking about the culture from the outside will yield the insight that comes through familiarity from involvement in the culture. By being in the culture we develop a sense or familiarity with it.

In accounting for Welch's insight into GE, it is often said that Welch had an "insider's knowledge" of GE. In Heideggerian terms what this means is that he had a non-cognitive, non-analytic knowledge of GE. This knowledge was based on a feeling for GE. The feeling for GE emerged out of his involvement in GE. Through his involvement in GE he became familiar with GE. Through his familiarity with GE he was able to see GE in a way that someone who had only a cognitive knowledge of GE was not able to see. In Heidegger's language, his familiarity with GE "disclosed" GE to him in a way that someone who was not involved in GE did not have access to. For example, someone coming from Mars will not be able to see the world in the way that humans do because from Heidegger's perspective, they are not familiar with the world in the same way as we are. They have not been involved in the world in the way that we have. Because we have been involved in and are familiar with the world in a certain way, the world is disclosed to us in a certain way. We can read the world through the way in which we are familiar with it. If we were not familiar with the world, we would not be able to read it. Reading, making sense of the world, being able to notice things in the world – all presuppose a way of being familiar with the world based on our sense of involvement in the world.

From Heidegger's perspective no amount of cognitive reasoning can give us this sense of familiarity with the world. This means that no perspective from the outside can see what we see in the world from the inside; no amount of scientific or rational analysis of our world from the outside will reveal the world in the way it is disclosed from the inside. Jack Welch's insider knowledge opened the world of GE to him in a way that it could not be opened from the disengaged outsider's perspective – whether this be the perspective of a consultant or social scientist.

Heidegger is making clear that knowledge gained through involvement cannot always be accounted for in theoretical terms and that it is mistaken to believe that theoretical knowledge is superior to experiential knowledge. The sense of familiarity established through involvement – through experience – cannot be reduced to theoretical terms. Another way of putting this is to say that we do not acquire conventions or habits for doing things in a cognitive way. We acquire our conventions in an implicit way, through our ways of acting and interacting in our own culture. The conventions in terms of which we make sense of experience are not gained in a cognitive way but are formed through the sense of familiarity that emerges out of our ways of being involved in the world. We do not, for example, sit down as children with a dictionary and learn the meaning of "mum" and "dad." It is in the context of our experiences with, for example, our parents that we acquire the meaning of "mum" and "dad." We may well go to a dictionary to formalise the meaning of these words but we acquire a sense of these words through being involved with mums and dads.

Similarly, the conventions underpinning the roles that we may play in life are not acquired in an explicit way but emerge out of the familiarity gained by being involved in the world. The role of being a child is acquired not by explicit thought but by being a child. Although we may study to be a doctor at university, the "know how" involved in being a doctor emerges in the context of our practice as a doctor; our sense of what it means to be a manager emerges out of the practice of management. The sense or know-how that emerges out of our practice cannot be taught to anyone else in a purely cognitive mode. It is the feeling of familiarity that arises as we practice our profession. We acquire our sense of the roles that we play by being involved in those roles.

For Heidegger, it is not only the conventions of behaviour that are defined through our involvement. Our conventions of thought are also defined through the way in which we are involved in the world. The conceptual categories in terms of which we think, the language in which we think, the way in which we reason all emerge out of the conventions in which we have been socialised – as was demonstrated in the way in which children acquire the sense of "mum" and "dad." These values we aspire to emerge out of the way we are involved in the world.

Because we do not acquire our conventions for behaving and thinking in a cognitive way, we have what Heidegger calls an "average everyday" understanding of our conventions. This means that, at best, we have a "common sense" understanding of our own conventions. We do not tend to think about them but to think and act in terms of them. They form the taken for granted horizon in terms of which we think and act in the world. We get "married," we go to "work," look for a "job," "go out" and have "fun" on a "Saturday evening" because that is the way in which we do things. We go to the movies, go shopping, on a picnic because that is the way of doing things. We do not tend to think of the meaning or purpose of going to the movies or of going to work – we tend to need to get on with the job rather than thinking about getting on with the job. Because our conventions guide our activity and thinking without themselves being the explicit focus of our thinking, we have a common sense understanding of them. They form the background in terms of which we engage in the world. They are not the foreground. And, indeed, from a Heideggerian perspective, it would be dangerous if they were constantly in the foreground of our attention. For then we would never get on with doing anything but would be constantly preoccupied with the meaning of our conventions.

However, Heidegger is by no means an "experientialist" privileging experience above thoughtful attunement and believing that all knowledge derives from experience. Experience, from the Heideggerian perspective has its own form of blindness. There are limits to the value of operating purely out of familiar ways of being involved in the world. Relating this to the context of Welch, it could be maintained that in Heideggerian terms knowledge through familiarity was not enough to transform GE. For it could reasonably be maintained that many people in GE were familiar with GE but did not transform it. Indeed many who were familiar with it, did not have insight into GE. This suggests that while familiarity may be a necessary condition of insider's insight into GE, it is not a sufficient condition. From Heidegger's perspective the additional step that is required is a care for GE. We can be familiar with something but not care for it, that is we can be complacent in our familiar way of doing things. We become so habituated to a way of doing things, that we cease to be attentive or to notice our own complacency.

To function in our familiar ways of doing things is to function within our "comfort zone." In our comfort zone we tend to lose our sensitivity to the world outside of our way of functioning; we tend to be impervious to the changes in the context outside of us and thus do not notice how we need to change in response to changing circumstances. We tend to function on automatic in a routine and repetitive way. We tend to do things because that is the "way in which things get done." In this way we lose touch with the original experience for doing things in the particular way we do them. This is often the case in organisations which tend to be founded on the experience of its creators or heroes. As they are creating the way of being of the organisation there is a vitality underlying the rituals and reasons they create for the organisation. However, as time progresses the rituals and reasons become ends in themselves and the organisation loses the vitality – the sense of spirit – underlying the rituals and reasons.

In this context we do things without having a firm sense of why we are doing what we are doing.

A second limitation of the familiar for Heidegger is that every mode of being familiar with the world allows us to see and act in the world in one way and not others. To put this in Heidegger's language, every way of being familiar with the world "discloses" the world in one way and "closes" it off in other ways. We can read the world from our perspective and not from others. We are locked within our Platonic caves and cannot see other possibilities. It is vital in times of change to be able to go beyond our familiar ways of seeing the world.

A third danger of familiarity is that we tend to see our ways of being familiar with the world not as one amongst others but as a privileged way of relating to the world. We tend to think that the way in which we do things is the way in which things are. It is the "best" if not only way of doing things – the most natural way of doing things. To think in this way closes off new possibilities and tends to be dismissive of other ways of doing things.

But perhaps most importantly from the Heideggerian perspective, we cannot assume that the world will remain familiar, that to put it in the Humian language developed in chapter four we cannot assume that the future will repeat the past – the very basis for stability. In fact Heidegger tells us that the future will not always repeat the past. There will always be moments in which the future disrupts the past.

Heidegger contrasts the experience of being familiar with the world with experiences of feeling strange in the world. Experiences of strangeness refer to those moments in which we cannot take our familiar ways of doing things for granted but as yet do not have a new way of doing things. It is the experience of being caught between the old and the new. The death of a loved one is occasion on which our habitual ways of doing things are disrupted and so for Heidegger is a moment in which we experience the strangeness of being. Going to a foreign land involves an experience of strangeness for here we see ways of doing things that are other than ours and we do not have the conventions for reading the situations of the new culture. Things seem strange and we do not know how to account for this strangeness. In chapter one we saw the effect of the disruption of the familiar. There we saw how when our familiar cultural patterns for social distancing are disrupted we come to notice them. When we are at home in our own culture, we tend not to notice our own ways of relating to people. It is when we bump up against different ways of relating that we come to be aware of our own ways of doing things. What was implicit now becomes explicit.

9
Welch's Outsiders Perspective from the Inside

I

In many ways Welch's philosophy emerged out of the way in which he responded to his not fitting into the culture of GE. He felt like an outsider in the culture of GE. For in his early years at GE, Welch was deeply disillusioned with the GE ways of doing things. It was within the first year of being at GE that, as he puts it "... The romance that brought me to GE was evaporating." (Welch, 2001, p. 22) He could not accept the GE way of doing things. He could not find a home for himself in GE. So frustrated was he with the GE way of doing things that he decided to leave GE – even though, it seems, that he did not want to leave GE.

It is important to highlight that he was "besides himself" with frustration. GE's ways of doing things were driving him "crazy." He was not a little crazy but was consumed by a frustration with the GE way of doing things. In philosophical terms that go right back to Plato to be "besides himself" with fury or frustration is to be in a state of mind that is ready to be philosophical. For, from this perspective philosophy begins in those emotional states that take us "outside ourselves." It is when we are "beside ourselves" or "outside of ourselves" that we are no longer trapped in the common sense ways of doing things. We are outside of common sense. It is precisely by being outside of common sense that we come to experience the limitations of the common sense way of doing things. Welch does sometimes refer to himself as being "mad" in the Platonic way of being outside of the customs and conventional ways of doing things: "One of the things about leadership is that you cannot be a moderate, balanced, thoughtful, careful articulator of policy. You've got to be on the lunatic fringe." (Welch, 1997)

Fury and frustration are moods that are well placed to take us "outside of common sense." Interestingly enough Welch's view at this point is not so different from Anita Roddick's view of entrepreneurship: ""An effective woman entrepreneur is a combination of a crazy person with a delinquent mind". (Roddick, 1996) In both cases being on the lunatic fringe or being a delinquent should not be seen in a clinical but in a philosophical sense of standing outside of the common sense ways of doing things. By standing outside of common sense the world appears, is disclosed in a different kind of way.

However, I am jumping the gun. Because of his frustration with the GE way of doing things, Jack Welch could not, in his early days at GE, take the common sense ways of doing things at GE for granted. He could not simply get on with the work but was attuned to and questioning the ways in which GE worked – so much so that he wanted to leave. As Welch was about to leave GE, he was persuaded to stay at GE. Staying at GE, however, did not resolve the frustration he felt at GE. He did not simply fit into GE but was able to stay in GE while feeling antagonistic towards it. This was not an easy or comfortable position in which to be. He was caught in a contradiction. As he says, he neither wanted to continually be a critic of GE nor did he want to lose himself by playing at being a "yes" man. He was constantly torn between the desire to express himself and the desire to get on with the job. Sometimes he expressed himself and on other occasions he shut himself up. Describing this experience he says: "In my early years, I tried desperately to be honest with myself, to fight the bureaucratic pomposity, even if it meant that I wouldn't succeed at GE. I also remember the tremendous pressure to be someone I wasn't. I sometimes played the game." (Welch, 2001, p. 47)

In Heideggerian terms Welch's not fitting in but remaining within GE is crucial for deepening his appreciation both of GE and of his own perspective on GE. For it is as an outsider who remains inside that he can see things in GE that those who are at home in the culture cannot see. It is as an outsider on the inside that he can refine and deepen his appreciation of GE conventions for doing things. If as outsider he simply left GE, he would not have had an opportunity to deepen his understanding of GE. And as someone who is simply on the inside, he would not be able to see the familiar and taken for granted conventions for doing things. The trick was to remain as an outsider on the inside. And Welch had the resolve to do this.

The tension between being on the inside and not fitting in, also enabled Welch to develop an appreciation of the assumptions in terms of which he was disillusioned and frustrated with GE. For when we are frustrated with something, we are frustrated with it in terms of something else. Welch was not frustrated with GE from a neutral position. There were certain expectations and values which he held that encouraged him to experience GE as frustrating. To be sure, these were not clear and developed at the outset but became clear and crisp as he dwelt in the tension of being an outsider on the inside. His critical perspective on the habitual ways of doing things at GE, enabled him to see his own way of seeing GE.

What shocked Welch in his early days at GE was the culture of indifference. He saw the source of the indifference as lying in standardisation. In order to convey Welch's experience of standardisation rather than just the concept of it, I will quote at length from his autobiography: "In 1961, I had been working at GE for a year as an engineer making $10,500 when my boss handed me a $1,000 raise. I was okay with it – until I found later that day that I got exactly what all four of us sharing an office received. I thought I deserved more than the "standard" increase. I felt trapped in the pile near the bottom of a big organisation. I wanted out. ... The standard predetermined raise was just a part of my irritation at what I saw as the company's stingy behaviour. ... The "standard" $1000 raise was the last straw." (Welch, 2001, p. 21)

That everyone was treated in a standard way, indicated, to Welch, a deep sense of indifference in the organisation. This sense of indifference was to be found on multiple levels within the organisation. It was to be found in the way in which senior and middle management interacted with each other. It was to be found in the way in which managers in GE thought about their business, making as Welch would comment presentations in a mechanical and routine way rather than being existentially involved in and passionate about their work. The attitude of indifference permeated the entire organisation. Meetings, reviews, conferences all were just going through the motions of doing things.

Welch's response to standardisation and indifference was not disengaged and analytical. It was passionate and guttural. In coming to terms with his fury and madness he begins to develop his own perspective on GE, a perspective which involves terms such as differentiation and caring.

Whereas standardisation had promoted an attitude of indifference, differentiation enables an attunement to, what Welch called, the "real stars. " It allows for a care and attunement to the human dimension of the organisation. This is not always care in the sense of "kindness" but care in the sense of discernment. For to differentiate is to be able to notice and distinguish between the "best" and the "ineffective." To be able to make such a distinction requires an attunement to the workforce – one that is absent in a standardised response. It is also in this context that "business feel" becomes important. For standardisation has robbed work of its feel, reducing it to a disembodied routine. Welch has always wanted to put the feel back into business.

As his venom for indifference grew, so his perspective on differentiation became more and more refined. He did not know in advance of his encounter with standardisation that he had a strong commitment to differentiation. It was not on his "philosophical radar." And so he could not think it out in abstraction. It was in the context of his experience at GE that it began to emerge. Only once he came to see what drove him mad, could he begin to unpack the terms in which he did not like what he did not like: "I was lucky to get out of the pile [of standardisation] and learn [the value of differentiation] [in] my very first year." (Welch, 2001, p. 25)

Thus we begin to see how Welch's philosophy develops – not by abstract thought but by insights formed in the field of experience. It was through his immersing himself in the field of GE experience that Welch bumped up against the limits of GE. The disruption at these limits enabled him to become attuned both to the habitual, common sense ways of doing things as well as to develop the framework for an alternative way of doing things. For his frustration enabled him not only to see what was wrong with the culture but to see the terms in which he felt the system to be wrong.

Frustration is a mood that is uniquely placed to do this. Because when we are frustrated with something we can neither let it go nor simply accept it. We are caught in a tug of war about it. Welch could neither leave nor simply be at home in GE. He stayed with his frustration in order not only to examine GE as an institution with which he was frustrated but to unpack the terms in which he was frustrated with GE, the terms which would become the basis of his vision for GE.

Ironically then the frustration which nearly led Welch to leave GE is in Heideggerian terms the basis of his attunement to GE. The frustration that nearly led to his leaving GE was also the condition in terms of which he could gain a "helicopter" perspective into GE. Paradoxically Welch's frustration also indicated how attuned to GE he was. For to be frustrated with something shows an involvement in something. We can only be frustrated with what we are attuned to. We do not get frustrated with what we are not attuned to. This makes sense in the Heideggerian terms developed by Patricia Benner when she says that for Welch GE would not "show up as [frustrating] unless [it] mattered. If the person (Welch) does not care, an event (GE) cannot be [frustrating]." (Benner and Wrubel, 1989, p. 1)

Although Welch was on the verge of leaving GE, he was never indifferent to GE. He had a very powerful emotional response to GE – right from the very beginning. Paradoxically, many of those who stayed at GE, who accepted the GE way of doing things were indifferent to GE. For they did not care about the culture of indifference that permeated GE. They simply got on with the job. They were indifferent to the culture of indifference that permeated GE. They did not challenge the culture of indifference. It guided their activities in GE without becoming an explicit theme of concern.

Whereas for most employees the GE way of doing things formed the background against which they did things, for Welch, in his early days of being in GE, the GE way of doing things had become the foreground. Whereas most of the employees were simply involved in doing their work, Welch was finely attuned to the implicit culture of the workplace. Thus while most employees could "get on with the job" within the context of the culture of GE, they did not make the culture an explicit theme of concern. They accepted it as the common sense way of doing things. He was continually caught in a tension between getting on with the job and being attuned in a critical way to the way in which GE did things.

Michael Gerber has developed an idea which helps clarify the position of Jack Welch. He maintains that we need to distinguish between working "in" our business and working "on" our business. We work in our business when we are simply absorbed in the work that we are doing. We get on with the job. We work "on" our business, when we stand back from "getting on with the job" to think and reflect on our way of working in the business, that is to think about our ways of doing things. For the most part, he maintains we tend to be involved "in" our work rather than being concerned with reflecting "on" work. What we see in Welch as an employee of GE is that he was caught in simultaneously being involved in the work and was concerned with reflecting "on" the GE way of doing things. Whereas most of his fellow employees were simply concerned with getting on with the job, he had a dual attunement. Putting this in Heideggerian terms, whereas his fellow employees simply got on with the job, Welch was attuned to the conventions or common sense culture which underpinned the GE way of getting on with the job.

It is crucial to understand that the switch between working in and on the job did not happen in a routine way. We cannot simply switch our minds from working "in" a job to reflecting "on" our way of working in the job. From the Heideggerian perspective, it is a disruption in our way of doing things that enables the shift from working in a job to reflecting on our way of working to take place. It was Welch's frustration with GE's way of doing things that enabled him to move from a position of being involved "in" the work to reflecting "on" the GE way of doing things. His frustration took him out of a taken for granted relationship to GE's way of doing things. It made the taken for granted common sense conventions explicit.

Furthermore, Welch's attitude towards this frustration enabled this transition to be a constructive rather than a destructive experience. Rather than attempting to resolve the frustration, Welch was able to "dwell" in the frustration. Once he decided to stay at GE, he also stayed in the contradiction between his desire to be at GE and his frustration with GE's way of doing things. For he could not settle down at GE and was able to stay in an unsettled state. This unsettled state was both a virtue and a vice. While he constantly risked losing himself in GE, he was also able to see things through the eyes of his frustration that others were not able to see.

Thus we see that Welch's frustration starts off with specific incidents at GE; incidents in which he rallies against GE's practices of standardisation. Throughout his years at GE this frustration does not go away but refines his critique of existing GE conventions and provides the basis for an alternative vision of GE. The frustration extends its scope to not only include

GE but the conventions and practices of management which, in general is dominated by a scientific management account of organisations. Even when, as CEO of GE he goes about reconstructing GE, it is frustration with the standardisation of bureaucracy that drives him through moments of uncertainty. It is his hatred of bureaucracy that allows him to deal, in a resolute way with those who criticise and seek to undermine him. Thus he says that he hated being thought of as "Neutron Jack" but "I hated bureaucracy and waste even more. The data-obsessed headquarters and the low margins ... were equally offensive." (Welch, 2001, p. 125)

Again the language is strong and his conviction is again underpinned by a mood or business feel. We have already seen how central mood is to philosophical experience, that it underpins the experience of disruption. In the context of Welch what we can say is that the passion which drove him both to deconstruct and reconstruct GE was a deep frustration with GE, a frustration which did not let him rest or find an escape from but which tormented him in such a way that he could neither simply stay in nor leave GE but was released only when he began to reconstruct GE.

Summarising the central theme: In Heideggerian terms our "feeling" or way of caring shapes what we do and do not see in a situation. Parents who care will be able to see what needs to be done for their children. Parents who are indifferent will not notice what needs to be done. Similarly Welch's feeling of frustration attunes him to taken for granted dimensions in GE. It was in terms of Welch's attunement to GE that he was able to see things in GE that those who were indifferent to the indifference were not able to see. His attunement to the culture of indifference at GE enabled him in the long run to shift the culture of indifference from the margins or background of concern at GE to the foreground of concern at GE. He shifted it from the margins to the foreground when he became CEO of GE. Now nobody would be able to be indifferent to the culture of indifference. The practices used by Welch to shift the culture of indifference from the margins to the centre of attention at GE will be discussed further on. For now the philosophy that emerges out of Welch's being beside himself in GE will continue to be developed.

We can also see that a feel for something reveals things about that thing that cannot be gained through detached observation. Welch in the context of his feel for GE could see things that those operating out of a detached and analytic perspective could not see. No matter how much we examine a culture from the outside, its mood will not reveal itself.

II

As Welch climbed the GE ladder so his philosophy for GE began to crystallise. What started out as a vague and overwhelming frustration with GE became a guiding force in the way that he as CEO of GE undertook a bold revisioning and restructuring of GE. For the duration of his period as an employee of GE, he kept his critique and emerging vision of GE to himself but when he became CEO it burst out of him. He began to express his frustration with standardisation and called for an organisational attunement based on differentiation. Both the language and disposition in terms of which he expressed his critique of the traditional GE and his alternative vision of GE had become more sophisticated. No longer could he simply be seen as a voice undermining the traditional practices of authority in GE. He had become the voice and driving force behind a new GE. He had moved from being a corporate rebel to being a leader of a new way of doing things for GE; from simply being a destroyer of the old order to being a "creative destroyer;" someone who destroyed the old and opened up new possibilities and ways of being for GE.

His critique of the old and his vision for the new GE did not emerge overnight. It had been bubbling in him for decades. Now, as CEO, it would be legitimate to express the frustration and open up new possibilities. Throughout the development of his critique and new vision he was guided by the same frustration which expressed itself as a tension between the conventional or habitual ways of doing things at GE and the need for a new way. As his frustration led him to critique the traditional ways of doing things, so his alternative began to emerge with more clarity. As we have seen in his early days at GE, he opposed the attunement of differentiation to the indifference of standardisation. This contrast would take on many different forms as his philosophy began to develop. In order to adjust to differentiation, corporations would need to move away from the indifference of bureaucratic ways of thinking to the flexibility of a values based way of thinking. For the regulations of bureaucracy did not allow for the flexibility and spontaneity required by differentiation. It entrenched standardisation. A values based way of thinking opened up these possibilities. As Welch says: "We took a bureaucracy and shook it ... I believe the GE I'm leaving is a true meritocracy, a place filled with involved and excited people, with good values and integrity." (Welch, 2001, p. 431)

Note the language he uses in the quotation: the notion of "shaking" a bureaucracy is suggestive of the same frustration that plagued him all along at GE. It is almost that in shaking the bureaucracy, he is undergoing a catharsis, a release of the tension that has built up in him over the years of being critical of GE but finding no outlet for the expression of his frustration. When, however, he becomes CEO of GE, his relation to his frustration changes. No more does he need to keep it in and hidden. It becomes the mood and driving force behind the way in which he transformed GE.

We also see a maturing of his philosophy. As the last quotation suggests, instead of contrasting standardisation and differentiation, he is now contrasting bureaucracy and a values based approach to organisational leadership. Bureaucracy falls on the side of standardisation while a values approach is seen to underpin differentiation. Bureaucracy is associated with indifference while values enable differentiation and infuse the organisation with passion – or what he calls "excited people." This is because, in Welch's terms, values are not rigid and prescriptive. Whereas bureaucracies operate in terms of standard procedures always working towards greater regulation of activities, a values approach enables employees to bring their own attunement into their work. A values based approach enables employees to take initiative, be entrepreneurial and care for their work while the standardisation involved in a bureaucracy encourages employees to function as "cogs in the machine." Values, from Welch's perspective are broad and general enabling employees to interpret them in ways that are appropriate to their circumstances. Bureaucracies, through the encouragement of uniformity, produce a mood of indifference: "Organisational layers were another residue of size. I used the analogy of putting on too many sweaters. Sweaters are like layers. They are insulators. When you go outside and you wear four sweaters, it's difficult to know how cold it is. … In the 1970's and 80's big business had too many layers …" (Welch, 2001, p. 96)

In a bureaucracy nobody knows how cold it is and nobody cares – this is because employees are robbed of their function as "carers." Bureaucracy produces an insensitivity to the context of work and a focus on the procedures of working. Values, on the other hand allow for a dynamic interaction between employee and situation. The detailed prescriptive rules of the bureaucracy are not mediating the employees relationship to their situation. They have decision-making power. Within the framework of the values, they are called upon to be responsive to the situation in which they are employed.

The tension between standardisation and differentiation underpins Welch's distinction between managers and leaders. The language in which Welch expresses the difference between leadership and management is underpinned with his frustration with the latter and his belief in the former. As we have already seen, from Welch's perspective managers are cold and uncaring whereas leaders care and are highly attuned to their workforce. Managers work with the numbers. Leaders work with developing self-confidence in the workforce. Managers are disengaged. Leaders are engaged.

The same frustration experienced in his early days at GE is reflected in his first mission statement to GE and in his recollections on his thinking behind it. In his recollections on writing the mission statement he shows his disdain for Wall Street analysts who were listening to him. These analysts "expected a detailed breakdown of the financial numbers. They could then plug those numbers into their models and crank out the estimates of our earnings by business segment. They loved this exercise. Over a 20-minute speech, I gave them little of what they wanted and quickly launched into a qualitative discussion around my vision for the company." (Welch, 2001, p. 105)

We can see his disdain for the standardisation, the formulaic model in the analysts' way of doing things. We can see the same frustration that caused him to want to leave GE. Now, however, it has been developed and is starting to work in his service. We also see how he is moving from a quantitative to a qualitative underpinning for his philosophy of organisational function. We also see a frustration with the routinisation of standardisation in the notion of plugging numbers into models rather than being responsive to Welch's talk. Indeed, none of the analysts present at the meeting did respond to Welch.

In the mission statement we see a frustration with standardisation in the form of what he calls a "paint by numbers" approach to organisational thinking, and in his rejection of what he sees as the rigidity and emptiness of developing a grand strategy for GE. In contrast to such a strategy, Welch would like to cultivate an atmosphere of openness in GE. To do this, rather than having a detailed strategic plan, he believes in the value of what he calls a central idea rather than a strategy at its core. In the context of developing his vision for GE he says: "What does relate and will enhance the many decentralised plans and initiatives of this Company isn't a central strategy, but a central idea." (Welch, 2001, p. 448)

The difference between a central idea and a central strategy, for Welch, is the difference between what he calls a "lengthy action plan" and the evolution of a "central idea through continually changing circumstances." An action plan assumes that reality can be defined through a blue print that is developed in advance and then implemented; where all that managers and employees need do is match the numbers and not to respond to situations out of their own initiative or concern. A central idea, on the other hand does not assume that reality can be defined in advance but provides a framework in which the idea can emerge according to the situation. The difference between the two is a difference between "implementation" and "emergence." Action plans are "implemented" while an idea is given the opportunity to "emerge." Implementation means modelling according to a blue print while emergence allows for responsiveness according to the situation.

From a leadership perspective, the latter involves setting the "broadest of objectives" in which people can "shine," thereby allowing the company to grow. Whereas in an action plan power is concentrated at the top, the evolution of a central idea calls for empowerment throughout the organisation. In the context of a broad idea, what holds the organisation together is not a bureaucracy or even structure but a set of values. It is by living and internalising the values of an organisation that focus and cohesiveness is achieved. Values allow different parts of the organisation to work towards common objectives in different ways. From Welch's perspective a values based approach allows for unity (or shared objectives) and differentiation – a lengthy action plan produces only conformity and sameness. Because values are the glue which hold an organisation together, it is crucial that those in the organisation share the same values. Again, for Welch this does not mean conformity. On the contrary shared values allow for differentiation at the coal face of the work front.

A further dimension in which Welch expresses the tension between the indifference of standardisation and the care of differentiation is in his attitude towards the philosophy that has dominated organisational thinking, scientific management. He sees scientific management as perpetuating the reign of indifference and not providing a framework for the care of differentiation: "We need to drive self-confidence deep into the organisation. A company can't distribute self-confidence, but it can foster it by removing layers and giving people a chance to win. We have to undo a 100-year old concept and convince managers that their role is not to control people and stay 'on top' of things, but rather to guide, energise, and excite." (Lowe, 2001, p. 41)

In this quotation we see Welch moving from a concern with only GE to a concern with the philosophical context in which business is conducted. The transformation required of GE is not specific to only GE but requires a transformation in the basic conventions and concepts in which organisations have made sense of themselves: "Like most major corporations, GE previously relied on the doctrine of scientific management: the theory that any work process – including its human element – can be broken down to its component parts and then reassembled in an efficient or 'scientific' manner. That sort of thinking fostered assembly lines and military-style hierarchies, which produced enormous wealth but generally, alienated employees. By contrast, the values-based organisation that is emerging at GE derives its efficiency from consensus: Workers who share their employer's goals don't need much supervision." (Tichy and Sherman, 1993, p. 4)

Workers who share their employer's values and goals can be left alone. They do not need to be bogged down in myriad's of details in which their practices are prescribed. A final dimension upon which the tension between the indifference of standardisation and the attunement of differentiation expresses itself is in terms of what I shall call the "ethics of authenticity" in Welch. In Welch the ethics of authenticity resolved around two pillars: a hatred of what he called "superficial congeniality" and the need to face reality. Superficial congeniality is linked in Jack Welch's mind with the disengaged practices of scientific management. It is embedded in a set of practices that had historically underpinned the culture of GE: "GE's culture had been built for a different time, when a command-and-control structure made sense. Having been in the field I had a strong prejudice against most of the headquarters staff. I felt they practised what could be called '**superficial congeniality**' – pleasant on the surface, with distrust and savagery boiling beneath it. The phrase seems to sum up how **bureaucrats typically behave**, smiling in front of you but always looking for a 'gotcha' behind your back." (Welch, 2001, p. 96)

For Welch, superficial congeniality covered all acts of corporate deception, experiences in which what people said was not what they meant. It also covered those kinds of acts in which people avoided the **tensions and anxieties of work responsibility** by going through the motions of the work. Anything which had been reduced to a formula but actually required a dynamic interchange was seen in terms of superficial congeniality. For example Welch says: "I didn't like sitting and listening to canned presentations or reading reports, preferring one-on-one conversations where I expected managers to know their business and to have the answers."

For Welch "canned presentations" produced "superficial congeniality" because they reduced interactions between people to empty rituals. Everyone was polite to each in such a way that what was really going on was covered up. This made it impossible to feel the climate of the organisation. Any plan that was presented as a "rosy picture" drew the scepticism of Welch. In the context of "superficial congeniality" people in an organisation are concerned with protecting their own position rather than facing business reality: "An awful lot of ritual goes on in companies. A lot of what I call 'selling hats to each other,' They come in with big thick boots, make presentations to each other; no customers know you're making it, the market doesn't know you've tied yourself up in a room preparing charts for weeks; so I constantly say, 'don't sell hats to each other,' go out and do business." (Lowe, 2001, p. 44)

Superficial congeniality makes candour difficult and produces self-delusion which he believed "can grip an entire organisation and lead people in to ridiculous conclusions." Superficial congeniality is dangerous because it can blind an organisation in a way that it cannot see the wood from the trees. It loses sight of its purpose and of its feel. Welch came to believe that the culture of GE was underpinned by the ethics of superficial congeniality, that it was eroding GE and that it needed to be changed. He offers the following experience in his early days at GE as a description of how deeply entrenched superficial congeniality was in the culture of GE: "Holt and Farnsworth [two of his colleagues at the time]... knew how the GE system worked. This was my first real look inside the 'traditional' GE."
...In Fort Wayne, one day during an HR review, Fred was giving a glowing appraisal of a guy I knew. [Welch asked]:"Fred, how the hell can you write this? He's not that good. We both know that this guy is a turkey. This appraisal is ridiculous." To my surprise Fred agreed.

"Do you want to see the real one?" he asked. "I can't send this to head-quarters. They'd want me to kill this guy." Fred wasn't alone in those days. He thought he was being a nice guy, protecting people who weren't up to their jobs. That's just the way it was. No one wanted to deliver bad news. In those days it was standard to fill in your appraisal form by writing that your career objective was at least your boss's job. The boss's response usually was "fully qualified to assume next position" – even if they both knew it wasn't true. Many of these "kind" performance appraisals would come back to haunt me in the early 1980's when we had to downsize the company. That "false kindness" only misled people and made their layoff an even greater shock than it should have been. "… I learned the importance of people, supporting the best and removing the weakest." (Welch, 2001, p. 58)

"False kindness" is another phrase for superficial congeniality. It occurs where the desire to protect someone gets in the way of people seeing who they are and of allowing the organisation to place people in a way that maximises their potential. From Welch's perspective kindness is not simply a good in itself, there are occasions on which kindness is a deception and is inauthentic. This inauthenticity is not simply moral but has devastating effects both for the individual and for the organisation. While it feels like a person is being protected by it, it actually creates more uncertainty in that no one really knows where they stand in relation to the organisation and the organisation loses sense of the purpose for its existence, – or, as Welch puts it, these acts of false kindness came back to haunt him when he was CEO of GE.

Welch believed that GE was historically underpinned by a culture of "superficial congeniality," that it had been entrenched in the bureaucracy and supported and created by the management of GE. If it was not changed, GE would not be able to be responsive to its own environment, let alone the changes that Welch saw coming. The concept that he opposed to "superficial congeniality" was what he called "facing reality." Speaking about facing reality he says: "Facing reality sounds simple but it isn't. I found it hard to get people to see a situation for what it is and not for what it was, or what they hoped it would be." (Welch, 2001, p. 103)

From Welch's perspective to face reality is to see through the conventions of superficial congeniality that are blinding GE to its changing circumstances. It operates in terms of a principle of, as he puts it, "don't kid yourself." It is to be able to stop going through the motions of doing things and recover the purpose or meaning behind doing them: " I wanted to break the cycle of these dog-and-pony shows. Hierarchy's role to passively 'review and approve' had to go."

To face reality was to respond to situations in terms of corporate feel, to embrace ownership of the work, to be engaged in it, to challenge and be challenged in the work. It was to encourage dialogue, risk taking and questioning. It was to see things through fresh eyes. It would be to care for our work – just as we care for children, so we need to care for our work. Without caring we are not properly attuned to our children; so too without caring we are indifferent in the workplace, are not responsive to opportunities and possibilities in our work environment. Only as people care can they innovate and be involved. Only as people are involved with their whole being in what they are doing can they be alive to their work context. As one employee at GE put it: "For 25 years you've paid for my hands when you could have had my brain as well – for nothing." (Welch, 2001, p. 183)

Finally, putting this in Heideggerian terms, the dynamic interchange between superficial congeniality and the need to face reality were the generative forces of Welch's deconstruction of the conventions of organisational life. They enabled Welch to highlight the way in which conventions had become ends in themselves, deprived the people in organisations of their vitality and created a blindness to reality. Through the use of these generative forces, he was able to undermine established conventions in such a way that members of the organisation – both those who stayed and left – were able to begin to see doing business and organisational life in new ways.

In other words, it was his "ethics of authenticity" that allowed for a re-enchantment of GE. It was by deconstructing the conventions of GE that new possibilities were opened up for GE. The tools in terms of which Welch deconstructed GE were his hatred of superficial congeniality and the need to face reality. To be sure, as we shall soon explore in greater detail, the closing down of the old ways and the opening up of the new ways were underpinned by much uncertainty. And sometimes it is hard not to say that this uncertainty was paralysing and despairing. But it was and still is the basis of rethinking what it means to be in business, to work in an organisation in the new century.

It should be noted that neither Heidegger nor Welch are against conventions themselves. For the most conventions are enabling devices. They allow us to get on with work by taking the sense of work for granted. If we did not have conventions we would be permanently stopped in our tracks – witness a migrant in a new country who does not know how things are done. Heidegger and Welch are concerned with conventions becoming ends in themselves. When we go through the motions or when it becomes valuable to do the right rituals. Al Dunlap has summarised the dangers with this approach: "So many companies, for one reason or another, totally lose their way. Many were great household names at one time. Along the way, their own people forgot the entrepreneurial spirit that created them. The managers became custodians. They lost the ability to lead." It is precisely when the managers become custodians that there is a need to "face reality" and get beyond the conventions.

From Welch's perspective the fundamental problem that GE faced was not a technical or rational problem but an existential one, one of moving from an indifference to one in which people cared for their work. What had prevented them from caring was the practices of scientific management which had taken the heart and thus the care out of work for people.

We cannot care if we are reduced to machines. It is precisely our attune-ment, our caring that differentiates us from machines which can be switched off and on, do not feel things as urgent, are not attentive, do not notice possibilities and opportunities in situations, are not committed to their work (as though they have work). For GE to succeed in the future it had to develop these non technical but human dimensions in its leadership and people.

Here we can begin to understand the significance of a philosophy for Jack Welch. The process of shifting GE from its conventional ways of doing things to a new way was a philosophical process.

10
Turning Intuitions Into Visions

Jack Welch's philosophy did not come with any scientific guarantees. It was not first developed in a laboratory and then applied in the world of practice. Indeed it was never developed in advance as a blue print which was then implemented in practice. As he undertook the transformation of GE, Welch had nothing more than an intuitive understanding of – a feeling for – what he wanted GE to look like. His appreciation for GE would become clearer only as GE was itself transformed. The language through which he would come to understand GE developed only as he committed himself to transforming GE. For example, we have already heard him say: "I did know what I wanted the company to "feel" like. I wasn't calling it culture in those days, but that's what it was." (Welch, 2001, p. 92)

This phrase suggests that he had a feeling for GE but not the language in which to express his feeling. It was only as he committed himself to transforming GE that the language to understand the transformation developed – not in advance of it. Welch compares his process to that of an innovative scientist who follows the path that his intuition has set up for him. Describing an instance of the way in which he develops his perspective, he says: "I was sitting on the beach under an umbrella in Barbados in December 1989 on a belated honeymoon with my second wife, Jane. ... Work-Out had become a huge success. We were kicking bureaucracy's butt with it. Ideas were flowing faster all over the company. I was groping for a way to describe this. ... Sandy Lane in Barbados was a great place. I'd never experienced a Caribbean Christmas – it was different. Seeing Santa Claus pop out of a submarine while I was lying on the beach may have been just the jolt I needed. That day I got the idea that would obsess me for the next decade. ... **Suddenly**, the word boundaryless popped into my head. It really summed up my dream for the company. I couldn't get the word out of my mind. Silly as it sounds, it felt like a scientific breakthrough. A week later, all wound up with my newest obsession, I went directly from Barbados to our operating managers meeting in Boca Raton. ... I called boundaryless the idea that 'will make the difference between GE and the rest of world business in the 1990's. ..." (Welch, 2001, p. 185)

There are a number of issues to be highlighted in the quotation. Firstly, we see again how the language to express his understanding of practices in GE did not develop in advance but only afterwards did he find the language to express the practices. As he says, he was "struggling" to find the language to express the already existent practices. Secondly the language did not arise out of rational deliberation but emerged, as he says "suddenly" as if out of nowhere. His attention was in fact directed elsewhere – at Santa Claus on a beach in Barbados. In this context the idea of boundarylessness seized him. He could not get it out of his mind. It could be said that the idea "dawned" on him. It came over him. The similarities of this process to the process of scientific discovery are worth noting. Describing his process of scientific discovery Isaac Newton has said: " I keep the subject constantly before me, and wait until the first dawnings open slowly by little and little into the full and clear light." (Westfall, 1994)

What is significant in Newton's quotation is the idea of "dawnings." Rather than imposing his descriptions on objects, he waits for it to become clear. He lets it be. The process of developing an idea through allowing it to "dawn" on one is known in terms of Heiddegger's philosophy as phenomenology. Heidegger quite explicitly uses the idea of "dawning" to describe the phenomenological process. New ideas are not produced but "dawn" on us. The phenomenological process is pivotal to allowing the new or that which is not yet visible to emerge. We cannot force the frenzied intuition of the artist or creative artist to express itself. We cannot use analytical reasoning to encourage the intuition to emerge. An interesting case is the mathematician, Henri Poincare who tried through rational deliberation to refute a set of mathematical theorems only to find that the set of theorems dawned on him: "For 15 days I strove to prove that there could not be any functions like those I have since called Fuchsian functions. I was then very ignorant; everyday I seated myself at my worktable, stayed an hour or two, tried a great number of combinations and reached no results. One evening, contrary to my custom, I drank black coffee and could not sleep. Ideas rose in crowds; I felt them collide until pairs interlocked, so to speak, making a stable combination. By the next morning I had established the existence of a class of Fuchsian functions, those which come from the hypergeometric series; I had only to write out the results, which took but a few hours." (Poincare, 1946)

Again we see that the new ideas came over him. This is very interesting because we could expect in the rational domain of mathematics that it would be by reason that a new way of doing things would announce itself. Instead what we see is that the ideas announce themselves in him. They do so in a frenzy; in a way that will not let him rest or sleep. He needs to be attentive to the frenzy that is occurring in him. He needs to listen to the turmoil that is going on in him. As he is attuned to the frenzy in himself, so the ideas emerge in him. Then, all that he has to do is, as he himself says, is "write them down," – no systematic and detailed rational analysis. Thus he was attentive and vigilant, waiting for the new to emerge, allowing it to reveal itself but not imposing ourselves upon it.

We need to be able to follow the path of intuition in encouraging it to express itself. Instead of attempting to seize it, we need to allow the intuition to express itself in a sketch which is vague and opaque at first but becomes clearer as we sketch. In the process of sketching, we are not forcing the end result but playfully continue with the sketching until the painting completes itself. Welch sees this phenomenological process as central to his leadership style. He calls it wallowing: "For me, "wallowing" has always been a key part of how we ran GE. Get a group of people around a table, regardless of their rank, to wrestle with a particular tough issue. Stew on it from every angle – flush out everyone's thinking – but don't come to an immediate conclusion." (Welch, 2001, p. 141)

"Stewing on it," "flushing out" the ideas, not coming to a conclusion – these are all central elements of the phenomenological process; a process that can be defined in contrast to an analytic process which attempts to force out a conclusion. Phenomenology is a process in which we allow the thing to seize us and for our understanding to emerge out of being seized by the subject matter. Anita Roddick of the Body Shop describes this process in terms of the entrepreneur. She uses the idea of being obsessed to describe the way in which an entrepreneur is seized by an intuition or idea. To say that the entrepreneur is seized by the idea is to say that they do not initially have control of the idea or intuition. It overwhelms them and compels them. Regardless of whether they want to or not, they are preoccupied with the intuition. It does not let them rest or turn their attention elsewhere. In Niezschian terms, it drives them to a frenzy. As much as they may want to be rational and continue with their everyday work, they cannot but help be involved in their "obsession." Yet even when they do not resist the intuition, they still do not know what will emerge from it. They do not have clarity regarding the obsession. They cannot force it out; cannot reason it out but must allow it to emerge – just as the artist needs to allow the painting to emerge from the sketch. To allow it to emerge, they need to learn to listen to the frenzied intuition. Only then will they begin to have control over it.

Wallowing should not be confused with brain storming. It has less of an element of brain in it. Rather, wallowing is identified with a certain mood. When we wallow in something, we are usually seized by a powerful mood, something that has got hold of us and instead of forcing ourselves out of this seizure, we allow ourselves to wallow in it. Brain storming is far too rational. It does not presuppose an experience of being seized by a mood or intuition. Wallowing and phenomenology are a process of encouraging the mood to express itself. Instead of berating ourselves for being in a mood, we learn to listen to what the mood is expressing. Brain storming or the storming of ideas does not presuppose a mood. Wallowing occurs where we are overwhelmed by a mood – in this case, the mood of confusion. When we can allow ourselves to wallow in the mood of confusion, we open up the possibility for new ideas to dawn on us. The importance of mood is that it expresses what we feel.

Instead of forcing a conclusion to emerge, Welch emphasises the process of allowing ideas to emerge. Forcing conclusions can prevent an attunement to the ideas that would emerge throughout the process of wallowing. Not only is this similar to the process of scientific discovery, it is also very similar to the process of artistic creation. The Impressionist painter Vincent van Gogh's understanding of his own artistic process sheds some light on Welch's process. Describing his process van Gogh says: "But you will ask: What is your definite aim? That aim becomes more definite, will stand out slowly and surely, just as the rough draft becomes a sketch, and the sketch becomes a picture, little by little, by working seriously on it, by pondering over the idea, vague at first, over the thought that was fleeting and passing, till it gets fixed." (van Gogh, 1997)

Van Gogh tells us that only as the artist commits himself to the canvas does the art object and the artist's understanding of the piece of art develop. It is not that the artist has a complete understanding in advance of the art object. They have an intuition – a "frenzy" as Nietzsche calls it, that is, something calling for expression but not even they know what is calling for expression. It is only through the leap into sketching that the frenzy begins to work itself out and take form. It is in this process that the artist's understanding of what he is doing becomes refined. He knows what he is doing by doing it – not by thinking about it in advance. What is vague at first becomes clearer through the process of sketching. The artist needs to leap into the frenzied process of sketching without a definite idea of the art piece. He needs to be able to allow the piece of art to develop through his process of sketching.

So too in the case of Welch, it was only as he committed himself to transforming GE that GE took the particular shape that it did. But more than this, it was only through the commitment to resketching GE that Welch's understanding of it developed. His thinking about GE was, like the sketching of the artist, vague and frenzied at first but clarified and expressed through his actions in GE. Welch's artistic frenzy was his frustration with GE. GE was the canvas upon which his frustration would turn into an artwork. The art work became clearer as he worked on GE.

The process of allowing the new to dawn is central to the artistic process. Art, as Paul Klee tells, us is the process of allowing that which is not visible to be made visible. In this sense art is to be contrasted with normal science. Normal science, historically speaking, is concerned with analysing that which is observable. In its positivist context, only that which is observable is meaningful from a scientific perspective. In contrast to this, art is a process of enabling that which does not yet appear to be made apparent. In the context of science Newton was allowing that which was not visible to be made visible. In the context of art, van Gogh was allowing that which was not visible to be made visible. And in a corporate context, Welch was shining a light on that which was not yet visible.

As the CEO of GE Welch encouraged this artistic process amongst his employees. He believed that he could not dictate the way in which employees implemented his vision for GE. The most that he could do was define the idea in terms of which GE would operate. What would emerge through these ideas would depend on how employees interpreted them and worked with them at the coal face of work. Welch's ideas were like the rough sketch of the artist. What emerged through this rough sketch would depend very much on the workers at the coal face. They would be responsible for what they created. He would encourage them to create, would not know in advance what they were going to create but would set them free to create. Through this process their work of art would emerge: "I wanted to create a company 'where people dare to try new things – where people feel assured in knowing that only the limits of their creativity and drive, their own standards of personal excellence, will be the ceiling on how far and how fast they move." (Welch, 2001)

To do this he needed not to impose his will on the people but to encourage them to bring the creativity out in themselves. This meant a shift from "management" to "leadership" for management had historically been concerned with imposing the organisational blue print on employees whereas leadership was concerned with bringing out the creativity of people: "We need to drive self-confidence deep into the organisation. A company can't distribute self-confidence, but it can foster it by removing layers and giving people a chance to win. We have to undo a 100-year old concept and convince managers that their role is not to control people and stay 'on top' of things, but rather to guide, energise, and excite." (Lowe, 2001, p. 49)

The company develops by bringing out the creative potential in its people. This process of "bringing out" is central to the phenomenological process which is defined in contrast to the scientific management approach of the manager imposing a blue print. Scientific management works by ordering the work of employees in terms of a blue print. The phenomenology of Welch works by allowing workers to create in terms of a broad idea that takes shape in action: "The people closer to the work know the work best. They own it and decide how far to delegate the spending authority. They become more accountable." (Welch, 2001)

The phenomenological process can be seen at work in the development of Welch's notion of "Work-out," a process of corporate dialogue between managers and workers. The concept was not developed in advance of its practice. It occurred to Welch in the context of worker scepticism regarding his desire to establish honest communication. Workers had complained to him that his desire for corporate honesty was noble in theory but was laughable in practice. Instead of taking offence at their critique, he acknowledged their perspective, did not know what to do about it immediately, "wallowed" in it, and out of his "wallowing" emerged the process known as "Work-out".

The very process of work-out operates phenomenologically. Work out is a process of listening to the frustration of workers and for turning these frustrations into new possibilities for GE. It operates on the principle that "those closest to the work know it best." Historically worker frustration with management was ignored. In the context of the "Work-out" process workers frustration with management becomes the basis of a dialogue between workers and management. Out of the tension of the interaction between workers and management, the frustration of workers are turned into new possibilities for GE. In this way through listening to workers the shape and identity of GE emerges and is formed.

It also seems that the work-out process mirrors the early experience of Jack Welch at GE. Where his frustration was not provided an avenue to be expressed, work-out provides a framework for his staff to express their frustration in a productive way.

Finally, it is important to re-iterate that in Welch we detect a central theme of existential thought: there is a certain kind of knowledge that emerges through our commitments and activities. It is, again, a non cognitive basis to cognitive knowledge. Only as we commit ourselves do our ideas develop. Ideas do not develop by thinking in an ivory tower but in the context of action. This is the way in which Welch developed his philosophy for GE and for business in general.

Welch had neither the support of public opinion nor the backing of scientific evidence to support his call for organisational transformation at GE. Yet he undertook and persisted with the changes. How do we understand what made it possible for him to trust his own judgement in the absence of support and without him having objective certainty that what he was doing was the right thing. Is it not irresponsible and reckless of Jack Welch to undertake a transformation of one of the world's most successful companies on the basis of an untested intuitive knowledge? Yet could it be any other way?

Initially, Welch tried to convey his vision in a rational way, in a way that would appeal to the common sense of the business community and to employees within GE. To have done this would have made it possible to debate the vision in a public way. In his address to Wall Street market analysts he attempted to set up a debate. On this occasion, he prepared a rational presentation which was clear, simple and elegant in its use of language. However, not only would no one buy into it, no one could even relate to it. It is not even that they objected to it, they could not even make sense of it such that they could object to it. In question time at the end, no one could even formulate a question to be asked.

Welch's common sense and that of the analysts did not match each other. They thought he was crazy. Each were in different "mindspaces." He could not appeal to them or anyone else for support. He was on his own, alone, without backup. Welch shattered the common sense understanding that GE had of itself and that organisations have of themselves. This is an extremely difficult task to perform. Common sense is highly resistant to change. It has an air of authority about it. It is rational. It is legitimate. It undermines those who transgress its boundaries, by making them feel foolish. He or she who transgresses it, is made to feel an outsider. There is no doubt that Welch was made to feel an outsider because of his beliefs. Yet, he persisted in spite of being made to feel an outsider.

It is time to highlight the existential journey of Welch. The existential journey is one in which a person commits themselves to a path without support either from other people, from a belief in an absolute such as God and without objective scientific or rational confirmation that they are on the correct path. Indeed there is no way of knowing that they are on the "correct" path. They have made a decision to follow a certain path but there is no way of knowing that they have made the correct decision. Sartre brings out the anguish and resoluteness involved in this process when, to paraphrase him, he says that "If an [intuition] speaks to me, it is still I myself who must decide whether the [intuition] is or is not a [creative one]." (1975, p. 31)

This was very much the experience of Welch. He had an intuition of a new way for GE. He had to decide whether to trust the voice of the intuition. And he had to do this being fully aware that there was so much objective evidence and pressure from the mainstream counting against him. A major episode in this respect was the years of the early 1980's, years of downsizing in which hundreds of employees were forced to leave GE. On the one hand many argued that this created a spirit of demoralisation within the organisation and created widespread uncertainty in the industry and the businesses world in general. Jack Welch recognised this: "In the early 1980's you didn't have to be in a GE business that was up for sale to wonder if Jack Welch knew what he was doing. The turmoil, angst and confusion were everywhere … Throughout the company, people were struggling to come to grips with the uncertainty." Continuing he says that "people weren't buying [his vision]. For them, it was total disconnect. They saw him as Neutron Jack, as a person who "removed the people but left the building standing." (Welch, 2001)

In the midst of the turmoil, when the stability of the present is collapsing and the future way of doing things has not yet emerged, who do we believe? How could Welch himself have known that he was doing the right thing? Was he a Neutron Jack or the father of a new way of doing things? Even in retrospect there is still much discussion on this issue. To complicate matters many people were downsized on the grounds of financial scarcity but at the same time Welch built expensive training facilities for employees that would stay on at GE. How could he in one and the same breath say that there was not enough money to maintain the status quo and yet build lavish facilities for existing staff? This seemed to be a contradiction. Yet instead of experiencing it as a contradiction, he experienced it as a paradox: (Welch, 2001, p. 124)

What Welch does say is that he trusted his gut – or to put it in existential terms, he took a leap into "faith" where faith means that inward certainty in the face of objective uncertainty." And the energy for his faith or for trusting his gut came from his frustration with bureaucracy. Thus he says that he hated being thought of as "Neutron Jack" but "I hated bureaucracy and waste even more. The data-obsessed headquarters and the low margins … were equally offensive." His frustration was the cornerstone of what made living worthwhile for him and it was something that he was prepared to die for. Again what we see is how it was the emotional energy of his frustration that drove him forward, that underpinned his willingness to commit his energy to transforming GE in the face of no objective support for his position. It was his fury that gave him focus.

The willingness to act on a powerful conviction without any objective knowledge or the support of public opinion is known in existential terms, as resoluteness. Resoluteness we may define, along with faith, as subjective certainty in the face of objective uncertainty. It is the feeling of certainty in the absence of any reinforcement from the outside – whether this be in the form of other people agreeing with one or proof through scientific testing or even rational persuasion. This is an experience that we may identify again and again in the biography of Welch. He was able to act on the basis of his convictions without support from external and objective sources. As we have seen, when he presented his ideas for a transformed GE to analysts on Wall Street, they thought that he was crazy, that he did not know what he was talking about. Yet the lack of support did not undermine his convictions but strengthened his resolve: "I was sure the ideas were right. I just hadn't brought them to life. They were just words read on stage by a new face." (Welch, 2001)

Inward certainty comes not from objective or analytic thought but from an existential commitment to a belief, a commitment that precedes rational deliberation. In the case of Welch, this commitment is rooted in a frustration that he is prepared to die for. To fail to be true to his frustration would be to deny himself. This he could not do. It would have been easier to give up GE than to give up his frustration. He would have lived in self deception if he were to stay at GE and simply deny his frustration. He could not choose not to be frustrated but he could choose how to live out his frustration. So no matter how objectively uncertain his vision was, his frustration inspired him and pushed him forward to express and act.

The strength of Welch's inward certainty in the face of objective certainty, was made possible by a commitment to a set of principles which guided him into the unknown. The central guiding force through the unknown, a place in which all objective certainties had been surrendered was what I have called Welch's "ethics of authenticity." As we have seen this was his hatred of "superficial congeniality" and his commitment to "face reality." The ethics of authenticity guided him in the destruction of the old and the emergence of the new vision. Here again we see how a philosophy develops as he engages in the unknown and how this philosophy supports him in traversing the unknown in which he has disrupted the old way of doing things. Welch's philosophy does not predate his transformation at GE but emerges through the process of transforming GE.

How was Welch to communicate his vision? It should be borne in mind that Welch was not operating in the same common sense horizon, set of conventions or mindset as his employees in GE and the market analysts on Wall Street. It was precisely their conventional mindset that he was changing. How did Welch convey and open up a mindset that was different from the one that analysts and employees were accustomed to? He cannot appeal to their common sense to change their common sense. He cannot appeal to their conventions or mindset to change their conventions. For it is their very common sense and their conventional patterns of thinking and doing that he is wanting to change. As we have seen when Welch tried to be rational, analysts laughed at him and employees looked at him with a quizzical astonishment.

Just as frustration brought the complacent way of doing things to the centre of Welch's attention, so Welch would bring it to the centre of the organisation's attention with very powerful moods; moods of angst and uncertainty. Rather than using rational persuasion, it was through moods of disruption that he enabled employees at GE to begin to think about their work and place in the organisation in new ways. An example of the way in which Welch uses disruptive moods can be seen in the way he highlighted the importance of GE as a values based organisation. It was by firing four corporate officers who did not live up to the values of GE that Welch enabled employees at GE to see the importance of values. He made the reasons for firing the Officers public: "In front of 500 people ... I explained why four corporate officers were asked to leave during the prior year ... "When I wanted to make a point, I'd never use the traditional 'left for personal reasons' excuse. ... I explained that one Officer was removed because he wasn't a believer in [our values] ... We can't be talking about reality, candour, globalisation, speed, and empowerment and have people who don't embrace these values. Everyone must walk the talk." Continuing he says "You could hear a pin drop. When I used the lack of [congruence over values] as one of the principal reasons for a manager's reasons for leaving, the idea really hit home. **You could feel the audience thinking**, This is for real. They mean it." (Welch, 2001, p. 189)

This quotation highlights the way in which Welch uses disruptions to transform the way in which people in the organisation think about that which the organisation takes seriously. We should emphasise the phrase: **You could feel the audience thinking.** In order to change peoples' ways of thinking, they need to feel that way of thinking. It is no good that they simply have a conceptual understanding of the new categories. They must have an embodied sense of the new way of doing things. In order to get them to feel that way of thinking, there is a need for a disruption in the routine ways of doing things. They need to be taken out of the norm or conventional habits in order to experience a new way of doing things. Again we also see that feel is the basis of vision. For now the members of the organisation began to see and experience the organisation in a new way. They became aware of the importance of values in the organisation. We also see that feeling and thought are not simply separate from each other – as scientific management has encouraged us to believe. We feel and think at the same time, a thought underpinned by a feeling is attuned while a thought without a feeling is disengaged.

It should be mentioned that Welch was not unaware of the negative effects of the uncertainty that he was creating. In response to it, he tried to provide what psychodynamic psychologists call a "holding" environment. A holding environment is one in which a client or patient who enters psychotherapy is provided with a safe environment in which to express their insecurities. They feel secure enough to open up their insecurities. Welch attempted to provide such an environment by not simply asking employees but by changing the psychological contract with employees: instead of sacking them, he tried to provide them with the life skills that would ensure employability rather than employment as such. For people within the organisation, the holding environment was provided by leaders who encouraged the growth of self-confidence in employees. In both cases anxiety was contained through strategies that would enable employees and ex-employees to continue to develop.

What we see is that Welch generates insights into GE out of the contradictory relationship that he has to do GE. What does this mean on a methodological level? What does the notion of "business feel" mean on a methodological level?

John Kotter has maintained that the difference between leaders and managers on a methodological level is that the former tend to be inductive while the latter tend to be deductive in their style. Inductive thinking is that kind of thinking which proceeds from facts to theories or conclusions. The theories are generated from observation of a number of facts. The repeated observation of facts allows one to make generalised statements which are theories. Kotter claims that leaders, in an inductive way, are able to develop visions or "theories" based on their observations of the organisation and the market context in which the environment is situated. They are able to see patterns and through articulating these patterns can form a vision. The manager does not form visions but is able to implement the visions of the leader. From Kotter's perspective the process of implementation is similar to the process of deductive thinking. Deductive thinking is that form of thinking in which theoretical claims are applied to particular cases. Managers as deductive thinkers operate out of a blue print that they apply to their particular circumstances.

The interesting issue in the case of Welch is that he was neither an inductive nor a deductive thinker. A deductive thinker requires a theory in which to operate. While Welch was formulating his philosophy, he did not have a well expressed theory or universal vision in terms of which to operate. He did not have a blue print that he could apply to GE. His vision was being developed as he dealt with his frustration at GE and not in advance of his operations.

Welch was not an inductive thinker because he did not have a well developed hypothesis in terms of which he saw GE. Inductive thinking requires an hypothesis in terms of which to make significant observations. In his frustration Welch felt very deeply that GE could be another kind of organisation but he did not have a clear idea of what this other kind of organisation would look like. Indeed, even when he was CEO of GE, he did not always have a well developed cognitive understanding of what he wanted GE to look like. He had what we have already referred to as a "feel" for GE. It was as his feel was expressed that the shape and language in which to make sense of GE became clear in his mind.

Unlike an inductive scientist, Welch was not simply showing people what was already there. He was changing peoples thinking, their "mindset" about that which was already there. This would enable them to see what was already there in a new light. The process of shifting mindset or conventions is not an inductive but a destructive activity. It requires destroying the existing mindset or conventions for doing things. The destruction of the existing mindset opens up the possibility for a new mindset. It allows the world to be reformed. To the extent that Welch offered a new mindset, his process was one of creative destruction and not just one of destruction.

Thus we see that while both the organisational practice of Jack Welch and the philosophy of Martin Heidegger can be articulated in terms of the convention-disruption-vision model of philosophical experience, this model does acquire a depth of detail in both. It becomes the convention-disruption-dawning-disclosure model of philosophical experience. As we shall see for Heidegger, not all disruptions lead to new "visions." Heidegger helps us to understand how disruption leads to new possibilities. It is through a process of what he calls "**dawning**." This refers to our willingness to allow new ideas to "**dawn**" on us. Finally Heidegger would be sceptical of the notion of a "vision." From his perspective, we do not "have" a vision. "Visions" are not things that can be put in a package. Rather, Heidegger would point us in the direction of the activity of envisaging, an activity that does not box possibilities into a thing. He calls the activity of envisaging, "**disclosure**." It is a process of "**disclosing**" new ways of seeing things.

It was only as Welch acted that his philosophy began to develop. It did not develop in advance of his actions.

11
Leading out of Confusion: Grove's Crisis at Intel

I

How does someone lead when they are themselves confused and uncertain? This is a question that Andrew Grove of Intel enables us to address. For unlike Welch, Grove himself underwent the changes that he took Intel through. Whereas Welch steered GE through a transition in which he, as CEO, had, at the outset, a strong intuition of the direction of the change, Grove did not, at the outset of Intel's crisis have a strong intuition about the direction in which he was taking Intel. Indeed, faced with the threatened collapse of Intel, he was overwhelmed by confusion and uncertainty. He lost his bearing. Yet he was able to think creatively and productively in the experience of having lost his bearing. The shock of the crisis at Intel enabled him to listen to the mood or feel of the organisation in a way that he had taken for granted before. Through turning what he saw and heard into action, he was able to transform the threat to the existence of Intel into an opportunity which opened up new possibilities. More than this, in spite of being in the unknown he was able to take Intel with him on the journey towards a new way of doing things for Intel. It was in the way that he dealt with confusion and uncertainty in himself that paved the way for envisaging Intel in a new way.

What are the conditions under which a life threatening experience becomes in an organisational context an opportunity to see new possibilities for the organisation? What are the conditions under which a leader who himself has lost direction and is not sure of the new direction that he is taking, able to guide those who work for him into the new direction?

What we shall see is that it was precisely by giving up the need to find direction that Grove allowed a new direction for Intel to become clear to him. The more Grove tried to find a direction for Intel, the more frustrated he and Intel became. However, that moment in which he gave up the need for finding a direction – at that moment in which he gave up the need for trying, was the moment in which a new direction began to emerge.

In this chapter I will situate the experience of Andrew Grove's transform-ation of Intel in the context of Heidegger's philosophy. In fact I will be using the work of a Heideggerian psychoanalyst to bring out the per-spective of Grove. This is the work of Viktor Frankl, an existential psycho-analyst who developed his views in response to his experiences in a concentration camp during the Second World War. Based on the philo-sophy of Martin Heidegger, he calls his form of psychoanalysis, logother-apy. One of the techniques that is central to logotherapy is what he calls "paradoxical intention." This idea is grounded in the belief that the human cannot will itself out of a disruptive experience. He gives as an example an insomniac. He notes that very often when people have difficulty sleeping, we try to will ourselves to sleep. However the more we try to sleep the more we reinforce a lack of sleep. Willing requires an active mind. The more we will ourselves to sleep, the more we are watching ourselves trying to sleep. And the more we are watching ourselves trying to sleep, the more attentive we are to ourselves trying to sleep. The more attentive we are to ourselves trying to sleep, the more awake we are. Thus the more we watch ourselves trying to sleep, the more awake we are.

For Frankl, rather than trying to sleep, the insomniac, needs to be able to embrace their difficulties in sleeping. The more that they can embrace their difficulties in sleeping, the more they can change their relationship to sleep. Instead of being dominated by a fear of not sleeping, they are able to develop a more playful relationship to sleep. They are open to the possibil-ity of the night being experienced in other ways.

An interesting example of Frankl's logic can be found in the experience of Fredric Taylor the founder of scientific management. Commenting on the experience of Taylor, Gareth Morgan has said: "Fredric Taylor, the creator of scientific management was a man totally preoccupied with control. ... From about the age of twelve, Taylor suffered from the most fearful nightmares and insomnia. Noticing that his worst dreams occurred while he was lying on his back, he constructed a harness of straps and wooden points that would wake him whenever he was in danger of getting into this position." 221 *Images of Organization* by Gareth Morgan (Sage Publications Newbury Park, CA 91320 (1989)

Through controlling the positions in which he slept, he attempted to have control over his nightmares. Indeed it seems that by creating the conditions for waking himself, he avoided having nightmares. However, much of his life was spent avoiding having nightmares: "The insomnia and sleeping devices stayed with him in one way or another throughout his life. In later years he preferred to sleep in an upright position, propped by numerous pillows. This made spending nights away from home a rather difficult business, and in hotels where pillows were in short supply he would sometimes spend the night propped up by bureau draws." (222)

Thus while he might have avoided nightmares, he never escaped the imminent threat of nightmares. In a sense he had "nightmares" or sheer terror about nightmares. He was bedevilled by the anticipatory anxiety of having nightmares. He was always dominated by the threat of nightmares. No wonder he suffered from insomnia. He was too concerned with his way of sleeping to allow himself to sleep. In contrast to this, embracing his nightmares in (for example) the context of Frankl's existential psychotherapy would have enabled him to overcome domination by them. Rather than trying to avoid the nightmares, acceptance of them would have encouraged a new relationship to sleep. He would have been able to detach himself from his nightmares. And in his detachment he would have been able to examine them.

In the context of Grove's experience at Intel what we will see is both attitudes. Firstly, we will see how Grove "tried" or "willed" himself and Intel out of the disruption. However, the more he willed or tried to pull Intel out of the disruption, the more he entrenched the disruption. Secondly, we shall see how it was only when he embraced the nightmare of the disruption that he began to free himself from it. We shall also see how the embracing of the nightmare of disruption was the basis upon which Grove became philosophical and how it was through this philosophical moment that a new way of envisaging Intel was made possible.

Grove's experience will allow me to bring out two different responses to dealing with disruption; what I shall call an attitude of managerial control and an attitude of philosophical reflection. In the attitude of managerial control we attempt to control the disruption that we are in. In this attitude we believe that only as we have control of the disruption can we get out of it. On the other hand, in the attitude of philosophical reflection, we embrace our lack of control of the disruption. We embrace the uncertainty of being in the unknown. In Grove's experience of philosophical reflection what shall be seen is that the very letting go of control became the basis for going beyond the disruption and opening up of a new way of being for Intel.

It should also be pointed out that Grove's experience at Intel allows us to see the human dynamics involved in Schumpeter's entrepreneurial philosophy of creative destruction. Whereas Schumpeter outlines the theory of creative destruction, in the experience of Grove at Intel, we shall see the thinking and feeling that occurs in the experience of the destruction of an habitual way of doing things and the creation of a new way of doing things. As we shall see the moment of turning destruction into creation is the moment of paradoxical intention. For paradoxical intention is a way of detaching ourselves from the nightmare of what is threatening so that we can experience things in new ways. It is this moment of detachment that is crucial in the transformation from destruction to creativity. We shall see the range of emotions that occur in the moment of paradoxical intention.

These range from despair to excitement, feelings of loss of confidence, moments of denial and the exhilaration of new commitments.

What we shall also see is that the crisis that Grove experienced at Intel led not only to a transformation of Intel but to a transformation in his way of thinking about management and organisations. He underwent a "paradigm switch" in which he moved from seeing organisational activity primarily in terms of "managerial control" to a more paradoxical position of being sensitive to the need to both let go of control and being able to assert control where necessary or where demanded by the situation.

Let us have a closer look at the way in which Grove and Intel turned an experience of despair and confusion into a new set of possibilities for Intel. The central event in Grove's paradigm switch was a crisis at Intel generated by a threat from Japanese competitors. This crisis occurred in the early 1980's when Intel dominated the microchip market. It had taken years for Intel to build itself up to be the dominant player in the market. It was proud of itself, having put much effort into building itself up. As Grove says: "We worked day and night to design the chip ... We worked as if our life depended on it, as in a way it did."

The emotional nature of Grove's language should be noted. Through the intense effort and commitment of employees at Intel, a way of doing things – the "Intel" way of doing things – emerged. Intel was proud of its problem solving practices and of its practices of dialogue in which ferocious arguing whilst remaining friends developed. It was proud of its excellence in research practices. It also developed a strong identity and culture. In this culture "Intel stood for memories; conversely, memories meant (usually) Intel." (1997, p. 85) So deeply rooted were the practices of Intel that they had the character of what Grove calls "religious dogmas." (1997, p. 90) They were imprinted in the very being of Intel. They gave Intel a sense of confidence and certainty in the world of microchips. Intel just knew what it was doing. Its convictions allowed it to go from strength to strength, enabling it to focus on becoming more efficient and taking its culture for granted: "People were pleading with us for more parts. ... We were scrambling to build more capacity." (1997, p. 88)

This was an exciting period for Intel. They were extremely goal focused – until it came to the Japanese who were able to produce better quality microchips in larger volumes and at less of the cost. This sent shock waves of fear through Intel. But in the early stages Intel dealt with the threat as a challenge to develop its own efficiencies. And so it attempted to deal with the competition on the basis of its cultural strengths. It relied on its practices of problem solving, research and dialogue to become more efficient in its production of microchips. However, the more efficient it became, so the more efficient became the Japanese competitors. Every time Intel improved, its competitors improved. Not only did this frustrate Intel but it caused widespread panic in Intel. For Intel tried everything that it knew to deal with the threat, yet each effort resulted in failure: "We fought hard. We improved our quality and brought costs down but the Japanese producers fought back." (1997, p. 87)

Senior management at Intel realised that they did not have the know-how to beat off their Japanese competitors. In fact they were quite stunned by the way in which Japanese know-how surpassed theirs. As Grove says, the "quality levels attributed to Japanese memories were beyond what we thought were possible." (1997, p. 85) They saw that the Japanese were, to use the words of Grove "taking over the world semiconductor market" and they saw this happening, to use Grove's expression "in front of our eyes."

In Socratic terms they were at this point experiencing a moment of "aporia." The word aporia comes from the Latin a poria which means to be without a path. For Intel the experience of the powerhouse of Japanese competition was one in which they felt that they had been knocked off their path. They had lost their way because they could no longer rely on their way of doing things. They could not rely on their way because they had seen in the Japanese a more effective way of doing things, one which they lacked both the know-how and resources to match. They felt overwhelmed by the power of Japanese competition: "All this was very scary from the point of view of what we still thought of as a little company in Santa Clara, California." (1997, p. 85)

Although they felt overwhelmed by the efficiencies of the Japanese, this did not stop them trying to compete with the Japanese. Indeed their primary response to the threat was to work harder. However, hard work was also no solution. For hard work in the absence of a clear direction is self defeating. Even though Intel could see that it did not have the means to compete with the Japanese, it would not give up "trying." Even in the face of failure they continued to try. But none of their trying helped them escape the threat to their existence: "During this time we worked hard without a clear notion of how things were ever going to get better. We had lost our bearings. We were wondering in the valley of death." (1997, p. 89) No matter how defiant Intel was or how intensively it believed in itself, it had lost its way. It was confused: "We had meetings and more meetings, bickering and arguments, resulting in nothing but conflicting proposals." (1997, p. 88)

They were in a state of existential denial – like the insomniac who tries to sleep while knowing that they cannot get to sleep. In the midst of its bickering and disillusionment Intel continued to be caught in the contradictory position of both experiencing itself going downhill yet believing in its ability to take on the threat of the Japanese. It developed all sorts of fantastic alternatives to try and outmanoeuvre the Japanese: "There were those who proposed what they called a 'go for it' strategy: 'Let's build a gigantic factory dedicated to producing memories and nothing but memories, and let's take on the Japanese. ... ' Others proposed that we should get really clever and use an avant-garde technology." (1997, p. 89) Yet at the same time they knew that they were not getting anywhere: "Meanwhile, as the debates raged, we just went on losing more and more money." (1997, p. 88)

Here we see what the philosopher Kierkegaard called the "despair of defiance," that despair in which we defy the realisation of our own weakness and vulnerability. Even though we feel our resources to be under threat, we feel that we are strong enough to do anything. Intel knew that its way of doing things was not working for it but it still relied on its way of doing things to cope with the threat. In many ways they were much like a young child fighting with an older child. Even though the younger one has no hope he or she does not give up. They are constantly defying their own weakness, refusing to recognise the strength of the older child. So Intel, focused on beating the Japanese rather than acknowledging that they were experiencing themselves as a little child – or, as Grove puts it, a "little company in Santa Clara, California." This was too much for them.

Senior management at Intel were desperate but could not face their own desperation; vulnerable but could not face their own vulnerability, unable to talk to each other but unable to face that they could not talk to each other – indeed they kept on shouting at each other. They realised that they were not getting anywhere but could not face that they were not getting anywhere and kept on "trying" to get somewhere – kept on exerting their will. They were denying the inevitable – just like the insomniac who cannot sleep but nevertheless still tries to sleep.

Existential denial has an ambiguous structure: we do not deny what someone else says or sees. We deny what we ourselves are seeing. Denial is the experience of a contradiction: realising that its ways of doing things had been undermined, Intel still kept on relying on its way of doing things to see it through. Existential denial occurs on those occasions in which we feel threatened and powerless to deal with the threat. Rather than embracing our experience of powerlessness in the face of a threat, we believe that we can rely on our own resources. However, as we see in the case of Intel, it is the very resources on which they are relying that are under threat. For it is the very practices and processes in terms of which they were producing memory chips that were under threat by the Japanese – yet it is these very "abilities" that they believed that they could find direction and security. Thus it was their research practices, their forms of communication, their style of production that was under threat – yet they kept on attempting to rely on these to see them through.

It is important to highlight the state of mind or attunement in which existential denial emerges. It emerges not when we are in the comfort zone of our familiar ways of doing things but when the familiarity has been disrupted in such a way that we can see no way of carrying on; no way of going forward. In existential terms, we often find it difficult to embrace the experience of having no way to carry on. In Grove's terms we find it difficult to embrace the valley of death. Instead of embracing the valley of death, we "try," we "make an effort," and exert our will. We believe that the power of our will, will see us through. And yet when we rely on our will or make an effort we rely on our familiar ways of doing things – the very things that have been undermined.

The crucial danger of denial is that it takes a person or group deeper into the very experience that is threatening them and which they are trying to avoid. So the more Intel attempted to rely on its practices to respond to the threat, the more vulnerable and uncertain it became. The more we attempt to will ourselves out of the anxiety, the more intense becomes the anxiety. An example on an individual level is an insomniac. The more the insomniac "tries" to sleep, the more vigilant they are of themselves and the less able they are to sleep. So the more Intel attempts to will itself out of its anxiety, the more it plummets into the valley of death.

Furthermore, the deeper into denial we go, the foggier our vision of reality becomes. We stop seeing clearly – and more than this, stop seeing that we stop seeing clearly. Indeed it is often in the experience of denial that we may become rationally and intellectually very sharp or clear but this is often at the expense of a balanced view of reality. For example, during this period Grove found that his intellectual resources were focused on outwitting his colleagues in clever and smart ways rather than being focused on the "broader picture." Indeed he had lost sight of the broader picture.

II

If we cannot succeed by "trying," "making an effort" or by "willing" ourselves out of the dead end experienced when we cannot rely on our familiar ways of doing things, how can we relate in a constructive way to the "valley of death"? Is there an attunement or attitude other than "trying" which is possible in this experience? The way in which Andrew Grove went about freeing himself and Intel from its experience of being locked into their habitual ways of doing things suggests that there is. For Grove, together with Gordon Moore, developed a new way of seeing Intel and thus a new set of possibilities for Intel. Instead of seeing Intel as being locked into the production of microchips, Grove and Moore steered Intel towards the production of microprocessors. They enabled Intel to shed its old way of doing things and begin to develop a new way of doing things.

What needs to be highlighted is the mindset or attunement that underpinned this shift. I want to describe this as a shift from a "trying" mentality to a "philosophical" mentality – from a mentality of pragmatic "busy-ness" to quiet reflection. And I want to pose the following question to elaborate the point: How is it that Grove who was so caught up in a "trying" mentality was able to shift to a "philosophical" mentality? What enabled him to move from the one to the other?

The existential psychiatrist Viktor Frankl has developed the concept of "paradoxical intention." In terms of this idea, he believes that there are certain things that are thwarted by a "trying" mentality. As we have already seen in the case of an insomniac, the more they try to sleep, the less able they are to sleep. Similarly, he believes that for those people who have lost a sense of direction in life – the more they try to find a sense of direction, the more frustrated they will become. For a sense of direction is not something that we can "try" to find. We cannot go to the store and find a sense of direction. By giving up "trying" to find a sense of direction, we can change our relationship to a sense of direction. Indeed, giving up the need to find a sense of direction opens up the possibility of a philosophical attitude, an attitude in which instead of "trying," we come to reflect on life. We come to see new possibilities in life.

Although this may sound strange, it does provide a theoretical framework in which to describe the experience of Grove at Intel. It was precisely when he gave up "trying" to find a direction for Intel, that a new way of being for Intel opened up. There came a point in Grove's struggle that he realised that he could not struggle any more, that struggling was futile. He contemplated both his own end at Intel and the death of Intel. Yet at that very moment he entered into a qualitatively different mindset. He moved away from a mindset of "trying" or "willing" to one of "resigned reflection." In this mindset he began to ask different kinds of questions about himself and Intel: I remember a time in the middle of 1985, after this aimless wandering had been going on for almost a year. I was in my office with Intel's chairman and CEO, Gordon Moore, and we were discussing our quandary. Our mood was downbeat. **I looked out the window** at the Ferris wheel of the Great America amusement park revolving in the distance, then I turned back to Gordon and I asked, "If we got kicked out and the board brought in a new CEO, what do you think he would do?" Gordon answered without hesitation, "He would get us out of memories." I stared at him, numb, then said, "why shouldn't you and I walk out the door, come back and do it ourselves?" (1997, p. 89)

As this quotation indicates, Grove and Moore were no longer trying to fight off their aimlessness. They had given up "trying." They accepted their lostness. Grove accepted the possibility of his own end at Intel. However, the moment they gave up a trying mentality, they entered a different mode of attunement; a reflective mode of attunement; one in which they stood outside of a dogmatic commitment to the habitual way of doing things at Intel. Their minds were now free to roam; to be responsive to other possibilities. Here Grove could pose a speculative "what if" question to himself and Gordon Moore about Intel, that is, he asks Moore and himself to answer the question: what if they were replaced by another CEO?

As indicated in the quotation, the way in which Moore answered this question renewed both Moore's and Grove's sense of hope. It opened up new sets of possibilities for them; one that they could not imagine whilst in a "trying" mentality. They moved very quickly from a sense of resignation and despair to one of excitement. To be sure the excitement was mixed with much uncertainty. For they did not have a well-developed sense of the new journey that they were about to embark on. But, in the face of the unknown, they had openness to a new direction that they did not previously have. The combination of excitement and uncertainty was more hopeful than despair and resignation.

As part of their new attitude towards Intel, they began to see that Intel had already been moving in a new direction but because of their preoccupation with a "trying" mentality they had been blind to this new direction. At a grass roots level a shift had already begun to take place. Middle management, Grove notes, had for a long time been shifting production from microchips to microprocessors: "By the time [senior management] made the decision to exit the memory business, only one out of eight silicon fabrication plants was producing memories. ... Bit by bit [middle managers had been allocating] ... our silicon wafer production capacities to those lines which were more profitable, like microprocessors..." (1997, p. 97)

Paradoxically, the acknowledgement by Grove and Gordon Moore, the chairman of Intel, that they could not meet the threat posed by competition in terms of their historical strengths did not lead to the demise of Intel but enabled Grove and Moore to begin to see Intel in a new way. The moment of acknowledging their lostness was also the moment in which they were able to see new possibilities. Their moment of greatest despair was also the occasion for much hope and a new way of being. They embarked on what Grove called a "new journey." On this new journey they began to see things in their organisation that they had taken for granted. They became more attuned to the mood of the organisation. They began to realise that as senior managers they had drifted away from the coalface of the organisation's activities. They did not even know that they had drifted away. The threat of the Japanese highlighted for them that they had moved away. It made them stop and look at what in fact was occurring within Intel – and they saw how detached they had become from the various levels within Intel.

We could well articulate this as an experience in corporate therapy, a form of therapy in which an experience of fragmentation of the Intel "psyche" becomes the occasion for becoming attuned to the mood of the organisation and refocusing the technology, energy and mindset of the organisation. Indeed Grove in his post Intel crisis reflection urges senior management to learn how to listen to the fears and uncertainties emerging out of middle management. The process of listening to the fears of middle management is a therapeutic process – something that is quite foreign to the rationalist training of managers. And so what we begin to see is not only that Grove's perspective on Intel begins to change but his perspective on managing in an organisational context begins to change.

Why is it that an acknowledgement of their lostness became the basis for a new way of seeing Intel? This was because they were no longer dominated by their lostness. They were no longer "trying" to avoid their lostness and thus they were no longer motivated by their lostness. By accepting their lostness, they freed themselves from its hold over them. Once they were no longer motivated by a desperate need to escape their lostness, the sense of being lost, lost its grip on them. They could begin to see beyond the horizon of being lost. Putting this in terms that Heidegger borrows from the German poet Holderlin we may say that there where the danger is, so the saving power grows. Instead of avoiding the danger, we need to embrace it.

It was not Intel that they were killing but their old attitude towards Intel that was dying. They were freeing themselves from a historically powerful mindset. Instead of trying to meet the competition in terms of their historical mindset, they began to question the mindset in terms of which they had been habituated. The more they were able to question their habitual mindset, the more they were able to see new possibilities for Intel. Although Grove had no definite sense of the new direction for Intel, his mood was transformed from despair to an excitement mixed with a great deal of uncertainty and guilt.

Part of the process of moving from a "trying" to a "philosophical" attunement lay in both Moore's and Grove's ability to see Intel from the perspective of an other. Hence Grove's questioning in the above quotation, asking Moore how he thought a new CEO would see Intel. This shook them out of their habitual mindset and freed them to see in a new way. As we have already noted the experience of the gaze of the other is a condition for philosophical reflection, that form of reflection in which we come to question our habitual ways of doing things as a basis upon which to open up new ways of doing things.

The experience of Grove at Intel shows how difficult it can be to develop a "helicopter" perspective. For we are so locked into our habitual ways of seeing things that in the face of a threat to our way of doing things we tend to rely on them more rather than rise above them. We need to go beyond a trying mentality to develop a helicopter perspective. Going beyond a trying mentality often means embracing the anxiety of losing our path, the anxiety of not knowing where we are going. The human tends to resist this. Yet, as we see in the case of Grove, it is by accepting the loss of path that he is able to rise above the frenetic and frenzied but pointless "trying" attitude. The acceptance of the loss of path allows his mind to open up to new possibilities for Intel. And so paradoxically, it is by letting go of Intel rather than by "trying" to save it, that he allows for it to be saved!

Heidegger calls the attitude needed to embrace the anxiety of losing our path "resoluteness." In this context resoluteness is the power to affirm rather than deny our own powerlessness and limitations. It is the strength of the person who can accept his own limitations – like Socrates who acknowledged rather than denied his own ignorance. For Heidegger such experiences occur on occasions in which we are ready to embrace our own death. It was precisely on an occasion in which Grove was ready to embrace both the death of Intel and the end of his journey at Intel that he was able to move from a state of denial into a state of accepting that Intel had lost its way.

A beautiful scene that vividly depicts an experience of resoluteness is given in the video "The Dead Poet's Society." In this particular scene Professor Keating, the teacher takes his students into the vestibule of the school and shows them photographs of past generations of students all of whom were now dead. In bringing the death of past generations of scholars to "life" for the students he invokes in them a sense of their own mortality. In the moment of an experience of their own mortality, he tells them to "seize the day" and they feel the sense of opportunity and possibility he is evoking. Putting this in terms of Heidegger's notion of resoluteness, it was precisely in the moment of embracing their limitations – their mortality – that the zest for life could emerge in them. In a similar experience Grove at Intel, begins to feel excitement when he has accepted the mortality of Intel. This transformed him from an attitude of resisting the Japanese to a new one; one in which he began to "seize the day" for Intel again.

Thus we begin to see how the threat posed by competitors shifted the attunement of Grove and Moore. It shifted their attunement from one of being aggressive like warriors, trying to beat the competition to one of philosophical reflection on the habitual but taken for granted conventions and assumptions behind Intel's functioning. First they attempted to meet the competition in terms of their strengths. When realising that they could not, they began to question the conventions of their own strengths. This form of questioning was not easy. It was like questioning the unquestionable. They were seen as and experienced themselves as traitors. But it was by being able to continue with this process of questioning that they were able to envisage Intel in a new light.

III

It would be mistaken to think that just because Grove had realised that a new direction for Intel was needed that he had this direction at his fingertips. What we shall see is that just like Welch at GE, Grove did not have a blue print for the new way of doing things at Intel. He did not instantly have a new plan for the new way of doing things at Intel. He could not manufacture, produce or "will" the new direction but needed to allow it to emerge. The idea of allowing the new to emerge may sound fuzzy but Grove developed a concept which makes it concrete and grounded. He says that in the experience of disruption we need to first allow chaos to rein and then be willing to rein chaos in. In allowing chaos to reign we are simultaneously freeing ourselves from the old way of doing things and opening ourselves up to new possibilities. In reigning chaos in, we are executing a new direction for the organisation: "Much as management has been devoted to making and keeping order in the company, at times of [fundamental change] they must become more tolerant of the new and the different. Only stepping out of the old ruts will bring new insights. The operating phrase should be: 'Let chaos reign!' Not that chaos is good in general. ... But the old order won't give way to the new without a phase of experimentation and chaos in between." (1997, p. 130)

The process of allowing chaos to reign and then reigning it in follows Frankl's logic of paradoxical intention: we allow chaos to reign when we have given up the need for managing the situation; when we have given up the need to "try" and contain the threat. To allow chaos to reign is to allow the threat to overwhelm us. In allowing the threat to overwhelm us we are freed from domination by the threat and open ourselves to new ways of relating to the threat. Once we have allowed chaos to reign, we are ready to find a new focus and thus are able to reign chaos in.

From Frankl's and Grove's perspective a new way of doing things emerges by first allowing chaos to reign and then reigning chaos in. Grove's crisis at Intel allows us to see the emotional dimensions of this experience. It allows us to see the process of moving through the uncertainty of chaos to the certainty and focus of a new way of doing things. More exactly, the process that Grove went through can be expressed as movement from subjective uncertainty, through intuitive certainty and culminating in objective certainty. The experience of subjective uncertainty occurred, as we have seen, in the moment of loss of direction. Once Grove has a sense of a new direction for Intel he moves into an experience of intuitive certainty, that is, a certainty in which he sees and feels a new direction for Intel. He "knows" that the new direction is right for Intel. But because it is not yet **embodied in the world** in any way, it is nothing more than an idea or an **intuition**. While it may have intuitive certainty, it does not have objective certainty, that is it is still an idea or vision rather than a concrete reality that is expressed in all the practices of the organisation. It is when the intuition becomes embodied in the practices of the organisation that it acquires an objective certainty. It is no longer something simply in the minds of the leaders. It becomes a way of doing things. Everyone has a sense of what to do and how to be in the new way of doing things.

As we know the first sign of change was Grove and Moore's realisation that they needed to get Intel out of memories. This was a liberating thought for them. However, at this stage they knew what they were getting out of, but not what they were getting it into. They were in a between moment; between the collapse of the old ways of doing things and the not yet of a new way of doing things. This was an experience of being caught in the unfamiliarity of the unknown in which the "rules of business ... have not yet been formed" (1997, p. 139) and in which one doesn't "know exactly where they are going; they only know that they can't turn back." (1997, p. 140)

In the space between the collapse of the old and the not yet of the new, Grove and Moore began to both construct a new direction for Intel and discover that this direction was already being implemented in Intel. As we have already seen they began to see that middle managers were already shifting away from memory chip to micro processing technology and they began to build a vision around this as the new direction for Intel. They were advocating a commitment to micro processing and discovering that many of the production plants in Intel, under the instructions of middle managers had already shifted to the production of microprocessors.

In this process both Grove and Moore were themselves being transformed. They were changed by the changes. While they could see that Intel was going in a new direction, it was an unfamiliar direction to them. They thus simultaneously embraced and felt odd embracing the new direction at Intel. So while they felt much excitement they also experienced much uncertainty: "I suppose that even though our minds were made up about where we were going our emotions were still holding both of us back from full commitment to the new direction." In this state there is simultaneously conviction and tentativeness regarding the new direction. At this stage "even the shape of your desired goal is not completely clear." (1997, pp. 91–2)

Grove was on an emotional roller coast. He was caught between guilt, uncertainty and excitement. He felt **guilty** because he felt he was betraying the history and identity of Intel: "Intel equalled memories in all of our minds. How could we give up our identity?" (1997, p. 90) The experience of guilt made him hesitate in the development of his new way of seeing Intel – again showing not only how emotions cloud our business judgement but that we need to free ourselves of our old way of seeing things, that they are part of us and that to surrender them is like surrendering a part of ourselves. For we experience guilt on those moments when we give up that which is part of ourselves. From Heidegger's perspective we cannot but mourn the death of a part of ourselves.

The new emerges as we get rid of the old and the old dies as we enter the new. Leaving the old creates guilt. Entering the new is filled with uncertainty. It is an experience of being tossed between waves of guilt and uncertainty. Grove felt uncertainty because even though he knew that Intel had to get out of memories, he did not at this early stage have a strong sense of what Intel would get into. Every new idea felt strange and unfamiliar to him. As he says, he had a hard time experiencing Intel in a new set of terms. He was torn in himself because even though he knew that Intel had to get out of the memory business, he was still drawn to the memory business as a part of his history. He was caught between the new and the old. Referring to an occasion on which he challenged existing beliefs he says, "One of [the senior management team] attacked me aggressively, asking, 'Does this mean you can conceive of Intel without being in the memory business?" In response, Grove felt anxious: "I swallowed hard and said, "yes, I guess I can.' All hell broke loose." (1997, p. 90)

However, he also felt excitement because, he now had a mindset that was attuned to new possibilities. Prior to the realisation he was overwhelmed by the despair of not being able to see possibilities. Now he was open and hopeful. Once Grove opened himself to new possibilities the new direction of Intel became obvious to him. As he puts it: "if we are not doing memories, what should our future focus be? Microprocessors were the **obvious** candidate." (1997, p. 93) Microprocessors were the obvious candidate because small teams within Intel had been developing the technology for Intel. This technology, however, had been developed on the periphery of its main business which was memory chips. Once it had accepted the collapse of its main business, it was able to see what was occurring on the periphery of its business: "We had now been supplying the key microprocessors for IBM-compatible PC's for nearly five years, we were the largest factor in the market." (1997, p. 93)

As Grove became more aware of the central role of micro processing technology at Intel, he became more and more confident in the development of a new focus and identity for Intel. No longer was he plagued by feelings of guilt and uncertainty but was very much outer directed, focused on developing a new way for Intel. He became confident in the way he began to challenge those at Intel to embrace the new direction. He began to reign chaos in. He began to develop what he called strategic actions through which to bring those still habituated in the old mindset into the new way of doing things.

There are times for trying and there are times for being philosophically attuned.

12
From Control to Reflection in Management

I

Not only did the crisis at Intel lead to the transformation of Intel, it also led Grove to rethink his understanding and practice of management. Whereas prior to the crisis, he had assumed a rational understanding of the theory and practice of management, through the crisis, he became acutely aware of the non-rational dimensions of management. This includes the role of judgement, intuition and emotion in being a manager. In times of crisis, he maintains that managers have got nothing more than their intuition and judgement on which to rely. Rather than analysis, they need to rely on their ability to read situations. This leads him to conclude that rather than seeing management as primarily a technical activity, it needs to be seen as an activity which involves the person as a whole, that being a manager presupposes being a well developed and well rounded person.

Underpinning sound judgement in management from Grove's perspective is a sense of what he calls "paranoia." Managers in order to thrive need to be paranoid. Of course, he cannot mean this in the clinical sense of the word. For people who are paranoid tend to project their own feelings onto others. They do not see or read other people well at all. Grove wants to convey the opposite, namely an acute ability to read situations. What he is getting at through the idea of paranoia is that managers need to always be attuned to threats to the existence of the organisations, that being attuned to threats is the basis of being vigilant and that vigilance allows managers to be attuned to new opportunities and possibilities. They need to be able to discern different kinds of threats and real from imaginary threats. It is by being attuned to threats that they are able to anticipate and be attuned to changes in their environment.

For Grove, managers need to know how to worry correctly. It is his ability to worry that allows him to be attentive and attuned to what is occurring at the coalface of the organization. It is worry that prevents him from taking his own assumptions for granted. Worry is the basis of his curiosity: "I worry about products getting screwed up, and I worry about products getting introduced prematurely. I worry about factories not performing well, and I worry about having too many factories. I worry about hiring the right people, and I worry about morale slacking off. ..." (1997, p. 3)

Why is worry so important? It was Freud who over a century ago articulated for us the way in which fear and anxiety are states of heightened arousal in which we become more attentive to the situation in which we are. For Grove, it is his sense of worry that allows him to be constantly scanning his environment to see what is occurring: "It is fear that makes me scan ... searching for problems: news of disgruntled customers, potential slippages ... Simply put, fear can be the opposite of complacency. Complacency often afflicts precisely those who have been the most successful." (1997, p. 118)

Of course not all worry is productive. It can be paralysing. Too much worry, as Freud and other psychotherapists can tell us, leads to a numbing of our attunement. This point is reiterated by Grove who says that an environment of excessive and uncontrolled fear will "cut off the flow of bad news from the periphery." And as we have seen too little worry leads to complacency. But he who knows how to worry correctly is alive to that which is taken for granted in the complacency of routine. To be able to worry appropriately is a virtue and a sign of practical intelligence. As Kierkegaard puts it: "Whoever has learned to be anxious in the right way has learned the ultimate." For whoever has learned to be anxious in the right way is not bogged down by threats but always sees possibilities in them.

Grove believes that it is his ability to worry appropriately that allows him to see beyond the conventions of the day. It is worry that allows him to be attuned to new possibilities for Intel. For worry shakes him out of the complacency of conventions and encourages a reflective relationship to the situation we are in: "If we fear that someday, any day, some development somewhere in our environment will change the rules of the game, our associates will sense and share that dread. They will be on the lookout. They will constantly be scanning their radar screens." (1997, p. 117)

Thus what we begin to see is the role of emotional attunement or business feel in Grove's understanding of the manager. In terms of the Heideggerian language developed in the context of Welch, it is Grove's worry that allows him to "care for and be attuned to the organisation." Without this sense of care no amount of technique or even theoretical knowledge would attune him to the organisation. Paraphrasing the Heideggerian scholar Patricia Benner, our worries indicate what matters to us. We are concerned with what we worry about. It is Grove's sense of worry that allows him to feel what is occurring in the organization. Making sense of the organization requires not only analysis of data but a feeling for the organization. Feeling makes possible an attunement that cannot be attained through rational analysis of data: "But data are about the past. ...

By the time the data showed that the Japanese memory producers were becoming a major factor, we were in the midst of a fight for our survival." (1997, p. 117) In contrast to the rational analysis of data, their sense of worry had already alerted them to this fight. But, as we have seen, they denied the reality that was emerging through their worry.

This is not to say that there is no place for the analysis of data. Rather, as Grove puts it, "you have to know when to hold your data and when to fold them." (1997, p. 117) A manager needs to be able to discern situations in which they need to be rational from situations in which it would be appropriate to operate in terms of business feel. They need to be able to respond accordingly.

It is tempting to say that in the language of Daniel Goleman, Grove came to see emotional intelligence as the underlying dimension of being a manager. However, Goleman's notion of emotional intelligence does not adequately express the role played by emotion in Grove's new perspective on management. Let us have a look at why this is the case.

In terms of Goleman's idea of emotional intelligence, someone who is emotionally intelligent is aware of his/her emotions and is able to manage his/her emotions well. Thus Goleman says: "Emotional Intelligence refers to the capacity for ... managing emotions well in ourselves and in our relationships." What such a definition fails to take into account is the kind of experience that Grove had. As we have seen, Grove went through experiences of being lost, confused and in fact unable to manage his emotions. As he indicates, there were times in which he became quite infantile. To condemn him as not emotionally intelligent at this point would be to dismiss the main point, that is, that Grove was able to work himself through and out of his confusion. It was his ability to work through his own ignorance turning it into a new way of being in touch with Intel that was decisive. He went in and out of being in touch. He lost sight and then regained insight. This process of losing touch and then regaining it is part of the creative process. As Frank Barron says: "The truly creative individual stands ready to abandon old classifications and to acknowledge that life ... is rich with possibilities. To him, disorder offers the potentiality of order. ... The creative individual not only respects the [unknown] in himself, but courts it as the most promising source of novelty. ... They have more contact than most people do with the life of the ... imagination. ... The self is strongest when it can regress (admit primitive fantasies, naïve ideas, tabooed impulses into consciousness and behaviour), and yet return to a high degree of rationality and self-criticism. ... The strong self realises that it can afford to allow regression, because it is secure in the knowledge that it can correct itself." (Barron F. "The Psychology of the Imagination", 1958, p. 63)

What we see is that creative people let go of their emotions. They are not afraid to be unable at times to not manage their emotions. Indeed, they are strong enough to let go of managing them; not as an end in itself but for the sake of a qualitatively different form of being in touch. In confusion they can see new possibilities. Grove espouses the same belief. As we have seen, he talks about managers being able to allow chaos to reign in times of crisis and that allowing chaos to reign in times of crisis allows for the emergence of new possibilities.

Instead of managing his emotions and the situation in which he was in, Grove actively refrained from managing the situation. By allowing chaos to reign, he allowed the new to emerge, to show itself. He allowed himself to go through what he calls the "valley of death" in which he recognised and embraced the fact that he did not know where Intel was heading. It was by embracing it that he enabled it to move forward. Many of the most interesting leaders in the history of thought are not those who have been able to manage their emotions but who, from the depth of being lost and confused, have developed new ways of being attuned to the world in which we live.

Again we turn to the figure of Socrates whose own sense of being perplexed and ignorant was the basis of his very powerful attunement to life. He could ask all sorts of questions not because he managed his emotions but because he acknowledged and embraced his confusion. He was able to turn his confusion into a practice of questioning in which he took nothing for granted. Similarly Grove was able to turn his confusion into a way of questioning Intel and allowing it to be seen in a new light. Managers need to be able to let chaos reign in times of crisis because they need to be able to relinquish their habitual mindset. This is always an experience of chaos, because it means letting go of the stable and familiar conventions through which we have experienced the world.

It is the manager who attempts to hold onto and manage his emotions in times of disruption that demonstrates a lack of attunement to the changing situation. Here Grove would speak about the defensive manager who is in denial. Indeed, we have seen the futile attempts of Fredric Taylor to manage his nightmares. The effect of his activities was to perpetuate his need to contain his nightmares.

In the context of disruption management and leadership are not so much about managing emotions but about allowing them to speak, very often by letting go. Here we have the antithesis of the traditional view of management which was centred in always maintaining control. For historically the role of management has been seen primarily as one of control. However, Grove is maintaining that there are circumstances in the life of an organisation in which things are beyond the control of managers – like the paradigm shifting experience that was generated by the experience of Japanese competition. In such moments both control and planning would be counter productive. They would preclude management from coming to terms with the situation that they are in. For they would be controlling in terms of an old and inappropriate mindset. For, as we saw in this situation senior management tried to control and plan their response to the Japanese. But the more they tried to plan, the more threatened and chaotic things became – the more out of touch they became with their own situation. Rather than planning or controlling in the face of being overwhelmed, management needs to recognise and be attuned to the chaos that it is in. It needs to learn to listen and to acknowledge that it does not know what is going on – rather than control or plan. It is only as it acknowledges its own ignorance in chaos that it is open to new possibilities.

Under conditions of stability, control and planning might be the rules in terms of which management functions. For here order and predictability are possible. But in the face of change, as already outlined, we cannot assume that the future will repeat the past. Control is simply not possible. In the face of a paradigm switch, control is a defensive strategy which far from transforming the situation intensifies the very uncertainty that a manager may be attempting to go beyond. In order to see new possibilities we need to let go of existing mindsets. New mindsets do not emerge through controlling and planning but as I have suggested, they emerge in an artistic way, a way in which we allow the new to emerge. It is by allowing chaos to be that the new emerges. From Grove's perspective it is through experimentation that we emerge into a new way of doing things: "Loosen up the level of control that your organisation normally is accustomed to. Let people try different techniques, review different products, exploit different sales channels..." (1997, p. 130)

In times of disruption managers need to become philosophical, allowing for the questioning of habitual ways of doing things as the basis for opening up new ways of doing things. This means not that there is no terror or uncertainty but it does mean accepting it – going through it, seeing it as the basis for questioning habitual ways. It should be pointed out that Grove is not advocating allowing chaos to reign as an end in itself. Rather once chaos has allowed a new direction to emerge, it needs to be reigned in: "The time for experimentation is over. The time to issue marching orders – exquisitely clear marching orders – to the organisation is here. And the time to commit the resources of the corporation as well as your own resources – is upon you." (1997, p. 153)

The idea of a philosophical experience offers a way of working with emotions that does not reduce them to states needing – as Goleman claims – to be managed. Rather the idea of a philosophical experience enables us to understand how states of not managing can be turned into opportunities for seeing things in new ways; how ignorance and confusion can become sources of insight and vision. There is a rich tradition in the history of philosophy that would allow us to develop the idea of philosophical experiences. For example, Machiavelli's notion of the relation between chaos and virtu. Like Grove, Machiavelli believed that we cannot always manage disruption, that we need to have the strength of character to allow disruption to reign so that we can reign it in. This aspect of Machiavelli's philosophy is expressed by Gabriel who contrasts a Machiavellian with a traditional manager: "Machiavelli tried to show how rulers or managers may rule in an environment which alternates between disorder and order, not by pretending that everything can be controlled but by accepting randomness and arbitrariness. At the broad level, Machiavelli ... was operating within an implicit and occasionally explicit paradigm that life is at times chaotic." (1996 ISPSO)

Both Machiavelli and Grove define chaos in terms of the "winds of change." We have already expressed Grove's view on this. Machiavelli is quite poetic in his description of the winds of change: "I would liken her to one of those wild torrents which, when angry, overflow the plains, sweep away trees and houses ... Everyone flees ... and yields to the fury without the least power to resist. ... And yet in seasons of fair weather, men can ...construct dikes and banks..."

It is interesting to note that Joseph Schumpeter uses the image of a "gale" to describe the kind of change involved in the process of creative destruction. For in a gale our foundations are swept out from under us and we can no longer rely on our habitual foundation for doing things anymore.

The question is: what do we need to cope creatively in the "gale" force winds of creative destruction? For Machiavelli, we can never know how our fortunes are going to change but we can anticipate the fact that they are going to change. Similarly for Grove, as we have already seen, managers need to be attuned to the winds of change. He sees middle management as being attuned to the winds of change. In both cases the winds of change disrupt our habitual or conventional ways of doing and seeing things. They change the rules of the game. Machiavelli sees what he calls the hand of "Fortune" underpinning such change. Through this he conveys the idea that there are certain things that are beyond the control of managers, namely how and when things are going to change. For Machiavelli it is important that managers respect and become attuned to the limits of what they can and cannot manage. Where their ability to manage reaches its limits, they need to have the "humility" to realise their limits as a way of being able to respond in chaos. Gabriel goes on to maintain that what leaders need to cope with chaos is a sense of virtu: "What Machiavelli, along with some of his contemporaries counter-posed to Fortuna is neither management nor control, but *Virtu*." (1996)

Grove is constantly attuned to the possibility that things may change in a way that he does not and cannot anticipate. As we have seen what leaders need to be attuned to the possibility that things may change in unanticipated ways is a sense of paranoid worry. This sense of worry keeps one from being complacent. It allows one to see over the horizon and gives one the flexibility to shift one's way of thinking in line with the new changes. Corresponding to Grove's notion of paranoid worry is

Machiavelli's notion of virtu. Virtu, for Machiavelli consists in both the ability to "read" the "spirit of the times" in which we live and to have the agility of mind to change our perspective with these changes. He says that it is "necessary for [a leader] to have a mind ready to turn itself accordingly as the winds and variations of fortune force it."

Underpinning virtu, from Machiavelli's perspective is the refusal of a leader to take anything for granted. Leaders need to be constantly attuned to threats in their environment. They are constantly aware of the fact that things can be other than what they are or appear to be. They have a sense of doubt of the status quo that keeps them alive to other possibilities: "Nor let it be supposed that any state can choose for itself a perfectly safe course of conduct. On the contrary, it must reckon on every course it may take as being doubtful; for it happens in all human affairs that we never seek to escape one mischief without falling into another."

Like Machiavelli, Grove says that a leader needs to be constantly attuned to threats: "I attribute Intel's ability to sustain success to being constantly on the alert for threats, either technological or competitive in nature. The word paranoia is meant to suggest that attitude, an attitude that constantly looks over the horizon for threats to your success."It is possible to conclude that there is a relationship between Machiavelli's notion of virtu and Grove's notion of paranoia: in both cases they believe that a leader needs to know how to worry in order to deal not only with objective threats but also with the unanticipated threats involved in the winds of change. It is safe to say that there is an interesting relationship between the experience of business feel in Grove and Machiavelli's notion of virtu, and therefore that underpinning the notion of business feel is a notion of virtu, that is, that to develop our business feel we need to develop our sense of virtu.

We could also look at Aristotle's notion of practical wisdom as a basis upon which to flesh out philosophical experiences. Practical wisdom is not concerned with developing theoretical conclusions but is concerned with acting in a wise way. For Aristotle practical wisdom refers to the attunement to "straightway" "do the appropriate thing at the appropriate time in the appropriate way." The example that is often quoted in this context is the experience of appropriate anger. Aristotle says, "Anyone can become angry – that is easy. But to be angry with the right person, to the right degree, at the right time, for the right purpose, and in the right way – that is not easy." Another permutation of this is Kierkegaard's claim about anxiety: "Whoever has learned to be anxious in the right way has learned the ultimate."

Practical wisdom does not occur automatically but requires the act of being resolved. No matter how intellectually bright a person is, no matter how much knowledge or information they have before them, practical wisdom requires a resolute individual – an individual who is decisive in action. This is a position that is brought out by Hubert Dreyfus in his writing on Aristotle and Heidegger. And, as we have seen resolve emerges out of the way in which we respond proactively to what Grove called "valley of death" experiences. It is, as we said, the willingness to seize the day in the face of the experience of our own mortality. It is this resolve that allows us to be decisive in action and forms the underpinning of practical wisdom. It is also vital to our appreciation of a philosophical experience.

There is a need to go beyond the literature of "emotional intelligence" in order to understand the role of emotions in attunement. What I am suggesting is that there are rich traditions in the history of philosophy that can give us access to the notion of business feel. A further difference between Grove's notion of business feel and Goleman's notion of emotional intelligence is that whereas emotional intelligence refers to an awareness of one's own or others emotions, emotions do not form the focus of attention in Grove's experience of business feel. Grove's sense of worry is a way of scanning the environment in which he is doing business rather than an awareness of his own or others emotions. Business feel here is a way of focusing on situations – just as a musician who has a feeling for music is not attuned to his feeling for the music but to the rhythm, so Grove is not attuned to his feelings but to the business environment in which he is situated. Emotions are vital in being attuned to the world in which we operate. In fact for Heidegger, they are central to being attuned to the world. Being attuned to the world is not just a cognitive state but an emotional state. When we "care" for something that care for something has an emotional underpinning. We develop a feeling for the world. But in such a moment we are not concerned with our "feelings."

On Heidegger's version we are not emotionally attuned when we are attuned to our emotions – if anything when we are attuned to our emotions we are in a state of existential withdrawal, turned away from the things of the world to the emotions in terms of which we are attuned to the world. From Grove's perspective the focus of the emotions is not the self or person but the business or organisation. A manager is not primarily attuned to his own feelings but to what Grove calls the "winds of change." They have well developed antennae for reading how business and organisational situations are changing.

There seems to be a circular argument involved in Goleman's definition of emotional intelligence as awareness of our own feelings. We do not define cognitive intelligence or IQ in terms of an awareness of our reasoning abilities. We do not say that we are intelligent when we are highly aware of our own intelligence. Rather we identify intelligent actions in the performance of these actions. Someone is intelligent when they are exercising their intelligence in pursuit of a goal. This goal may be solving a mathematical equation. It may involve an analysis of data or a report.

In a similar way "emotional intelligence" can be seen not in being aware of our own emotions as such but in the performance of acts which presuppose "emotional intelligence." Going back to Aristotle's example of anger: "Anyone can become angry – that is easy. But to be angry with the right person, to the right degree, at the right time, for the right purpose, and in the right way – that is not easy." In this example we see that someone who is "emotionally intelligent" is not primarily concerned with his or her own feelings. Rather, we see "emotional intelligence" exercised in wise performance. We are "emotionally intelligent when we are acting in emotionally intelligent ways. Furthermore "emotional intelligence" expresses itself in the appropriate proportion of emotion – to be angry in the appropriate amount is crucial.

Worry, vigilance, seeing experiences of threats as opportunities to open up new possibilities – all of these are part of the language of business feel. Grove is not, however, concerned with introspection, with a form of worry turned towards the "self" but to the horizon in which business is conducted. He believes that the role of emotion in attuning managers to the environment in which they are situated has been neglected both in the theory and practice of management. This is because management has been seen primarily as a rational discipline. Because rationality excludes emotions, managers have not been trained to be attuned to the mood of the organisation.

II

For Grove a sense of business feel is important in organisational communication. Grove became acutely aware of senior management's isolation in the ivory towers of headquarters and thus of its need to be attuned to the "coalface" of the organisation. He was aware of the way in which a rational approach to management perpetuates the sense of disengagement on the part of senior management. He came to see that in order to be attuned to the coalface of the organisation, senior managers needed to learn how to listen to the mood of the organisation.

The process of listening involved is crucial to understand. It is not a process of learning to listen to presentations of data or information by middle managers but as Grove makes clear, it is one in which he learnt to listen to the fears and vulnerabilities of middle managers. This is because middle managers are "outdoors where the winds of the real world blow in their face" whereas senior management is "more or less bolstered [at] corporate headquarters." (1996, p. 109) Because middle managers are "outdoors," they are more vulnerable and sensitive to change whereas senior managers are protected from experiencing the threat of change. If senior management rely only on data or documented information filtered through the formal channels of the organisation, they will not be attuned to the mood of the organisation.

For existentialists it is through our fears or anxiety that we learn to read the horizon or context in which we are situated. And now we see that for

Grove it is by learning to read the fears of middle management that senior managers can become attuned to that which is occurring at the coalface of the organisation. Through being attuned to our fears we are able to sensitise ourselves to the implicit and taken for granted dimensions of organisational life – none of this will be revealed through information that is presented for analysis. In learning to listen to fears, Grove notes that the tone of voice of middle managers, their conviction and their body language are just as important – if not more so than the content of the information they are conveying. Indeed, it is their mood and body language that indicates to him that he needs to shift from engaging in an analytic examination of the content of what they are saying to a questioning of his own perspective formed in the ivory towers of corporate headquarters. Commenting on an interchange between himself and one middle manager who warned him that things were not quite right, Grove says: "My immediate reaction was to shrug off the news. I feel much safer back here in California than he does in 'enemy territory.' But is my perspective the right one? Or is his. ... I could claim to have a better overall perspective on things. Yet I have learnt to respect changes in the tone of messages from people in the field." (1997, p. 109)

The process of listening to middle management requires a Socratic humility. As Grove says in the above quote, he could claim to have a better overall perspective than middle managers and thus could shrug his worry off. However, Grove also has the ability to not take his own perspective for granted – especially when the mood of the middle manager indicates that he should be taken seriously. This willingness to listen and suspend his own perspective is often thwarted by a sense of pride on the part of senior managers, a pride in their seniority of knowledge and thus the humiliation of feeling that they have something to learn from their juniors. Grove acknowledges that this is hard: "Admitting that you need to learn something new is always difficult. It is even harder if you are a senior manager who is accustomed to the automatic deference which people accord you owing to your position." (1997, p. 145) For if senior management does not fight their pride "that very deference may become a wall that isolates you from learning new things."

This is where we need to develop a Socratic flexibility, a flexibility in which we experience our ignorance not as something to be ashamed about but as an opportunity to ask new kinds of questions. It was precisely this ability to acknowledge that he did not know that gave Socrates his competitive advantage. Like Socrates, Grove often demonstrates the emotional attunement that allows him to turn embarrassing moments into opportunities for learning. On one occasion he speaks about moments of awkwardness in expressing the new direction of Intel to middle managers. They were asking him questions that he did not have an answer for. However, rather than shutting up or becoming defensive in the experience of awkwardness, he uses it as an opportunity to examine the limitations of his own perspective. He tries to see that which he is not seeing about the organisation. Indeed these moments of awkwardness become occasions on which he says to himself: "Grove, listen up, something is not quite right here." (1997, p. 129)

It is his Socratic humility that allows Grove to maintain a healthy curiosity for the business feel at the coalface of the organisation. For in developing such a curiosity their sense of ignorance is transformed into a positive attunement in a way that enables the middle manager to experience confidence in his or her own expertise.

There is also an interesting lesson here for the debate between strategy and execution which is now popular. In terms of this debate there is a growing emphasis on the role of execution above that of strategy in achieving corporate goals. Summing up the argument Bennett et al maintain that "... it is not the lack of a strategy that causes [CEO's] to lose sleep, but rather their organization's inability to execute against a strategy, often long after they think they have expressed that strategy with near-perfect clarity." One of the reasons they give for the anxiety concerning implementation is that there is an emotional distance between senior management and those *who are much closer to the relevant products and customers.*

In Grove's terms, in order to bring strategy and execution into alignment with each other, there is a need for senior executives to develop their business feel and for senior executives and those closer to the customers and products to learn to dance with each other. For it is in terms of their feel for the business that senior executives can become attuned to the lived presence of the workface. Furthermore, as Bennet et al point out, senior executives are often perplexed because they believe that they have expressed their strategy in a rationally clear way; that they could not communicate it in more of a clear way – yet there is a failure at the coalface to implement it in the expected way.

However, rational clarity and emotional clarity should not be confused with each other. It is well known that someone can be rationally clear but emotionally confused. Rational clarity conveys data and information. It does not convey passion, feeling or even meaning. Indeed sense and meaning cannot be conveyed rationally. It is through myth, story telling, poetry and narratives that meaning is conveyed. No matter how rationally clear senior executives' expression of their strategic vision is, the sense or feeling for this vision will not be contained in the document but requires a dynamic interaction between executives and those at the coalface such that they can "feel" each other's reality. Without this ability to "feel" the reality of each other, rational expression of a strategic vision occurs in a vacuum.

This is a danger with especially scientific forms of management because it, like all other forms of (positivist) scientific activity, is premised on management not being involved in the activity of workers but of analysing and observing their activity from a distance. They are able to see and observe the behaviour of workers but not to develop a feel for the experience of working at the coalface and thus preclude themselves from being able to read vital signs at the coalface of the workplace. Rather than standing at a disengaged distance, a feel for the workplace requires managers to "immerse" themselves in the experience of the workplace.

The concept of developing an understanding or business feel by immersing themselves in the workplace does not mean that they have to become workers at the coalface. The idea of immersing oneself in a field to understand it is drawn from existential philosophy. It requires forms of dialogue that presupposes empathy and humility. It requires that senior managers develop the empathy to enter the world of the workers – not because they have gone soft but because they wish to develop an attunement to the organisation at the coalface of the winds of change. It is through empathy that they will develop a feel for the organisation at the coalface. And it requires the humility of not taking their own assumptions about the organisation for granted – that is, that they take seriously the views of the organisation of those at the coalface, even when – or perhaps especially when – they contradict those of senior management. For it is precisely in this way that they will be alerted to the hidden and unexpected in their organisation. This was the experience of Grove at Intel who both saw and did not see microprocessing on the horizon.

For Grove communicating in times of disruption is not just a rational activity but requires the use of emotions. Managers and employees in an organisation cannot be forced to accept a new mindset. The process of creating a new mindset is a process of allowing the new to emerge – just as the new emerged in Grove, so the new emerges in the employees. Historically management has used strategic plans to convey the transformation in culture and way of doing things in organisations. However, because of the abstract nature of rationality, Grove turned away from the use of strategic plans in favour of what he called strategic actions to allow the change to emerge: "What's the difference? Strategic plans are statements of what we intend to do. Strategic actions are steps we have already taken ..." Strategic plans are conveyed in a cognitive way. They are underpinned by the belief that we can through rational persuasion change our minds and behaviour. Strategic actions are underpinned by the belief that our way of thinking changes when the practices and habits in which we engage are changed. Examples of strategic actions include the assignment of an up-and-coming player to a new area of responsibility; ... a cutback in the development effort that deals with a long pursued area of business." (1997, p. 147)

Strategic actions are those actions in which the mindset of staff are transformed through actions that disrupt the habitual routines of employees. These actions call them to realise things in a new way: "While strategic plans are abstract and are usually couched in language that has no concrete meaning except to the company's management, strategic plans matter because they immediately affect people's lives. They change people's work" (1997, p. 147)

When our lives are affected by strategic actions, the mood in which we are attentive is very different from that state of mind in which we are thinking in a rational way about a strategic plan. In the face of a strategic plan we can be analytical and picky. Indeed we are attuned to a document, a piece of paper. In the face of a strategic action, when our way of doing things has changed, we are thrown into a state of perplexity in which we need to struggle to come to grips with and make sense of our new situation. There is a very big difference in being attuned to a document which expresses a strategic plan and a new situation which expresses a reality that we are not accustomed to. Strategic actions "command immediate attention. ... They cause consternation and raise eyebrows..." (1997, p. 147)

Strategic actions take people off the path that they are accustomed to. In the moment of Socratic aporia which comes from being knocked off their path, they are opened up to new possibilities of being and doing. For they cannot rely on the habitual path anymore. Strategic actions are vital to the transformation of entrenched mindsets. They create the opportunity for what Grove calls "what do you mean?" questions. These are questions that clarify the focus of the organisation and an appreciation of people of their place in an organisation. These are questions which allow for the new mindset to grow. For questions of meaning are precisely questions of a new mindset.

As Grove points out managers have a tendency to cling to old mindsets as much as possible. The sooner strategic actions can be introduced, the sooner the transition to a new mindset becomes possible. Of course this does not mean that those who feel threatened by a strategic action cannot become defensive and embrace practices of denial – as did Grove and Intel at the beginning of their experience of being threatened by the Japanese. What this means is that managers need to be able to work the various forms of response to strategic actions. They need to be able to work with anxiety and denial.

Psychoanalytic psychologists have developed the notion of a "holding environment" to describe the experience of psychotherapy. A holding environment is one in which a client is given the opportunity to express their insecurities in a safe environment. It is an environment in which people feel safe enough – held –to open up their uncertainties. Without such an environment we risk tumbling in a sea of uncertainty. Managers need to learn to develop "holding environments" for their staff in the process of change, enabling them to express insecurity with a view to transforming the paradigm of business.

13
Organisational Nationalism at Intel

Organisations are not just means to an end. They also reflect who we are. When our organisational ways of doing things are disrupted or disturbed, so we are also disrupted or disturbed. Our sense of self-worth is affected by the crisis. This is a message that is reflected through the experience of Grove at Intel. Furthermore, we cannot deal with this disturbance in a purely technical or instrumental way but need to be able to "reframe" and reflect on who we are in order to come through the experience of disturbance – not only on who we are as individuals but who we are as an organisation. Yet can we speak meaningfully about an organisation as going through an existential crisis?

The experience of Intel having its way of doing things threatened can be understood in relationship to the politics of nationalism. Just as a nation experiences anxiety and panic when it feels its way of doing things, its culture and identity being threatened, so, according to Grove Intel felt its very existence to be threatened by competition from the Japanese. Indeed, as we have already seen, Intel's way of doing things was enshrined in it like a set of religious beliefs. The threat to both religious beliefs and to nationalist beliefs is felt as a threat to a nation's very existence – or in the case of Intel, an organisational cultures existence. Intel entered a period of feeling as though it was in the valley of death.

In the context of such a threat nationalists do not act on functional or rational grounds but on emotional grounds – on the desire to protect the nation and get rid of the threat to their existence. So, too, Intel did not react on rational grounds but out of the desire to protect its way of doing things and thereby to protect its life. It may be thought that this is unusual for a business or organisation. For we are accustomed to believing that businesses are primarily rational and instrumental concerns in which we do not invest much emotions. Grove refutes this and maintains that a threat to our business is also a threat to our existence. We do not stand in a disengaged and neutral relationship to our businesses. Our businesses are part of who we are. Our "lives," our livelihoods and identities are contained in our businesses. To continue with nationalist lines of description, much "sweat and toil" is spent in developing our businesses. Intel had created a prominent place for itself in the market. It had "spilt blood" for its way of doing things. Its psyche had been built out of its way of doing things. Its confidence in itself emerged out of its way of doing things. To threaten its way of doing things was to begin to undermine the confidence it had built up in itself.

Because business has historically been treated as a disengaged rational activity, this existential dimension of business has not been given its place of importance. Grove enables us to bring out the way in which business is an existential activity. He allows us to see that just as a nation emerges out of a struggle with existence, so a business emerges out of a struggle with existence: Grove makes this point in the context of the development of what he calls the "psyche" of Intel, showing that the psyche of Intel emerged out of the way in which Intel "struggled" to create itself: "As I think back, it's clear to me that struggling with this tough technology and the accompanying manufacturing problems left an indelible imprint on Intel's psyche. We became good at solving problems. We became highly focused on tangible results. And from all the early bickering, we developed a style of ferociously arguing with one another while remaining friends (we call this constructive confrontation)." (1997, p. 84)

Thus we see that Intel's identity did not precede its "struggle" but emerged out of its struggle. It is not that Intel first had a psyche and then struggled to find a place in the market. It is as it struggled to find a place for itself in the market that its psyche emerged – and hence its way of doing things emerged. The "imprints" of its psyche emerged out of its practices. To threaten its way of doing things, as the Japanese did was thus to threaten its psyche – not just its skills or techniques but its "mind" was under threat. There is no way that we can simply switch psyche's. Furthermore, we do not need a well-developed understanding of psychology to appreciate that when a psyche or mind is under threat, it faces fragmentation. It does not simply have the resources to stand back from the threat. For it's very resources are under threat.

The psyche or mind that emerges out of struggle is not something that can simply be replaced. It is a bond with the environment. Heidegger expresses the bond in terms of the idea of a "home." A home from Heidegger's perspective is not just a house but the familiarity of a way of doing things. We are at home in the world, when we are familiar with the world. When we are at home in the world we can make sense of our experiences. We know how to get around. The sense of being familiar with the world is for Heidegger to be contrasted with moments of being unfamiliar with the world. When we are unfamiliar with the world, it is experienced as strange. In moments of strangeness we do not feel at home in the world. We do not know our way about. We do not know how to read or make sense of the situation that we are in. In Heidegger's terms, the threat from the Japanese propelled Intel into a moment of strangeness, a moment in which they felt the coldness of homelessness.

This sense of familiarity could not in a rational and calculative way be exchanged for another way of being familiar with the world. We cannot exchange ways of being familiar on the shop floor – just as we cannot exchange one culture for another culture. We cannot even be trained in ways of being familiar with things. It requires the "struggle" or the involvement in a world to be developed. For it is through the struggle that our practices are formed and that we come to develop the feeling that underpins our way of doing things. Techniques that are taught in abstraction are not guided by the sense or feeling that underpins a way of doing things. This is why those approaches to management which reduce it to a set of techniques that are packaged and handed out at training courses do an injustice to management education. The sense of struggle and "feel" out of which those techniques emerge cannot be conveyed in abstraction. It is when we try to reduce a way of doing things to a set of techniques that we run the risk of turning them into "fads."

However, when we face the challenge of our particular environment, we open up the possibility of developing a way of doing things that is rooted in our way of being familiar with the world. It is through the way in which we struggle with our environment that our know-how is built up. To think that we can simply import a "know-how" as a formula or technique that has worked successfully elsewhere misses the point. For what comes to us as a technique or formula is something that has been honed through a struggle with the environment elsewhere. In the "struggle" with the environment a sense of familiarity with that environment emerges. We come to know our way about that environment without having to think about it. So it was with Intel: through struggling with its environment it developed an embodied way of doing things; one that its people had a "feeling for."

Businesses and organisations cannot just simply shake off their cultures' way of doing things and adopt new ways of doing things. As exemplified in Grove's description of Intel's experience, Intel could not simply shake off their old culture or way of doing things. And they could not simply put on a new way of doing things. The questioning of the habitual way of doing things threw them into an "existential crisis" in which they could not make sense of the reality which they confronted. They were in what Grove calls the "valley of death," a valley which he compares to crossing a desert. In this desert the old way has died but the new way has not yet been born. Their ways of doing things are not just means to an end but are the lens through which they experience reality including themselves and other people. Deprive them of their lens and their ability to make sense of the world in which they function evaporates. They are overcome by a deep-seated uncertainty and insecurity.

Just as a nation develops a pride in its way of doing things, so Intel, through the "blood it spilt" developed a pride in its way of doing things. Just as this pride underpins the sense of identity, security and well-being of a nation, so Intel's sense of pride gave it a sense of direction and purpose. Without this it felt lost. It had no sense of how to act. All of its technical abilities were intact but they had lost their significance or purpose. It was in an existential crisis.

The existential crisis of Intel is best understood in terms of what existential philosophers call existential anxiety. Existential anxiety is the experience of uncertainty that occurs where we feel we can no longer rely on or trust our own way of doing things. As reflected in the experiences of writers like Leo Tolstoy and Albert Einstein, in existential crises, we feel as though the ground on which we stand has lost its stability. In such an experience we feel overwhelmed by a threat without having a sense of a clear focus of what to do, how to interpret or make sense of a situation, what role to play or how to be. There is no doubt that Intel had lost its focus in this existential sense: "During this time we worked hard without a clear notion of how things were ever going to get better. We had lost our bearings. We were wondering in the valley of death."

Existentialists contrast anxiety with fear. In the experience of fear there is always an object that we are focusing on. For example, we experience fear when we are threatened by a dangerous animal. In such a situation we can either fight or take flight. We are capable of acting in a goal directed way. This is not so in the case of anxiety. Our will – our strength is rendered superfluous. No matter what we do or how hard we try, this will not return our focus or allay the feelings of being overwhelmed by being threatened. This does not mean that we cannot try. It does not mean that we cannot put effort into our activities. It does mean that our efforts will amount to nothing. As Intel found, no amount of effort would give it clarity of focus and a sense of well-being. The experience of powerlessness is frightening. It is paralysing. We are overwhelmed by panic and in a sense all we can do is watch ourselves being overwhelmed by it. There is no strategic action we can take to allay it. For everything we do just brings about the terror again and again. In this experience, as Grove says, "your people lose confidence in you and in each other, and what's worse, you lose confidence in yourself." (1997, p. 139)

Grove in fact distinguishes between two types of worries. They correspond to the distinction between fear and existential anxiety already developed. In Grove's terms the one type has already been covered. He worries, as he says about objective problems like products "getting screwed up". The second form of worry is qualitatively different. It is the form of worry that occurs where our way of doing things is threatened. This is a form of worry that occurs at the moment of a paradigm shift where the old habits have proved futile but no new way of doing things has emerged. A paradigm shift for Grove is a "point of time in the life of a business when its fundamentals are about to change.... They build up forces so insidiously that you may have a hard time even putting a finger on what has changed, yet you know something has." (1997, p. 4)

The distinction between fear and existential anxiety is crucial to an understanding of the logic of existential denial. It is well known that people will do anything to avoid existential anxiety. The most terrifying fear is far preferable to states of existential anxiety. This is because in moments of fear we can at least do something. We can fight or take flight. There is some degree of agency and control possible. This is not the case in existential anxiety. We are, as already said, deprived of all power and agency. We have no sense of a future before us.

In the case of Intel what this means is that even though its way of doing things was being undermined by competition from the Japanese, it was still emotionally easier to rely on its traditional strengths than confront the anxiety of no future. For even though its traditional strengths were no longer effective, it can still do and act – rather than be overwhelmed by the experience of the "valley of death." No matter how futile its actions were, at least it could act. In the valley of death of existential anxiety we cannot even act. We no longer know who we are or what we are capable of. There is no longer a future focus: "What were we going to use for technology drivers? How were our salespeople going to do their jobs when they had an incomplete product family?" (1997, p. 91)

Thus Intel was caught between a fear, a specific threat from the Japanese and an existential anxiety, the fundamental disruption to its habitual ways of doing things. Initially rather than confronting the trauma of the disruption to its fundamental assumptions, it focused on the threat from the Japanese. At least it had a focus in the context of the threat from the Japanese. To entertain the disruption to its way of doing things was initially to entertain too much: "How could we exist as a company that was not in the memory business?" (1997, p. 90)

But it is precisely the acceptance of this moment which is the opening up of a reflective relationship to our actions. The acceptance of the terror of powerlessness is the beginning of the process of existential detachment which is the basis for philosophical reflection. In the face of fear we need to know how to act. In the face of existential anxiety we need to be willing to reflect. A leader needs to be skilled in both practices of worry. In the face of a paradigm shift leaders need to be able to deconstruct and reconstruct the organisation. In the face of an objective threat leaders need to be able to attack the threatening object. Leaders need to be able to determine when they are facing a paradigm shift and when they are facing a fear or objective worry.

The process of reflection in times of disruption is crucial to understand. Stephen Covey, in his book *The Seven Habits of Effective People* tells us that what people need in order to function effectively in the transformation from one paradigm to another is the development of certain habits. He defines habits in Aristotelian terms as that which we do repeatedly. In contrast to this, the perspective that this book has taken is that in the space of paradigm switches, in the space between the collapse of old conventions and the not yet of new conventions we cannot rely on habits to guide us. For in the cracks of conventions repetition is not possible. Repetition occurs under conditions of stability whereas in the face of change, the future is unlike the past – the very conditions that habit requires. In the cracks of conventions it is precisely our habits and habit in general that we cannot rely on. We are deprived of the safety of our familiar way of doing things. We cannot function on automatic. In the absence of habit we have no system, no rules or regularities on which to rely. Without our habits we are stripped naked.

We saw this quite clearly in the case of Andrew Grove who in the face of the disruption at Intel could not rely on the habitual ways of doing things at Intel but did not have any new habits or ways of doing things to replace the old one's with. Rather he had to learn to read and scan his environment in a new way. As he says all he had at his disposal was his intuition and his intuition was grounded in his ability to worry in an appropriate way. For his worry allowed him to be attuned to what he had taken for granted. It allowed him to operate effectively in the space between the collapse of the old and the not yet of the new – the space in which we cannot rely on habits for doing things.

Similarly Welch's business feel at GE cannot be reduced to a habit. His business feel operated in the experience of disruption of the old way of doing things at GE and the emergence of a new way of doing things. Here there were no routines or habits and no fully developed way of doing things. All that he had was his business feel – or in his terms his willingness to trust his "gut," his instinct and his feeling for the business. We saw how his business feel was grounded in the experience of frustration and how frustration led him to question the habitual ways of doing things at GE, how it led him to a new way of doing things and how it inspired him to keep GE employees on their toes. We also saw that trusting his business feel meant trusting something of which he did not have any objective certainty.

In the cracks of conventions there are no rules or methods or formulae that we can use to give us guidance. Rather we need to be properly attuned to what Machiavelli calls the "spirit of the times." Machiavelli notes that one and the same method may lead to success for one leader while it may lead to failure for another leader. For example one leader may use TQM successfully and another leader may use the same method but not gain success. It is not so much the method but the attunement of the leader to the spirit of the times in which they live that is significant. Putting this in Machiavelli's own words: "Because men are seen, in affairs that lead to the end which every man has before him, namely, glory and riches, to get there by various methods; one with caution, another with haste; one by force, another by skill; one by patience, another by its opposite; and each one succeeds in reaching the goal by a different method. One can also see of two cautious men, the one attains his end, the other fails; and similarly, two men by different observances are equally successful, the one being cautious, the other impetuous; all this arises from nothing else than whether or not they conform in their methods to the spirit of the times."

So too we may see of business feel; that one leader gets there with one kind of feel while another leader will get there with the opposite kind of feel. Jack Welch outlined a vision for GE. Lou Gertsner said that the last thing that IBM needed was a vision. What both had in common was a strong feel for their work – or to put it in Machiavellian terms, they had a strong attunement to the "spirit of the times." This spirit cannot be rationally produced. It cannot be produced by consciously following habits. For example, Covey claims that effective managers begin with the end in mind, that is, that they begin first by outlining and defining their vision and then implementing it. However, if we look at many of the leaders used in this book, they did not begin by first outlining the end that they were pursuing and then act on it. Rather the end emerged for many of them only as they acted.

For example, as already quoted, Anita Roddick had no sense of herself as an entrepreneur at the beginning of her journey. It was only once she had become an entrepreneur that she had a sense of herself as an entrepreneur. If at the pre-entrepreneurial stage of her life she were to imagine herself from the perspective of her own death, it is highly unlikely that she would have come up with a vision of herself as an entrepreneur. She herself was surprised to find herself having become an entrepreneur. This is a perspective that is elaborated in the existentialism of Sartre. As we have already shown, a person finds out who he/she is through the way in which he/she lives his/her life – not by contemplating themselves in advance. Similarly Welch had a feeling for what he wanted GE to look like but it was not an explicit image that he had at the beginning. It was only as the journey unfolded that the details became clear to him. He did not begin with idea of a boundaryless organisation. It emerged only later in his career. At the beginning as he says, he had nothing more than a feeling of what he wanted GE to look like. He had the courage of his convictions. As he committed himself in terms of his convictions, so his explicit understanding of GE and the ends that he was pursuing emerged.

What we see is that there is no one correct way of working, that it is not the habit or method that produces success but what Machiavelli calls an attunement to the spirit of the times and what I have called business feel. In both cases we are relying on ourselves, on who we are rather than on a method. In both cases, it is our intuition, our attunement, and our judgement that forms the basis of our commitment. We need to develop ourselves in order to deal with moments of disruption. Development of ourselves means in Machiavelli's terms the development of virtu. We can call this the development of character. In Grove's terms, it is our ability to worry appropriately, the ability to read our worries and to have the strength to withstand and embrace worrying. This is the non-technical dimension of management. It is under-rated but vital in management. Put simply management is not only a technical activity but requires a well developed person; someone able to act wisely in the face of adversity and contingency.

14
Philosophical Education in the Context of Management

Just as the paradigms in terms of which management are being concept-ualised are undergoing change so too the conceptions of management education, and, indeed, of education itself is undergoing a fundamental change. We are moving away from top down theoretical practices of edu-cation to more experimentally grounded views of education.

What is the educational process through which we become managers? Do we first learn about it in theory, from a blue print of management, from a course in the skills of management or from the way we immerse and involve ourselves in the experience of management/leadership? What, indeed, is the relationship between theory and practice in the learning of management?

Historically, the dominant form of education in western societies was what I shall call a liberal arts education. A liberal arts theory of education operated in terms of a distinction between theory and practice. First we learn the theory and then we apply it in practice. So to be a good manager meant to first learn the theories of management and then to apply them in practice. Such a view of education underpinned scientific views of manage-ment. Education in the scientific view of management did not mean to learn from one's own experiences but from the general theories developed by the scientists. They had developed, along scientific lines, the "proven truths" about managers. Managers needed to accept that these manage-ment scientists had developed the true way of being managers, learn their theories and apply them in practice. Managers' experience was only rel-evant at the stage of application. They had to fit their experience into the boxes of the "true" way of management established by the scientists of management.

With the emergence of adult forms of education there has been much questioning of the liberal arts notion of education. A central focus of the questioning has concerned the relation – or indeed the absence of the rela-tion between theory and practice. Theory and practice do not necessarily reflect each other. To learn the theory of something does not necessarily mean we are equipped to handle practice. This is a point that underlies the philosophy of Gilbert Ryle who maintains that to be able to theorise about something does not mean to be a good practitioner in that thing. And conversely to be a good practitioner in something does not mean to be able to speak about it in a theoretical way.

This situation is exemplified in our understanding of leadership. To be able to talk about the theories and concepts of leadership does not necessarily make one a good leader and conversely good leaders do not necessarily know how to speak clearly about leadership. Indeed this perspective has been noted again and again. For example Jim Collins, in describing Darwin Smith as an exceptionally great leader because of the way in which he transformed Kimberly Clark from a failing organisation into a great organisation, notes that when asked to describe his leadership style, Smith was at a loss for words: "Shy, unpretentious, even awkward, Smith shunned attention. When a journalist asked him to describe his management style, Smith just stared back at the scribe from the other side of his thick black-rimmed glasses. He was dressed unfashionably, like a farm boy wearing his first J.C. Penney suit. Finally, after a long and uncomfortable silence, he said: "Eccentric." Needless to say, the *Wall Street Journal* did not publish a splashy feature on Darwin Smith." (Collins, 2001, p. 68)

Furthermore, even when leaders are articulate this does not mean that they are theoretically clear in their expression of what it means to lead. Exemplary is the following definition of leadership from Jack Welch. "Being a CEO is the nuts! A whole jumble of thoughts come to mind: Over the top. Wild. Fun. Outrageous. Crazy. Passion. Perpetual motion. The give-and-take. Meetings into the night. Incredible friendships. Fine wine. Celebrations. Great golf courses. Big decisions in the real game. Crisis and pressure. Lots of swings. A few home runs. The thrill of winning. The pain of losing." (Gottliebson, 2003, p. 21)

The language that Welch is using is obscure. We experience a sense of excitement but it tells us nothing concrete. Indeed, Welch goes on to say that leadership is something that cannot be defined – even though he has been a leader for years. Conversely a theoretician who offers a crisp and clear definition of a leader does not necessarily make a good leader. For example, the following definition of leadership is clear but gives us no sense of the mood and vitality that underpins leadership: "someone who occupies a position in a group, influences others in accordance with the role expectation of the position and co-ordinates and directs the group in maintaining itself and reaching its goal."

In Jack Welch's conceptualisation, we see a vitality expressed but it is not a disciplined or rigorous definition of leadership. It conveys a sense of what leadership is about. We feel it, more than being able to construct it in rational or linguistic terms. On the other hand the social science definition of leadership is linguistically clear and precise; yet it does not convey the same sense or feeling for leadership as does Jack Welch's understanding of leadership. There is, from the perspective of the actor, something missing in the social scientist's definition of leadership. It is disengaged while Welch's is engaged.

The leader talks about leadership from within the experience of leading. The social scientist talks about leadership from an objective distance. The latter is outside of the experience while the former is "immersed" in the experience. The former's attunement to leadership is characterised by scientific neutrality, objectivity, value, freedom, etc. while the leader's very being is existentially at stake in leadership. His or her identity is crucial to their understanding of leadership. They are talking about who they are and what they do. In Jack Welch's terms he is concerned with "being" a leader; not with leadership as a concept but with the "being" of a leader. Social scientists are concerned with discovering the true or essential features of the concept of leadership, standardising the behaviors of leaders. Leaders are concerned with creating and coping at the coalface of life. The one wants an abstract definition. The other wants an understanding of his or her experiential world.

Frustration with the liberal arts practice has been highlighted within the area of teacher education where it has noted that learning theories of teaching did not necessarily make for excellence in teaching. In fact, it often creates confusion amongst teachers. Making this point in the context of pre-service teachers entering service for the first time Widlack writes of what he calls the "real-life shock" experienced by teachers in the transition from university based training to the contingent reality of the classroom. He claims that newly qualified teachers often respond to the trauma of transition "by a change in attitude from one which is university based, progressive and liberal to one which is conservative." He also notes that this shock manifests itself in experiences of teacher helplessness, insecurity and a general loss of proportion and perspective which expresses itself in a skepticism towards theory in which newly qualified teachers are advised to "Just forget what you have learnt." (Widlack, 1980) Here we see quite clearly how the contingent reality of the classroom can transform the explicit "progressive and liberal" beliefs of pre-service teachers to the "conservative" practices of teachers at the "chalk face."

Here we see how prior learning of theory rather than enhancing practice actually creates a dissonance in new teachers, a dissonance between what they are taught to think about teaching and what actually occurs in practice. Indeed as the quotation suggests the real live conditions can induce people to hold a diametrically opposed view to the one they might have had in theory. Practice and theory each has its own logic and constraints.

This situation is not unique to the teaching of teachers but also occurs in the education of managers. Andrew Grove has observed that the theoretical training of managers is often not adequate to the emotional reality of the workplace and that in the emotional reality of the workplace managers will often jettison their rationalist outlook for a more emotionally attuned one: "When your business gets into serious difficulties, in spite of the best attempts of business schools and management training courses to make you a rational analyzer of data, objective analysis will take second place to personal and emotional reactions almost every time." (1997, p. 124)

Management educators have also noted the tension between learning the theory of management and the practice of management. Steers and Porter, for example, note that even though they have collected a rich texture of scientific evidence for progressive views of motivation in the workplace, managers at the coalface tend to disregard this advice: "As we have seen throughout this book, we have learned a fair amount about work motivation and leadership effectiveness in the last few decades. However, when we survey current management practices relating to these topics, we frequently discover a sizable discrepancy between theory and practice; many contemporary organizations simply do not make use of what we currently know about motivating and leading employees." (1997)

They go on to claim that at the coalface of the workplace managers tend to be conservative, holding on to traditional views of motivation. Indeed at the coalface of the workplace the thinking of managers is not guided by theoretical categories but in terms of the contingent realities of their practice. How are we to explain this discrepancy between theory and practice? Argyris and Schon provide us with some clues to understanding this discrepancy. They maintain that theories are developed and taught under ideal time conditions while practice occurs under real time conditions. Practices are formed under "real-time conditions," (Argyris and Schon, 1977) conditions in which managers and teachers have to come to terms with the risk of failure, feelings of helplessness and, as we shall soon see many uncertainties. Their identity and practices as managers and teachers emerge not simply out of their conscious expectations of themselves but in relation to the way in which they respond to the demands of the "real-time conditions" of the classroom. These real time conditions include, as the quotation from Grove suggests, the emotional dimensions of the workplace – something that theorists consciously distance themselves from. Indeed theories are developed in disengaged, value neutral, and unbiased ways.

Theorists stand at an objective distance from their subjective matter. They are aloof and uninvolved when developing their theories. In contrast to this managers and teachers are involved in their practices. They are not observers but participators in their action. They bring their selves into their activities. Rather than searching for universal truths, they are concerned with pragmatic decisions. Summing this up Argrys and Schon have said: "The old ideal of a working relationship between research and practice has yet to be realised. The technology of rigorous research works best when it does not deal with real-time issues – for example, when scholars take years to study a decision that took several hours to make. This technology ... is based on diagnostic techniques that ignore ... the properties of effective action under real-time conditions."

Thus we see that the attunement of the theoretician and the practicing manager are qualitatively different. There is, for example, a qualitative difference between the way in which a leader talks about leadership and the way in which a theoretician or social scientist talks about leadership. For the social scientist leadership is an object of study. For the leader it is a way of coming to terms with his or her experience of the world. The social scientist is talking about something that is outside of and at a distance from him or her. The leader is talking about a set of experiences in which they are immersed.

We also see that the language of theory does not necessarily address the concerns of the practitioner. This has led to a disillusionment with theory, with some saying that there is no need for theory at all. What we need, so the argument goes, are practical skills. Skills are taught in the form of techniques. To be an effective manager is to learn the appropriate techniques and skills of effective management. Hence we see a proliferation of management techniques. These techniques reduce management to a series of formulas. In terms of this approach, as Farson says: "Thinking loses out to how-to-do-it formulas and techniques ... as the principal management guides. I can understand their appeal. Considering the difficulty of the task before them, it is not surprising that managers accept a definition of management that makes it seem as if it could be simply learnt." (1997)

The problem is that a formulas based technique approach to management has led to what many writers call an approach that reduces management to a series of fads. As one writer puts it: "Welcome to the fad-surfing Age, complete with a seemingly endless supply of programs and mantras for accomplishing 'breakthroughs' in performance .... To review just a few of the options: you can, if you wish, flatten your pyramid, become a horizontal organization.... You can empower your people, open your environment, and transform your culture..." (Shapiro, 1995)

In this approach the language of management becomes a language of jargon in which nobody really knows what they mean any more. Expressing this point Ann-Maree Moodee has said: "Managerial language is the language of corporate life, and ideally it should be used to influence and persuade. Clear communication is an essential skill for a manager who must use it to fulfill the tasks of supervising and directing subordinates. More often, however, managerial language is little more than base rhetoric; simply jargon." (2004)

This perspective is deepened by Don Watson who maintains that the language of management is an 'assembly-line' language; it's a language to stop you thinking," He goes on to maintain that it is a "language deliberately without any possibility of meaning, emotion or humour." (2003) Indeed,

Heidegger writing in the 1920's maintained that it is the function of jargon to inhibit thought. It closes and shuts down the world rather than opening up new possibilities and enabling people to learn from their experiences.

It was precisely because of the ways in which the jargon and faddism of a techniques based approach to management deprived management of thinking and vitality that Welch and others turned away from a techniques to a philosophically based approach to management. He rejects a techniques based approach as a "paint-by-numbers" approach to management, claiming that it always fails – what he calls for is an approach based on the development of ideas. Business people must know how to work with ideas. Similarly, Lou Gerstner moves away from a manual based approach to management to one which is grounded in the thinking of questioning. From his perspective managers need to be able to question the status quo. It seems self-evident to suggest that questioning the status quo requires an appreciation of the art and practices of questioning and of the forms of thinking that go into questioning. These cannot be reduced to a technique. It is precisely in the absence of a formula that such questioning occurs. This is why Henry Ford could say that thinking is the hardest task: there is no prescribed or predefined way of doing it.

We need to reconstruct our understanding of the process of educating managers. One way of addressing this question is to contrast the idea of education with the idea of instruction. This is a point made by Bruce Wilshire who maintains that the word education comes from the Latin word 'educare" which means "to lead out, or draw out." (1990, p. 22) The word instruction comes from the Latin word instruere which means to "build in." Education is thus a process of drawing out the taken for granted habits, conventions and questions that shape a person's way of seeing and doing things while instruction "merely builds in information and techniques" (1990, p. 22) without the person necessarily questioning their own habits or ways of doing things. In the instruction process we learn the perspectives and skills of others without necessarily developing our own perspectives and skills. In the instruction process we may even challenge the assumptions and perspectives of the authorities but we do not bring up our own assumptions for reflection. Our own assumptions – and thus our own "mindset" remain in the background.

This notion of education is quite reminiscent of Plato's idea of philosophy as a process of being led out of the cave. In Plato's cave we are imprisoned by the ideas of others, by the conventions of a society, so much so that we do not even know that we are imprisoned. The process of being led out of the cave is a process of learning to think for ourselves. In being led out of the cave we are moving from what custom and convention dictate to what we ourselves feel and believe.

An interesting example of the relationship between education as a process of leading out and instruction as a process of building in can be seen in the way in which Steve Waugh, the captain of the Australian cricket team learnt to be the captain or leader of the Australian team. In the early days of being a captain he was awed by the position and responsibility that he had been given. Not having been the captain of a national team before, he was uncertain as to what to do or how to be. He was in the unknown. He attempted to deal with the uncertainty of the unfamiliar role by imitating previous captains. As one commentator puts it: "Waugh did what others before him had done. He listened – to former players, captains and commentators. He took advice from anyone who was willing to give it – and there were many. He collated it all in his head and the result was, well, uninspiring. Ian Chappell recalls, Waugh captained the side in a conservative fashion, and that is not the style best suited to Australian cricketers." (Stewart, 2001)

Although taking instructions from others may have alleviated his uncertainty, it did no good for the competitiveness of Australian cricket. Waugh needed a change of approach and attitude. This began to occur on a tour of Sri Lanka in which things had been going down hill for Waugh and Australia. On this tour Waugh broke his nose. This experience jolted him out of his complacency. He began to think differently about himself as a captain: "I was sitting in the hospital with my nose smashed everywhere thinking 'Jeez, if I never play a Test again, I haven't done what I wanted to do as captain. I haven't really got stuck in and led from the front the way I'd like to have led. I've sort of been a prisoner to other people and other ideas rather than going for it myself." (Stewart, 2001)

Now instead of being a prisoner to the ideas of other people and to the approach of the textbooks, he allowed his own instinct and intuition for the role of captain to take over : "I decided to go on my gut instincts, to believe in my ability and go with that. I wanted to be loyal to myself and follow my own instincts rather than someone else's ... that takes a while to work out." (Stewart, 2001) Waugh's resolve was the point of departure for someone who is now recognised as one of the greatest captains in Australian cricket. In fact he has recently been recognised as the Australian of the year.

In this example we see how relying on the advice of others and on the approach of the textbook suppressed Waugh's own instincts from developing. Similarly an approach to leadership development based on instruction, may build ideas and techniques into people but it does not allow their own intuition or sense of voice to emerge. Without our own sense of voice we have no internal compass through which to be guided. We lose our feel for our activity and at best function on automatic. What is required for our own voice to emerge is a process of education that enables our own voice to be "led out" of the cave of the "correct approach." This is not in any way to deny the value of reading of textbooks or seeking of advice from others. It is to throw into question a process of instruction which is concerned with building things into a person rather than enabling a person's own attunement to come out. Such a person may be crammed with all the knowledge of the textbook but have no feeling as to how to act in the contingency of particular circumstances.

To learn the theories of others is thus not necessarily to refine our own way of being attuned and acting in situations. Refining our attunement requires an educational approach in which we can allow ourselves out. The process of coming out of the cave is a process of action. Our perspectives develop not by pure theoretical contemplation but in the context of acting. Leadership knowledge is a knowledge that is learnt in action. Thinking emerges out of action. We do not first know who we are as managers and then act. It is only as we act, get involved and commit ourselves that we come to know ourselves as managers. Our styles and thinking about management emerge from the way we behave as managers. An example of this is to be found in the case of Al Dunlap who developed his philosophy of management by immersing himself in the experience of managing: "Sterling was my first real chance to turn something around, even though I didn't realise that was what I was doing. To be honest, I was just there doing a job instinctively, cutting costs, hiring better people. Intuitively, I knew the business was manageable as long as I kept operations simple and profitable ... Even though I didn't realize it at the time, I was beginning to formulate the four simple rules [of leadership]." (1996, p. 118)

What we see is that he did not have his "four simple rules" of leadership in advance of leading. It was only as he acted and committed himself to the leadership situation that his philosophy began to emerge. His conceptualisation of the process that he pursued intuitively only emerged much later: "By this time, I pretty well knew what I was doing as a turnaround specialist, but I still wasn't doing it as consciously as I would at my next job ... I didn't have a philosophy then; I was doing everything on automatic pilot, based on what **felt right** and what delivered the most value to the shareholders. But out of this madness, a method was beginning to take shape – one I employed in my next job as CEO of Lily-Tulip."(1996, p. 123)

What we see is that Dunlap did not have a philosophy or even identity as a leader before the act of leading. It was through his experience of leading that he developed a philosophy, set of practices and identity as a leader. This was also the case for Welch. It will be recalled that he said that his philosophy of leadership emerged through his journey as a leader and not in advance of it. Through the way in which he engaged with experience, his voice began to emerge. It is the philosophy of Sartre that allows us to crisply articulate this experience of leadership learning. For Sartre human beings are distinguished from manufactured objects in that they are not defined in advance of their being conceived. Only through their involvement in the world does their identity emerge. We do not know who we are before we act. Only as we act does our sense of who we are become clear.

We need to act in order to learn about ourselves and our practices: "If man, as the existentialist conceives him, is indefinable, it is because at first he is nothing. Only afterward will he be something, and he himself will have made what he will be." (1975, p. 28)

Another example of this Sartrian process is the entrepreneurial journey of Anita Roddick. She did not have an idea of entrepreneurship in advance of being an entrepreneur. In fact when she started off the Body Shop she did not know that she was being an entrepreneur. It was only afterwards that she saw herself as an entrepreneur: "I never set out to be an entrepreneur, I'd never heard of the word and I was not interested in its definition. But since those days I have had plenty of experience of the ups and downs of entrepreneurship and I've met many other entrepreneurs I have admired, so I feel I can discuss the subject with a little authority." (2000, p. 38)

Putting this in Sartrian terms: "Man makes himself; he is not found ready-made; he makes himself by [his actions]." Only as a person acts do they develop an identity and a philosophy that underpins their actions. The process through which man makes himself and develops his philosophy is not through abstract thought but through his commitments. Making this point Sartre says: "We define man only in relation to his commitments; ... There is no sense in life *a priori*. Life is nothing until it is lived." (1975, p. 28) This view is echoed in Bob Joss's view of how a person becomes a leader. It is through the way in which a person acts that they become a leader: "if you actively set out to be a leader, you will probably fail because you will be too self-focused. Leaders set out to accomplish some task or goal, and it is through the successive experiences of trying to achieve those tasks that leaders are made."

It is our commitments that define the way in which we think and not our thinking that defines our commitments. If Welch, Joss or Dunlap had not committed themselves in the way that they did, their thinking would not have emerged in the way that it did. That they committed themselves in the way they did was not based on a prior theoretical knowledge but on a leap into the unknown. This leap was in both cases grounded in an intuitive conviction – not objective knowledge. As they committed themselves the intuition developed and the language in which to express the intuition emerged.

Because the expression of the intuitive dimension involves risking ourselves in the uncertainty of the unknown, the human being has the desire to avoid developing the intuitive dimension. One of the ways of avoiding developing this dimension is what Sartre calls "bad faith." In bad faith we attempt to avoid the risks entailed in expressing ourselves by identifying with the role that we are playing. We saw this in the case of Steve Waugh's initial response to being made captain of the Australian cricket team. Because of the awe and uncertainty he felt in this position rather than express his own instinct and intuition for being a captain, he played the role of captain, imitating other captains. By imitating other captains he avoided the uncertainty of expressing his own as yet unknown intuition for the position. Yet while he may have gained security, he lost his vitality.

Another example of such bad faith can be seen in the experience of Jack Welch when he became vice chairman of GE. So overwhelmed was he by the unfamiliarity of the position, he did not know how to be or what to do. He decided that he would imitate or play the role of vice chairman. Describing his first few weeks as vice chairman at GE he says: "At one of my earliest board meetings in San Francisco shortly after being named vice chairman, I showed up in a perfectly pressed suit, with a starched white shirt and a crisp red tie. I chose my words carefully. I wanted to show the board members that I was older and more mature than either my 43 years or reputation. I guess I wanted to look and act like a typical GE vice chairman." (2001, p. xiv)

His "bad faith" is to be found in his desire to "look and act like a typical vice chairman" rather than being himself. The more he played at being a vice chairman, the less the spontaneity of his self could emerge and indeed the less attuned he was to the situation. It was only when it was pointed out to him by a trusted colleague that he realised that he was playing at being a vice chairman rather than allowing himself to emerge: "Paul Austin, a longtime GE director and chairman of the Coca-Cola Co., came up to me at the cocktail party after the meeting. 'Jack' he said, touching my suite, 'this isn't you. You looked a lot better when you were just being yourself.' Thank God Austin realized I was playing a role – and cared enough to tell me. Trying to be somebody I wasn't could have been a disaster for me.

Rather than risk himself, he wants to be a "typical" vice chairman. For it is in the role of being a typical vice chairman that he could find certainty in the face of the uncertainty of a new and unfamiliar situation. In this sense bad faith is a response to the uncertainty of the unknown. Rather than risking ourselves, we will do things in the accepted way, in the way in which "others" do things. The consequence of this is that we do not allow who we are to emerge; we do not allow our own voice to emerge. From the existential perspective without our own voice, we are submerged in the opinions of other people. We lack a narrative to guide our own thinking and action. We lose, as Welch and Waugh did, their attunement to the particular demands of our situation: in the case of Waugh this meant not being able to perform at his best as a captain and in the case of Welch, his performance as vice chairman suffered from a lack of spontaneity and vitality – the very things that he had prized himself on.

It was only when they both realised that they were not being themselves and resolved to allow their own intuition to develop that they became alive to the demands of their situation. Speaking with one's own voice is crucial for understanding, judgment and attunement. If we do not speak with our own voice we risk so much in communication and clarity. As Dunlap says: "You must have goals and objectives, but they must be your own ... Your managers and employees must be able to understand what you're talking about and what they're doing."

It is important to note that it is not being claimed that all role playing is an act of bad faith. It is our relation to the role that is important. Do we imitate the role or do we allow ourselves to be in the role? We saw Jack Welch and Steven Waugh playing the role of vice-chairman or captain. It was only when they could be themselves in the role that they were authentically present. In both cases this involved an experience of letting go of the role whilst in the position of vice-chairman or captain and risking the emergence of their own way of responding and acting in situations.

An example of a leader caught between bad faith and the desire to express himself is the early leadership experience of Ricardo Semler: "My first experiences in the executive suite distressed me. Everyone was as starched as their shirts. I **tried to fit in**, I really did. I even went to a trendy men's store and acquired a complete corporate outfit – navy blue suit with white pinstripes, white shirt with French cuffs, black shoes. **I didn't wear the suit – the suit wore me.**" (Semler, 1993, p. 21)

Just as the suit wore him, so we can see the role of CEO wearing him as well. The more that the role wears us, the more we play at being a CEO, the more we are in bad faith. The consequence of bad faith is that we do not think through our own experience, we do not grapple with our own experience but are too busy modeling our experience on the experience of others. It is as though we can simply adopt others' way of doing things in an automotive or recipe type fashion **without channeling one's own prereflective opinions.** The following is a quotation from a person coming off a leadership training program and quite aware of the dangers of following another style blindly: "The question I now put to myself is: How can I do this openness and honesty stuff with the troops? It would be stupid of me to try to do it the way Margot has done it with us – it just wouldn't work, I know that. Still, it's up to me, I'm the leader, so I must trust my skills, my insights, essentially – my experience."

This person recognises that he needs to develop his way of doing things – his intuition, that if, he does not, he cannot be open and responsive. Lou Gerstner also recognised the pitfalls in attempting to "train" people to become leaders. Precisely through training them to become leaders, we preclude their leadership attunement from emerging. For leadership requires an approach which allows people's voice to emerge out of themselves. Training is an approach which builds skills into people.

Through the emergence of our own voice we become what Martin Heidegger calls "authentic." Authenticity is a state in which a person is expressing and disclosing their own voice. When Welch or Waugh played the role of a leader, neither were they doing their job at its best nor were they doing justice to themselves. Only when, they embraced the uncertainty of the new situation in which they found themselves were they able to perform and live life at its best. In this sense performing at our best presupposes not only the technical skills and habits of a role but the expression of ourselves. Authenticity refines our attunement to situations in which we find ourselves. It allows us to be alive to the dynamism of situations, rather than resting in the habits of our comfort zones.

What is the basis upon which we become either authentic or inauthentic in a particular situation? As has already been hinted, the role of existential uncertainty or anxiety is pivotal. This was seen in both Welch and Waugh. In both cases they initially played the role of vice-chairman or captain because of the anxiety experienced in the unfamiliarity of the new situation in which they found themselves. Existential uncertainty is that uncertainty experienced in unfamiliar and strange situations such as a new role or being in a new organisation. It is the state of arousal experienced when we have not yet fully embodied a role or way of doing things in a situation. It is characterised by not yet being able to make sense of the way in which things get done in a particular situation.

Heidegger believes that the uncertainty experienced in the face of the unfamiliar can be met by a sense of resolve. Resolve for Heidegger is not simply determination to succeed. It is not simply the focus experienced in being determined. Resolve is the ability to let go in the face of the anxiety of the uncertainty. In an inauthentic mode we wish to hold on rather than let go – as was the initial experience of Waugh and Welch when confronted with the unfamiliarity of their new roles. However, once they were able to let go and embrace the unfamiliarity of their new situation, they allowed themselves to emerge. They embraced their sense of not knowing what to do but they embraced it with conviction in a way that allowed their own "instincts" for leading to emerge. So, paradoxically the resolve to let go in the face of uncertainty, allows for the emergence of a voice and philosophy of, in this case, leadership. The more we try to play a role, the less our sense of resolve. The more we let go of the role whilst in the role, the more our voice in the role emerges.

Jim Collins' notion of "Level 5" leadership offers an interesting exemplification of the idea of resolve. Collins maintains that Level 5 leaders are neither simply strong, "macho men" nor are they simply withdrawn and sensitive. Rather they have a paradoxical combination of humility and powerful determination. Their sense of humility emerges out of life's experience in which they have had deep experiences of their own mortality and vulnerability as human beings. However, these experiences of vulnerability have not made them reclusive but have given them a determination which allows them to be resolute and focused in the most anxiety provoking of situations. Describing Abraham Lincoln as a Level 5 leader, Collins has said: "Level 5 leaders are a study in duality: modest and wilful, shy and fearless. To quickly grasp this concept, consider Abraham Lincoln, who never let his ego get in the way of his ambition to create an enduring great nation. Author Henry Adams had called him "a quiet, peaceful, shy figure." But those who thought Lincoln's understated manner signaled weakness in the man found themselves terribly mistaken – to the scale of 250,000 Confederate and 360,000 Union lives, including Lincoln's own." (Collins, 2001, p. 68)

These people become strong by the way in which they deal with their weakness. Rather than playing the role of macho men, they embrace their weakness, turning it into learning opportunities, opportunities which deepen them in such a way that they are not panicky in the face of anxiety provoking situations. Another example is Winston Churchill who was, for most of his life, plagued by a profound sense of anxiety and depression and yet in the most threatening kind of situation, was so attuned that he was able to provide Britain an inspiring vision in the face of an experience of deep despair.

For Heidegger, resolve is the power of embracing our own sense of power-lessness in a situation. For when we go into a new situation we are power-less because we are not familiar with what to do or how to be. We are walking into the unknown. Resolve is the virtue of being able to embrace that uncertainty when walking into the unknown. The more resolute we can be, the more our authentic voice can express itself.

Authenticity is the basis of leadership judgment. When we lead from the position of bad faith we are not present to the opportunities and possibilities in a situation. When we are authentic it allows the best to come out of ourselves and those who we are involved with. In order to lead clearly a person needs to "know" what they are doing. Knowing what one is doing is not just an intellectual activity but involves the experience of allowing one's own voice to emerge. Being present in a situation, being alive to possibilities and opportunities requires the expression of one's own voice. And in order to speak in your own voice there is a need to risk yourself in the context of your own experiences. For our voice emerges in response to choices that we make. There is a need to allow your voice to emerge out of the way in which you grapple with experience. For just as Welch and Dunlop did not know themselves as leaders in advance of immersing them-selves in the experience of leadership, so too Waugh's leadership style and philosophy emerged into an objective reality through the way he risked himself in the experience of leading the Australian cricket team. Only once he had resolved to take the risk, the leap into experience, did his authority as a leader emerge. A voice does not grow automatically. Only as we accept the challenge posed by developing our own feeling for leadership and or management does our voice begin to emerge.

Sartre would maintain that an instructional approach to management is bound to produce acts of bad faith. For in such approaches we are building techniques and ideas into managers without allowing who they are, their voice and intuition to emerge as managers. In this approach management training is conducive to the production of fads and jargon with managers playing the "role" of managers and embracing the jargon without having struggled with their own experiences. In this sense training or instruction encourages a cookbook approach to management: "Operating on autopilot … allows a manger to fall into a cookbook approach: do what other companies are doing, do it in the way the gurus say, and thereby both avoid the pressures to make independent judgments and mitigate personal accountability for deciding on a course of action". (Eileen Shapiro, 1995: 15)

It should be pointed out that anything can become a fad – any language can become jargon. A fad is not the set of skills or ideas themselves but the kind of relationship people have to the skills or ideas. It is a set of practices or ideas that we have not acquired for ourselves but have done them because that is the way things are done. We have not examined our own experiences but accept what has been built into us by the experts or authorities.

It is important to note that expressing our own voice does not mean that we cannot learn from others. The crucial issue is that we cannot use the learning of others to avoid the need to negotiate our own experiences. For our own way of doing things to emerge, for our own voice to emerge, we need to challenge our own experiences. To be sure others can help us make sense of our experiences. Indeed, they are crucial for they can enable us to see that which we are blind to in our own experience. But they cannot substitute for our need to experience and to emerge through experiencing. Conversely, learning through our own experience does not mean learning something absolutely unique and original. It may mean learning something very old. What is crucial is that we have learnt it for ourselves.

What is crucial in developing our own voice is not knowledge but the will to allow ourselves to become. This may sound strange. It may sound elementary, that the human being has a natural tendency to become itself. On the contrary, it is much easier for the human being to adopt the herd mentality, to fit, to do things the way they are done and not in any way to rock the boat. An illustration of this is given in the movie the Dead Poet's Society where an adolescent is gripped by the desire to become an actor but this involves going against his father's wishes for him. His father wants him to become a doctor. In the face of his father, he cannot express and justify his desire to be an actor. He feels his confidence crumble. At the most he finds that he can express himself behind the back of his father. He was acting without his father's knowledge or permission. But when his father does find out, he condemns the child and forces him to commit himself to medicine and to refrain from acting. Caught between the father's desire for him to be a doctor and his own unwillingness to express himself, he chooses suicide.

One way of reading the movie is to condemn the father for not allowing and encouraging the boy to be himself. Another way of reading it is that in any form of self-expression there is carried what I shall call the "in spite of" experience. Expressing our voice, becoming ourselves does not mean going against routine but it does mean that we cannot rely on routine to guide us. We can neither rely on other people or on a deity to guide us in this experience. Because it is we who are choosing these beings as significant. We have no guide when our voice is emerging. We are existentially alone. So alone are we that Heidegger considers an awareness of our own mortality as a vital element of coming to express ourselves.

To express ourselves is to make a stand. We express ourselves in spite of the uncertainty of the unknown. We do not naturally have the confidence to express ourselves. Our confidence emerges, as Sartre will tell us, out of the way in which we commit ourselves, in the face of the unknown. It is in spite of not knowing in advance the route or even the direction that our voice begins to emerge.

For too long management has been studied and learnt in a disconnected way, as though it is a set of procedures or skills divorced from the person. It is the voice of managers that needs to be developed. For whether we like it or not managers bring their own histories into management. They carry their own mindset. It is crucial that these be developed. This does not mean blindly listening to the voice of their intuition. It does mean expressing it but also having a critical relationship to their own voice. This latter theme will form the central focus of the next chapter.

Finally it may be asked: what is the significance of being authentic today? The more choices we have, the less we can rely on the voice of the expert. For it is we who need to make the choice of expert. We need to choose which management fashion to go for. It is we who need to choose between possibilities. There is nothing other than ourselves upon which to rely in making decisions. As is said in the Clue Train Manifesto: "There may not be twelve or five or twenty things you can do, but there are ten thousand. The trick is, you have to figure out what they are. They have to come from you. They have to be your words, your moves, your authentic voice."

15
The Socratic Perplexity of a Leader: The Case of Mort Meyerson

The idea of education as a process of emerging out of caves or boxes has two dimensions. In the last chapter we discussed the first dimension, namely, the emergence of our own intuition out of the willingness to commit ourselves to a task or goal. We saw this in the case of Steve Waugh and Al Dunlap. The second dimension refers to the relationship that we have to the intuitions that have emerged. Do we trust them just because they are our intuitions? Or do we need to have a critical relationship to them? Can our gut not be wrong?

Here is an example: As we know Al Dunlap's philosophy led him into much trouble. For a few years he was sought after as a CEO but he soon fell into disrepute. It seems as if his gut instinct was for breaking organisations down and had not honed the skills of putting them back together again. And he celebrated this by saying that: "Eventually, I have gotten bored every place I have been. ... I honestly feel that the infamous Al Dunlap doesn't exist except when confronted with extraordinary difficult situations." (1996, p. 26)

A balanced and well rounded leader is not one who is focused only on what he calls "extraordinary difficult situations" but has the flexibility to be attuned in a whole range of situations. Indeed the way in which Dunlap phrases it, it is as though he is not able to be attuned in anything other than "extraordinary difficult situations," for in other situations he seems unable to experience his own existence, his own sense of self. He is suggesting that he is not emotionally present in other types of situations. For in existential terms to say that we feel that we do not exist in a situation is to say that we are not emotionally "there" or present. In anything other than extraordinary situations he loses interest and focus. This is dangerous for a leader.

Dunlap does not stand in a questioning relationship to this need for extraordinary situations. He does not even begin to imagine the possibility of another kind of attunement or relationship to the world. It is as though this is the only kind of relationship that he is capable of having – as though he was born to be only in this way. It is the only situation in which his intuition operates. The need for extraordinary situations shapes his leadership style but he does not question whether or not it should shape his leadership style or how different his style could be if he questioned these experiences. He does not question his sense of not existing. It seems that he covers it up by immersing himself in "extraordinary situations." It is almost that he needs it to feel alive. As such he becomes a slave to "extraordinary situations" – just like a drug addict becomes a slave to the high produced through a drug.

Because he does not question the one dimensional nature of his leadership attunement, he is dominated and limited by it. He is suggesting that he cannot be a leader in any other way. Furthermore Dunlap implies that there is nothing that he can do about this situation: he states it as a given fact that he is vital only in extraordinary situations. It is as though it is a fact of his nature. However, from the existential perspective, our ways of being attuned to situations are not inevitable or predetermined. We can question the feeling of not existing and free ourselves from being dominated by such feelings. Indeed this is the function of existential philosophy and much psychotherapy in general. Both take the feeling of not existing as the basis for an inquiry into life and the self. Both believe that through reflecting on the feeling of not existing we can open up new relationships to life; new forms of attunement. Indeed both see such experiences as the basis of empowerment – one of the dimensions that are so often associated with leadership. We saw Grove doing this. We see him changing his attunement through a process of questioning his assumptions about Intel and about management in organisations.

We are responsible for the attunement in which we respond to circumstances. But we need to be able to work on ourselves, to reflect and challenge our way of being in order to do this – as was the case with Grove and Welch. Both were able to relate to their experience of uncertainty as a way of questioning their attunements. This is something that Dunlap appears unwilling to do. In existential terms, he is not resolved, that is, does not embrace the power to confront his own powerlessness.

What we see then is that there is a danger to acting uncritically on our "gut feel," our intuitions. They may be appropriate in some circumstances and not in others. They open the world in one way and they blind us in other ways. From one perspective they are insights. From another perspective they are prejudices. This point is made most eloquently by Fernando Flores: "I have my *beloved prejudices*. All of us have them, and we call them convictions. Sometimes we call them knowledge. I prefer to call them my beloved prejudices. You cannot say something if you don't believe it. But every belief, science and philosophy have shown, has something wrong with it someplace. You need to live with both." (1997)

The danger of acting uncritically on our intuitive judgment, our "prejudices" or convictions is that we will not, in Flores' terms, be able to see that they have "something wrong with it someplace." In this case, we will be following our intuitive judgments in a blind way. In order not to be blinded by our intuitive judgment, we need to develop a critical relationship to it. This will enable us to appreciate the limitations of our judgment, and open up the possibility for experiencing the world in new ways. Thus the second stage of education, of being led out of our cave is the development of a critical relationship to our intuitions, a relationship in which we begin to understand and unpack the beliefs or assumptions underpinning the way in which we make judgments. Allan Bloom unpacks the significance of examining our way of making judgments: "Prejudices, strong prejudices, are visions about the way things are. They are divination's of the order of the whole of things, and hence the road to knowledge of that whole is by way of erroneous opinions about it. Error is indeed our enemy, but it alone points to the truth and therefore deserves our respectful treatment. ... Only Socrates knew, after a lifetime of unceasing labor, that he was ignorant." (1987, p. 43)

In a time in which more and more leaders are speaking about the role of judgment in leadership, we need to refine the art and practice of making judgments. Refined judgment is the basis of wisdom. It is not something that we simply do off the top of our head – that is recklessness. The discipline of refining our judgment is a philosophical process that dates back to Socrates. Socrates was concerned not just with making judgments but with getting people to understand the assumptions or frameworks in terms of which they made judgments. The more we can understand the basis in terms of which we make judgments, the more we can understand where our judgments are coming from – the more we can trust our gut.

Again it needs to be said that the practice of examining our judgments is a philosophical and not a scientific process. For we are not examining any observable material entity that exists at an objective distance from us. We are examining what we ourselves believe – our opinions or prejudices. Furthermore this philosophical process needs to be distinguished from a traditional liberal arts notion of education. As was suggested in the last chapter, in liberal arts practices we tend to examine the theories of other people rather than our own assumptions. Education begins with abstractions made by others, experts. It does not begin with an examination of our own opinions. Yet, Blits has argued that philosophical education as exemplified by Socrates begins not with abstractions but with peoples' concrete opinions. Socratic "inquiry begins not from theoretical constructions or scientific theories or definitions , but from commonly held opinions about things ... Our opinions about things are our only access to ... truth." (1989)

What does the process of examining our own opinions look like? The process of philosophical education will be elaborated through the use of a case history. The experience of Mort Meyerson who at the time was CEO of Ross Perot systems will be used. Meyerson came to change his intuitions and attunement as a leader through an experience of examining his own assumptions about leadership. It is important to note that it is not simply that he came to think about leadership in a new way. He came to be attuned as a leader in a different way. His gut instinct about leadership changed. And it is this process of change of intuition, gut or attunement that will be the focus of this chapter. What will be shown is that it was the existential experience of examining his habitual assumptions about leadership that enabled him to see leadership in a new light. To say that it was an existential experience is to say that examination and question was not done in academic detachment but in a mood of intense uncertainty. As will be seen the meaning of questioning shifts with the mood in which we ask questions. When we ask questions because we feel frightened or insecure our questions emerge with a different feel than when we ask the same questions in academic detachment. The case of Mort Meyerson will make these concerns more concrete.

The case of Meyerson will also enable us to see the practical context in which philosophical questioning arises. For Meyerson did not take on the job of CEO of Ross Perot Systems with the intention of questioning his perspective on leadership. This was the last thing on his mind. He was action-orientated, wanting to get on with the job; rather than thinking about the assumptions which framed his way of getting on with the job. So confident was Ross Perot in Meyerson's habitual ways of leading that he told Meyerson to simply "follow his nose" – that is, follow his intuitive sense. Meyerson had had a history as a top-down, no nonsense style leadership. He had grown up on an authoritarian style of leadership. And it was in terms of this style that he intended to follow his nose. Describing the no-nonsense style in which he had been habituated he says: "We shifted people from project to project and simply expected them to make the move, no questions asked." Continuing he says: "In terms of priorities work was in first place; family, community, other obligations all came after ..." (1996)

Yet very soon after beginning work at Ross Perot, he found that organisational and business practices had changed in ways that his assumptions and practices of leadership were thrown into question. As he puts it: "Everything I thought I knew about leadership is wrong." He found that both his philosophy and practice of leadership were now outdated and inappropriate for the new world of work. He felt that he had let Perot down and that he was unable to lead his organisation. Talking to Ross Perot he said, "I was telling him that everything had changed. Technology, customers, the environment around customers, the market – all had changed. The people in the organization and what they wanted from their work had changed." (1996)

It is crucial to understand the type of problem that Meyerson was experiencing. It was not a problem of efficiency or effectiveness but a crisis of sense or meaning. He had lost all feeling for what it meant to be a leader. To be sure, he knew the theories of leadership and he also had a well developed sense of the habits of leadership, having been recognised as a good leader – indeed he was head-hunted for his present position. However, much like a person in an existential crisis he had lost sense of what it means to be a leader under the new conditions. Albert Camus describes this kind of crisis as an experience of the absurdity of life: "A world that can be explained even with bad reasons is a familiar world. But, on the other hand, in a universe suddenly divested of illusions and lights, man feels an alien, a stranger. His exile is without remedy since he is deprived of the memory of a lost home or the hope of a promised land. This divorce between man and his life, the actor and his setting, is properly the feeling of absurdity." (1995, p. 9)

Meyerson was in the absurd. He felt like a stranger in a world that was once familiar. He could not make sense of the world that he once inhabited. He was deprived of the sense of his know-how – much like a depressed person who has the capabilities and capacities to perform but has lost the will or energy to perform. Every practice and idea about leadership that he had acquired felt misplaced. It just did not fit.

Thus we see that Meyerson was in an existential rather than a functional crisis; a crisis in which he had to find a new meaning to leadership rather than improving or developing a set of skills for a leadership role. Thus it is crucial to understand that Meyerson is asking a question about the "meaning" of leadership. And he is asking this question not out of idle curiosity; not in an armchair but in a state of near panic. And the panic is that he has lost all sense of what it means to be a leader.

It would be a mistake to see his existential crisis as a psychological crisis. For it is not something within himself that has been disturbed – not his personality or mind. It is not as though he is in internal conflict. Rather, it is his relationship to the world that has been disturbed. As he says the environment in which business is conducted and in which organizations have operated have changed but the conventions that have underpinned his mindset have stayed the same. There is a disjuncture between the conventions in which he operates and the changing business environment. His habitual conventions for doing things do not allow him to make sense of the new reality. Thomas Kuhn calls this a paradigm crisis. It occurs where we cannot fit new facts into our existing theoretical frameworks. In a paradigm crisis novelty challenges us to rethink our framework. This was the experience of Meyerson: "Technology, customers, the environment around customers, the market – all had changed. The people in the organization and what they wanted from their work had changed." (1996)

But Meyerson did not by either instinct or habit have the framework in which to absorb the changes. His conventional mindset did not prepare him for these changes. As he says: "But I do know from my own experience that the leadership techniques that applied 20 years ago don't apply anymore." He was accustomed to operating in a top-down, authoritarian format. This, he says was appropriate for the old but stable world. In terms of the changes in the business environment this way of operating was no longer tenable. Indeed he says that if he were to operate out of the old autocratic mindset in the new world, he would "make every wrong move in the book." (1996)

Initially he did not know what he would need to be or how to behave or even how to think in response to the changing conditions. He was clueless. But he did know that he would need to change. As Kuhn notes the way in which novelty challenges us creates intense insecurity, frequently accompanied by a sense of despair. Kuhn quotes the experience of the physicist Wolfgang Pauli, who in between the collapse of the old physics and the not yet of Heisenberg's physics, entered a profound state of despair in which he wanted to give up physics altogether: "At the moment physics is terribly confused. In any case, it is too difficult for me, and I wish I had been a movie comedian or something of the sort and had never heard of physics." Yet once Heisenberg discovered new foundations for physics Pauli's whole attunement shifts: "Heisenberg's type of mechanics has given me hope and joy in life. To be sure it does not supply the solution to the riddle, but I believe it is again possible to march forward." (Kuhn, 1970, p. 84)

Interestingly enough Pauli's despair is reflected in the experience of Heisenberg in that period in which he had not yet discovered the paradoxes that would underpin atomic physics: "I remember discussions with Bohr which went through many hours until very late at night and ended almost in despair; and when at the end of the discussion I went alone for a walk in the neighboring park I repeated to myself again and again the question: can nature possibly be so absurd as it seemed to us in these atomic experiments?"

The experience of the despair between the collapse of the old and the new is reflected in the experience of Einstein: "It was as if the ground had been pulled out from under one, with no firm foundation to be seen anywhere, upon which one could have built." (Kuhn, 1970, p. 83)

We can say of Meyerson that the ground had been pulled from under his feet and he did not know where to turn. For Kuhn, it is in such moments that scientists tend to become philosophical. He maintains that for the most part scientists have no need for philosophy. They tend to get on with their everyday jobs as scientists. It is when they experience the anguish of a paradigm disruption that they tend to become philosophical, that is, tend to think about the taken for granted conventions which guide their everyday activities as scientists: "Scientists have not generally needed or wanted to be philosophers. Indeed normal science usually holds creative philosophy at arm's length. ... It is, I think, particularly in periods of acknowledged crisis that scientists have turned to philosophical analysis as a device for unlocking the riddles of their field." (Kuhn, 1970, p. 88)

We could say the same about Mort Meyerson. Under conditions of stability, he did not need to question his philosophy of leadership. Indeed such a question would have been seen as a waste of time. He needed to get on with his job. However, when he could no longer take his way of being a leader for granted, the issue of leadership became an explicit theme of concern. It was an urgent question. He could not continue as a leader without being able to answer this question. Thus we may say that the concrete conditions under which the philosophical question of leadership becomes important is when we lose all sense of leadership. In this situation, no matter what we do we will feel powerless unless we face the question.

Paradoxically then we may say that the question of the meaning of being a leader becomes a meaningful or significant question in those moments in which we feel or experience the absence of what it means to be a leader. When, as in the case of Meyerson, we lose sense of what it means to be a leader, we find ourselves face to face with the question of the meaning of leadership. When we do not feel the absence of a sense or feeling for leadership then we do not even notice that the question of what it means to be a leader is a meaningful question. Indeed we would tend to think that it is a meaningless question – that it is nonsense and that it interferes with our daily tasks of being a leader.

Although he knew that his old style of leadership was wrong, he did not have a ready made idea or set of practices for a new way to be a leader. He felt lost: "When I returned to Perot Systems ... I had to accept the shattering of my own self-confidence. I couldn't lead anymore, at least not in the way I always had." (1996) Although Meyerson believed in the need to change, his own practices and beliefs about leadership belonged to an old world and were thus out of touch with the reality of the changing world.

He knew that he could not turn back but he did not have any firm foundation upon which to step into the future. Meyerson was caught between the certainty of the collapse of the old way of doing things and the uncertainty of the unfamiliarity of the unknown future. So deep was this crisis for him that he considered giving up the position of leader: "There was a time during that first year at Perot Systems when I would go home and look in the mirror and say to myself, "You don't get it. Maybe you ought to get out of this business. You're like a highly specialized trained beast that evolved during one period and now you can't adjust to the new environment." (1996)

Yet rather than "getting out of the business" his confusion became the opportunity for developing a new vision and set of practices both for himself as leader and for the organisation as a whole. He was able to see this experience not as the basis to turn away from being a leader but to raise the question of leadership in an existentially vital way. What he asked himself, "is the new definition of leadership?" This does not mean that he was no longer lost. It means that he began to experience a new attitude towards his lostness – one in which it became an occasion upon which to ask questions. And so his questions multiplied: "To get rich, do you have to be miserable? And to be successful, do you have to punish your customers?" (1996)

What we see is that in the face of a shock or crisis in his experience of leadership he comes to ask the question of leadership. This way of asking the question of leadership is very different from disengaged "academic" question. It was not a question asked in scientific or rational detachment. Rather, his very practice and identity as a leader was at stake in this question. He was scared. He did not know his way forward. It was because his very being as a leader was in question that he came to think about leadership. Furthermore, it was not so much the disengaged concept of leadership that was under interrogation as his experience of being a leader. He was not asking theoretical questions about leadership but attempting to make sense of the experience of leadership – as a leader; from within – not from the outside.

We do not always need to be philosophical – only when our existence is questioned or ruptured do we become philosophical in an existential sense. When our old way of doing things is working, we have no need to question the terms in which we are working. We need to get on with the job, not focus on our concept of leadership. At these points the assumptions underpinning our judgments remain in the background, taken for granted. When, however, we are jolted out of our everyday absorption in leadership – then we can begin to say in an emotionally and existentially alive way "what does it mean to be a leader?" It is under such conditions that our intuitions become explicit themes for questioning – or to use a phrase of Meyerson, it is under conditions of disruption that instead of simply following our nose, we come to question our way of following our nose. When things are working well we do not even notice our own way of doing things. It is under conditions of disruption that we come to notice our way of doing things. Indeed, it was under conditions of disruption that Meyerson came to notice both his old style of leadership and open the way for a new style of leadership.

The movement from "following one's nose" to reflecting on "following one's nose" is a shift of mindset. In this shift we are attuned to different things. It is a shift from "doing" or a "doing mentality" to being attuned to our "doing mentality." For in our "doing mentality" we are not attuned to our mentality – we're too busy doing to be attuned to our mentality for doing. It is in the kind of crisis that Meyerson experienced that we become attuned to the mentality in which we "do." One example of this is the way in which Meyerson comes to notice the language that was used at Ross Perot systems to describe their way of doing things. Instead of simply just using the language to describe activities in the organisation, he came to think about the language itself.. "I listened to some of our senior leaders talk about how they handled people on teams who didn't perform. I heard talk of "drive-by shootings" to "take out" non-performers; then they'd "drag the body around" to make an example out of them. They may have meant it only as a way of talking, but I saw it as more: abusive language that would influence behavior. Left unchallenged, these expressions would pollute the company's culture." (1996)

Language which was once a vehicle of communication, now became a theme of reflection in its own right. Instead of calling for "drive by shootings" or "dragging people's bodies around," he came to reflect on the meaning of talking in this way. Instead of "taking out" non-performers, he came to reflect on the significance of thinking about people in this way. Through his crisis, he had taken an emotional step back from the everyday reality of the workplace. Instead of being involved in the hustle and bustle of business, he became sensitive to the hustle and bustle of business. Meyerson's questioning of language signaled a shift in his attunement. In his prephilosophical past, he used terms such as "drive by shooting" to facilitate activity. He did not even notice that he was using such language – there was no need to think about the language. As Meyerson says: "We called our assignments "death marches" – without a trace of irony. You were expected to do whatever it took to get the job done" (1996)

However, after his leadership crisis in meaning, he became sensitive to calling assignments "death marches" and he did not like what he saw, for he saw a warlike culture. The way in which we use language reveals who we are. To examine the language that we use to describe the world reveals our identity. This is a point that is succinctly made by Lou Gerstner who during his time as CEO of IBM came to believe in the "power of language. The way an organisation speaks to its various audiences says a lot about how it sees itself. Everywhere I've worked I've devoted a good deal of personal attention to the organisation's "voice" – to the conversations it maintains with its important constituencies, both inside and outside the company." (2002, p. 196)

In examining our language we are turning away from simply using language to communicate or to achieve our ends, to reflecting on what language reveals about who we are. It was on this level that Meyerson was shocked. The organisation's language exemplified a kind of identity that he did not want to have. It was, as he says "polluting" the culture of the organisation, creating an organisation in which people were unhappy. The price of business no longer made sense to him: an unhappy culture was not a worthy cost. In a similar way Gerstner was shocked to see what the language in use at IBM revealed about the culture of IBM. It revealed, as he says a culture of "no," one in which people could stop initiatives without any debate or deliberation, one in which "no one would say yes, but every-one could say no." (2002, p. 193)

Another example of Meyerson's turn towards philosophical questioning through examining language can be found in the following example: as an old style autocratic leader, he had motivated employees by tying pay to performance. This had allowed him to create a highly focused and motiv-ated work force which achieved excellent results. At this stage he was not reflecting on the meaning of "pay-to-profit-and-loss performance." He was concerned with the working of the system. He was confident in his leader-ship style. In his leadership crisis, however, he stood outside of the rela-tionship between pay and performance and came to reflect on the culture that was being created through it. He did not like what he saw. The costs of the good results were too much. "The emphasis on profit-and-loss to the exclusion of other values was creating a culture of destructive contention. We were about 1,500 people, with revenues of roughly $170 million. Our people were committed to growing the company – but we risked becoming a company where the best people in the industry wouldn't want to work." (1996)

The shift in his relation to language is not just a rational shift. It is a shift in mode of attunement. It is when we stand on the outside that we begin to notice the way in which language is used. This was the case with Lou Gerstner. It was, as he says, being an outsider coming into IBM that he began to notice the way in which it used language. And he began to notice the way in which it used language because he bumped up against the limits of the language. He found himself unable to use the language that every-one at IBM used. It was a strange and unfamiliar language to him. Because he could not use it, it stood out for him, that is he noticed it and it became something that he thought about – whereas those who knew how to use the language simply used it. They did not think about it. They did not notice what it said about them. Indeed they could not even begin to notice what it said about them – no matter how rational they were, they were just not attuned to the dimension of language.

Meyerson was not an outsider at Ross Perot. But his leadership crisis pro-pelled him into a position in which he was emotionally distanced from the new reality facing Ross Perot systems. The emotional experience of stand-ing outside of the language of Ross Perot allowed him to notice the lan-guage in a way that those who felt at home in the language were unable to notice. He was able to stand outside what he was within. This is the paradox of philosophical rather than scientific notions of objectivity. Scientific objectivity is not about standing outside what you are already within but simply about being outside. It does not account for the move-ment from inside to outside, assuming that it is something that can be achieved simply by the will to stand outside. The difficult movement is moving outside what you are in. This movement is not accounted for in scientific terms but is the vital and crucial step; a step that is the focus of most wisdom traditions of thought; disciplining one to have an objective relationship to one's own concerns, fears, envies etc. It is this notion that is vital to leaders who need constantly to be insiders who can get a view of the situation as a whole and not get lost in their absorption in a particular sphere.

The crucial philosophical point is that instead of simply being involved in the use of the language, he came to reflect on the language that he had been involved in using. In general terms, instead of simply being absorbed or involved in business, he now stood in a reflective relationship to the business that he had been involved in. The focus on language was not simply a disengaged scholarly and cognitive exercise. What was very important was the mood in which the questioning of language took place. It was not in the mood of academic detachment but a vital mood in which Meyerson felt his very identity as a leader to be at stake. It was in the mood of having his confidence undermined, being worried about his ability and his future direction. As such it was an existential questioning of language, a questioning in which his very identity was at stake and this questioning gave a vitality to the questioning of language which is absent in disengaged, scholarly appraisals of the language of an other. Meyerson's concern was a study of something that he was within, the very means by which he made sense of the world became present to him.

Thus what we see is that the conditions in which we come to ask questions philosophically is when we have lost sight of the answer to the questions. When we as leaders experience ourselves as not knowing what leadership is all about, and when we can embrace – as Meyerson did – this experience of the not known, then we come to ask the question of leadership. Crucial to this experience is the embracing of our own ignorance, of our own feeling of being in the dark. Here we are questioning not in academic detachment but in the uncertainty and self doubt of a personal experience. The crucial issue is to be able to hold onto our self doubt. We have called this resoluteness. Meyerson was resolute in that he had the power to embrace his own sense of powerlessness. Socrates became philosophical not because he knew better but because he did not know and was able and willing to work with not knowing.

Furthermore, it was in a mood of anguish that the question was being asked – in contrast to an academic style in which we need to be in a neutral state of mind. This is a central theme in existential philosophy. The mood in which we ask a question shapes the question that we ask and the kind of answer that we receive. Take the experience of human mortality as an example. The way we would talk about the experience of our own mortality on say a battle field has a very different mood from the way in which we would discuss it in a philosophy seminar room. In the latter case we would tend to talk about it in the disengaged atmosphere of "pure" logic. We would look at it in the form of a deductive syllogism. On a battlefield, however, it would be in the mood of dread, in the imminent threat to our own mortality that we would talk about it. In the latter case we would be wondering about questions of the weirdness of life, the senselessness of death or battle, of the possibility of a life hereafter, and of the people that we would be leaving behind. Logical proof would not be uppermost in our mind.

Similarly when we ask questions about leadership in the context of a threat to our leadership know-how and identity – this is very different from asking theoretical questions about leadership. In the former case we have, as was the case with Meyerson, lost all feeling for what it means to be a leader. His intuitive understanding of leadership has been undermined and eroded. And he is concerned with making sense of the experience of leadership. It is no good to throw a series of leadership theories at him. It is not the cognitive content of ideas represented on paper that he needs. It is not abstract proofs that he needs. Rather he needs to rekindle his sense or feeling for what it means to lead. This means looking at himself as a leader. As Meyerson says of his experience: "To answer the question of leadership meant that "I would have to look deeply into myself, reinvent my concept of leadership. And in the process, we'd all have to reinvent Perot Systems." (1996)

Just as the soldier on the battlefield enters a mood of contemplation, so Meyerson entered a thoughtful and pensive mood. He likened the experience of looking deeply into himself to the experience of being in a cocoon "I told myself I was having the same experience as a caterpillar entering a cocoon. The caterpillar doesn't know that he'll come out as a butterfly. All he knows is that he's alone, it's dark, and it's a little scary. I came out the other end of the experience with a new understanding of leadership." (1996)

Metamorphosis is that process in which we shed our old mindset as the basis for allowing the new mindset to emerge. In the experience of being between the two mindsets we cannot draw on the resources of either mindset to cope. We have left the old and so cannot draw on it but we do not yet have the new and so cannot draw on it. We are caught in the between. So it was with Meyerson: in his experience of metamorphosis he was caught in between the break down of the old and the not yet of the new. Martin Heidegger names the experience of being between the old and the new an experience of "withdrawal." Indeed, in his experience of metamorphosis Meyerson, was protected by withdrawing from the world. However, Heidegger maintains that in this experience of withdrawal, it is not that nothing is occurring or going on. On the contrary, in withdrawing from the old way of being, we are simultaneously drawing towards a new way of being. Thus Meyerson was withdrawing from an old view of leadership and simultaneously he was drawing towards a new way of being a leader. Through the metamorphosis a new view of leadership began to emerge for him; a more democratic view of leadership.

The process of working in the experience of metamorphosis is crucial to understand – especially for those of us raised in a rational mind set in terms of which only that which is already reasonable is deemed as legitimate or justifiable. What happens in this experience of change is that the very basis of reasonableness is in doubt. For what is reasonable depends on the mindset that one is in. Reason is not neutral or impartial but is informed by a set of assumptions. What is reasonable from one mindset is not necessarily reasonable from another; what is reasonable from the mindset of an autocratic leader is not necessarily reasonable from the mindset of Meyerson as a "democratic leader." Thus the way in which Meyerson reasoned as an autocratic leader was fundamentally different from the way in which he reasoned as a democratic leader. From the autocratic perspective "To be a leader at EDS, you had to be tougher, smarter, sharper. You had to prove that you could make money." In contrast to this in a democratic mindset a leader needs to develop the reflective processes through which an organisation can come to understand itself: "When people ask me for a decision, I pick up a mirror, hold it up for them to look into, and tell them: Look to yourselves and look to the team, don't look to me." (1996)

Examining his "democratic mindset" in terms of his "autocratic mindset" he would see himself as "crazy" – as defying common sense. In terms of the autocratic mindset there is no room for reflection, for enabling the organisation to "know itself." There is just the hands on stuff of getting on with the job. In the democratic mindset, however, the "tougher, smarter and sharper" leader of the autocratic variety creates a culture in which people fear to express themselves. In the autocratic style there is no room for emotional and personal dimensions whereas the democratic style is grounded in the valuing of the person. Or as Meyerson puts it: "Business-the-old way told people to leave their personal problems at home. Now we make it clear that personal issues are our issues as well. Not long ago, one of our sales executives had a child born with a hole in its heart. Through e-mail, I knew about that child within four hours of its birth. Within eight hours we had a specialist working with the infant. The child will now be able to lead a normal life. Our company made that happen because it was the right thing. It's not the only kind of thing we should do – but it does represent what we should be, the kind of feeling our company should create." (1996)

From the democratic mindset it makes sense to see personal issues as company issues but no amount of reasoning from the autocratic mindset will allow this to make sense. For, grounded as it is, in scientific views of management, the distinction between the private and the public is paramount. And so anyone who operates in terms of the scientific management mindset will see Meyerson's activities as crazy. No amount of reasoning in terms of the principles of scientific management will change this.

Similarly from the autocratic mindset the leader is expected to have all the plans. But from his newly developed democratic mindset Meyerson did not believe that as a leader he was responsible for planning. This made sense to him in terms of his new mindset but it did not make sense to those who were accustomed to the traditional mindset. They thought that Meyerson did not know what he was talking about: "In my early days at Perot Systems, people came to me and asked for "the plan." When I told them, I don't know the plan, they got angry with me. All I would say was, I don't know the plan. If that disqualifies me from being a leader, then you'd better go get another leader. We're either going to figure out the company's future together or we're not going to do it at all." (1996)

There is no way of making this switch in the role of planning intelligible through a neutral and unbiased process of reasoning – because none exists. As Meyerson says "All I would say was, I don't know the plan." What Meyerson could hope for is that his statement would create a sense of perplexity and, as been demonstrated through this book, perplexity forms the basis for questioning our assumptions, that is instead of questioning Meyerson's judgment, their sense of perplexity would enable them to question their own assumptions. However, Meyerson's refusal to offer a plan could easily be dismissed as nonsense.

The switch from the autocratic to the democratic mindset creates a child-like wonder and excitement at seeing the world in a fresh way. Meyerson was excited at the way in which the world began to appear in a new way. "The way to be a leader today is different. I no longer call the shots. I'm not the decision maker. So what is my job as a leader? The essence of leadership today is to make sure that the organization knows itself." (1996)

He also began to see his old world in a new way and much of what he sees, he does not like including the dehumanised way in which staff and customers were treated. More than this he sees that those trapped in the old mindset do not even begin to see that they are treating each other in this dehumanised kind of way. Referring back to the use of language, whereas Meyerson comes to see that talk of "drive by shootings" reflects the culture of the organisation, those who are trapped in the old mindset do not begin to see what their use of language implies about them.

Not only did he see his old world in a new way but he begins to experience a world that he had not seen before. He began to experience the organisation from the perspective of employees within the organisation. In his autocratic leadership attunement it did not occur to him to think about what those in the organisation feel about the organisation. Their feelings were of no consequence. In his democratic mode he comes to see that employees' perspectives on the organisation are central to organisational success and is shocked into speechlessness by their experience: "We convened meetings of the top 100 people in the company and asked them long lists of questions: How did they feel about the company culture? ... The answers were a laundry list of horrifying bad news. Our people were angry, frustrated, irritated, deeply unhappy. If our company were entered in a 100-yard dash, I concluded, we were beginning the race from 50 yards behind the starting line." (1996)

The answer to this question was, from the democratic perspective, vital to organisational commitment and innovation. This is something that is common sense from a democratic perspective – but not from an autocratic perspective. It was only once Meyerson's scientific management assumptions had been shaken that he could begin to see the value of caring for human beings in the workplace. This is why Meyerson is astounded when he comes to value values – because in his autocratic mindset he could not believe that values are of value. Only when he switches to a democratic mindset can he feel that values are of value – and then he cannot understand why he could not see, in the past they were of value. Indeed, he is amazed at those who are still locked into an autocratic mindset who cannot see that values are of value. Furthermore in his new mindset he begins to see some of the things that he was doing in his old mindset as "crazy."

This means that in the transition from one mindset to another the very basis of reason itself is in question. Because of this we cannot assume that reason can guide us through this transition. Indeed there is no method that can guide us through the transition. Empirical observation cannot act as a guide. For the way in which we observe or perceive is itself dependent on a mindset. We cannot see the mindset of the new world from the old one. Thus we can also say that no amount of experiential observation from the vantage point of the autocratic mindset would allow him to see the Socratic mindset. For from the autocratic mindset the Socratic way of doing things is just not perceivable. It is in the disruption of the old mindset that the new one becomes a possibility

In the case of Meyerson it was not through rational deliberation that he moved from an autocratic mindset to a democratic mindset. For there is nothing in the autocratic mindset itself that would enable him to deduce a Socratic mindset. It was only as he left the autocratic mindset behind that the Socratic mindset could appear on the horizon of his possibilities. When he was locked into the autocratic mindset, it did not open up the world in a Socratic way.

We cannot control our new mindset from our old mindset. We need to be able to let go of the old mindset to allow the new one to emerge. Meyerson had no plan of what the end point was. Indeed he says quite clearly that he was uncertain of where he was going. He needed to let himself be overtaken by the experience and allow his thinking to emerge rather than attempt to plan it in advance. This is much like Einstein's contention that change is called for by a set of problems which causes us to change in a way that we begin to think about the problems in a new way.

Withdrawal is a dynamic activity. It is full of life. And Meyerson understands this. It is important to see that he not only forms a new understanding of leadership but he also forms an understanding of the process of lostness that he is going through when he is caught between the old and the new way of doing things. Even though he has no direction, he is able to embrace no direction as a meaningful event. He is in, as he calls it the "dark" but the process of being in the dark is vital to the lightness of a new vision emerging. Being in the dark is not a nothingness, an emptiness. Something meaningful and purposeful is happening, namely, he is in a process of allowing the new to emerge. To put this in the language of Heidegger: "What withdraws from us, draws us along by its very withdrawal, whether or not we become aware of it immediately, or not at all. Once we are drawn into the withdrawal, we are drawing toward what draws, attracts us by its withdrawal. And once we, being so attracted, are drawing towards what draws us, our essential nature already bears the stamp of 'drawing towards.' As we are drawing towards what withdraws, we ourselves are pointers pointing toward it."

In conclusion we can return to the distinction between education and instruction developed in the last chapter. Meyerson exemplifies the process of education rather than instruction, that process of being led out of the cave of his habitual ways of doing things and drawing out of himself a new way of seeing the world. In this new way of seeing the world, he did not so much learn the theories of the experts as challenge his own opinions about leadership. This did not mean that he could not use the views of theorists to examine his own perspective. There is no reason why he should not. But the point is not to learn theory as an end in itself but to use it as a basis upon which to examine his own opinions. It becomes a partner in his dialogue with himself rather than something that he needs to represent on paper for an examination.

The process by which an opinion becomes an explicit theme of questioning is also exemplified in the case of Meyerson. Whilst Meyerson was confident in himself as a top down autocratic leader, he did not question his assumptions about leadership. Indeed it did not appear on his horizon as a possibility. It was only when he experienced a disjuncture between his habitual way of seeing leadership and the new business environment that his opinions on leadership became explicit themes of questioning and that he entered the existential mood of questioning. Thus it was in the experience of disruption that he noticed and became existentially attuned to his own opinions about leadership. The disruption led him out of his complacency. It was the existential basis for the act of education which we shall recall is the process of being led out of the cave of our conventions.

It is also interesting to consider the case of a leader who does not question his own intuitions. This is the case with Al Dunlap. Whereas Mort Meyerson and others see their uncertainty as a basis for questioning their views of leadership, Dunlap remains trapped in his existential restlessness. From the existential perspective the human being is capable of a whole range of attunements. We are not condemned to feeling alive only in one or two types of situations. We are not condemned to having only one mode of attunement to the world. Whereas Grove and Meyerson question their uncertainties, Dunlap remains trapped within a one dimensional intuitive understanding.

For Dunlap to have developed a more rounded experience of leadership he would have needed to question rather than simply accept his own restlessness. He was pulled and pushed. It dominated him and clouded his judgment. In order to be free of it he would have needed to embrace it by questioning it – as Meyerson and Grove embraced and questioned their own uncertainty.

16
Ricardo Semler's Philosophical Experience

I

Mort Meyerson is not alone. Ricardo Semler CEO of Semco, a Brazilian company, underwent what I shall call a "sustainability crisis"; a crisis in which his habitual style of organisational management undermined his ability to manage his organisation. Thus his style of management prevented him from sustaining his practice of management. It was self undermining. Through the way in which he responded to the sustainability crisis, he was able to transform his practice of leadership and organisational management from an autocratic and top down approach to what he sees as a democratic style of management. This transformation enabled him not only to sustain his practices as a manager but it breathed new life and possibilities into his organisation, making it a model organisation which a number of companies have wanted to emulate. He turned a self-destructive style of management into a creative and dynamic organisation – one which increased the "bottom line" of the organisation.

Semler's sustainability crisis was precipitated by two events; one organisational, the other personal. On the organisational level, the experience which began to paralyse organisational functioning was a tension between two factions within management, each of which believed in different management styles, neither of which was prepared to compromise. The tension between these two factions led to a state in which they were unable to even talk to each other and were openly hostile. Describing this crisis Semler says: "Semco was divided and confused to the point of paralysis. Even small problems were difficult to resolve; big one's were impossible." (1993, p. 45)

In the face of the crisis, he says that he needed to act. But at the time he did not have a sense of what he needed to do. He asked himself how he could stop the crisis but had no positive answer, finding himself in a position in which he had to "manage wave after wave of personal problems and discontent." (1993, p. 45) He tried to resolve the crisis by getting the parties to speak to each other. But this did not work. And it did not work

180

because there were fundamental points of principle that were unbridgeable: " It was a case of what, "in German is called *weltanschaung* – how you see the world." (1993, p. 44)

The personal dimension of the crisis was an experience of stress in which he literally worked himself to a standstill. He would work up to 18 hours a day. His habitual way of doing things was self-destructive. He was being driven to do more and more but with ever decreasing resources of strength and energy. He thought that he was physically ill and booked himself into a clinic for a check up. The results showed that there was nothing physically wrong with him. He was stressed out. In fact the doctor told him that he had "the most advanced case of stress I have ever seen in a person of 25." (1993, p. 47)

Life – his body – would not let him continue with his way of doing things. This was not a matter of will power. He had been working, on average twelve hour days – sometimes more. He worked over weekends. He literally could not do any more – yet the present way of doing business demanded more and more work. This was the essential contradiction: as a CEO, the business demanded more and more effort from him but his body had gone beyond its limits. Indeed, he says that 24 hours a day was not enough time for a senior executive. Yet at the age of 25 he was unable to continue: "I was visiting a pump factory in New York when I suddenly felt ill and again passed out on the shop floor." (1993, p. 45)

Something had to be very wrong with a way of life that did not allow a 25 year old to feel vital, that in fact produced a state of physical exhaustion and mental distress in a young man who should have been in the prime of his life. And surely in such a state we need to examine our way of life rather than trying to do more and more. Today it is called "working smarter and not harder." Business that undermines our mental and physical health is not life sustaining – the very reason for business in the first place, that is, business is about sustaining life. This is why human beings labour to produce: to nourish and sustain our lives. A business or form of business practice that is not life-sustaining needs to be questioned.

But then it is possible today that much of business has, like a ship that has broken free of its moorings, lost its anchor in sustainability. Indeed the "bottom line" seems to have become an end in itself – a measure of all things but it itself is not up for measurement. It is the value in terms of which everything is looked at but it itself cannot be questioned. To question it is to question the "holy grail" of much business.

Nevertheless Semler's stress experience called him to question not only his way of doing business but the life-style implied in business – a way of life in which all of his time was consumed by business while having no time for play and family. And he came to see that a lifestyle which demanded more and more from him but which sapped him of his strength and energy was counter to the spirit of life. Indeed no matter how wealthy he may have got from it, he was alienated from himself in it. For instead of being the driver of the business, he was driven by it. Rather than being creative and expressing himself through his work, he found himself to be reactive, constantly coping with pressure. Thus he resolved to change his lifestyle and way of doing business.

This point is made most clearly by Jan Carzlon of SAS who maintains that the more responsibilities a senior executive takes on, the less he is able to discharge all of his responsibilities. The danger of taking on too much work is that he will not be able to attend to everything that needs to be done. Writing about the responsibilities of senior executives under an auto-cratic management style who believe that they need to make all the decisions, Carlson says: "This system made it look as if the chief executive was taking full responsibility, but actually almost the opposite was the case ... He was only making decisions about those issues that came to his attention. ... Many decisions were never made. No one in the company was able to keep in mind the overall vision. ..." (1987)

It was in this contradiction that Semler was placed: more work but less able to be attuned to the full range of his responsibilities. The consequence, as Carlson suggests, is that the business began to suffer. For the decisions needed to be made. And someone needed to keep an eye on the overall vision. For otherwise the organisation is heading somewhere but is not attuned to the place or direction in which it is heading – often realising this only when it is already too late.

But it was not only Semler's life that was undermined by his habitual practices of business. The business itself was undermined by its practices. The business' way of doing business was throttling its own functioning. He found that the traditional form of managing organisations was not yielding the very results it claimed to yield. No matter how well organised Semco was, it was not achieving its potential: "Semco appeared highly organised and well disciplined, and we could still not get our people to perform as wanted." (1993, p. 53) Semler is not questioning the efficiency of Semco as an organisation. It was efficient but the efficiency was not delivering the kind of results it could be expected to yield.

For Semler this meant that he had to question the relation between productivity, discipline and a highly organised organisation. He came to see that there was no necessary relationship between order, discipline and productivity and thus he came to question the long held assumption that a well ordered, controlled and stream-lined organisation is the basis of productivity. The questioning of this assumption opened up an alternative way of thinking about productivity; one which was not afraid of but embraced chaos: "When you eliminate rigid thought and hierarchical structure, things usually get messy, which is how our factories look. Instead of machines neatly aligned in long straight rows, the way Henry Ford wanted it, they are set at odd angles and in unexpected places. That's because our workers typically work in clusters or teams, assembling a complete product, not just an isolated component. That gives them more control and responsibility." (1993)

In terms of the traditional view of management what Semler was worried about was that order and control had become ends in themselves and that managers had lost sight of the context in which discipline and control were vital. As long as they were maintaining "control" they believed themselves to be doing their job. Yet for Semler more important than maintaining control was productivity. There was for him no necessary relationship between productivity and control. Indeed, as we have seen productivity can be achieved in a "chaotic environment, one which is not streamlined. Such a view is absurd to the traditional common sense of managers. So much the worse for managers common sense: This is why Semler says: "The key to management is to get rid of managers. The key to getting work done on time is to stop wearing a watch."

When managing or watching the clock have become ends in themselves, this is organisational relations gone wrong. It is self defeating, turned away from the context in which it is situated and become preoccupied with its own activities. Managers need to give up their preoccupation with managing – with playing the role of managers. It is always the relation to productivity which must shape management practices: if productivity requires order, so be it. But if it requires a sense of chaos managers need to be able to embrace this. Management that forces organisational relations into the straight jacket of scientific management undermines its own ends.

What we see is that, from Semler's perspective, the very practices of business undermine the potential success of the business. Its way of doing things undermined its own effective functioning. Semler came to see that the traditional practices of management nurtured the contradiction in which he was wedged. It continually demanded more of him while sapping him of his dwindling resources to cope. This was not only the case on a personal level but on an interpersonal level. The traditional way of doing business created more and more tension between layers in the organisation. Managers wanted to exert more and more control while workers felt more and more alienated. The more alienated they felt, the more managers wanted to exert control. The more managers wanted control, the more resistance workers displayed. It was a never ending spiral and an untenable situation. Paradoxically "managing" people made them unmanageable.

II

This meant that the traditional way of doing business had to go and a more life sustaining one was needed to replace it. Semler was to describe this as a transition from autocratic management to democratic management. This was a transition from the rules and regulations of autocratic management to the values and choice underpinning democratic ideals. From Semler's perspective the autocratic manager places a worker in what is called a double bind, a situation in which they experience contradictory demands simultaneously. On the one hand the autocratic manager deprives the worker of his freedom to think and take initiative; on the other hand he blames the worker for not caring for and being responsive to the demands of his work. The autocratic manager claims that workers are lazy but does not see that it's their assumptions about work that construct the worker in this way.

Initially, Semler did attempt to deal with the crisis in a formulaic way. He and his colleagues tried all the gurus on the circuit. They imported change methodologies from all over the world but none of them worked: "I tried all the pre-packaged ideas I could find, scouring every business book with a title that began with 'How to ...' ... but I just couldn't make them work in our office or factories." (193, p. 53)

This is not to critique the ideas or insights in the "how to" manuals. Rather it is to say that Semler needed to discover the problem and way of dealing with it for himself. The danger with how to manuals is not the ideas in them but the fact that they prevent thinking for ourselves from taking place. They offer light in a way that encourages an avoidance of darkness. Yet it is by being able to grapple with the darkness that we come to terms with problems. It is by embracing the dizziness of the unknown that we can begin to emerge from it. Only as he owned the problem could he think through it: "I began to suspect that Semco's problems went deeper than I realised." (1993, p. 53) The more he realised how deep Semco's problems went, the more he owned them and the less he attempted to rely on a pre-packaged formula. It is crucial that literature helps us work with our darkness and not just offer light.

More than this there are types of problems that cannot be reduced to a formula or method. There is no program for dealing with the unknown. If anything the new way of doing things emerged out of the way in which Semler dealt with the contradictory nature of the traditional forms of business organisation. However now, instead of simply being overwhelmed by this contradiction, he developed an acute awareness of it. Whereas prior to the stress crisis, he was simply thrown from side to side, now he became aware of being thrown from side to side. Instead of simply living his stress in a kind of "what can I do about it?" attitude, he made coming to terms with stress a central part of his life. This allowed him to think about rather than be lost in the contradictions of the business.

It is again crucial to point out that the experience of embracing contradiction is crucial to enabling a new way of doing things to emerge. And the willingness to embrace contradiction is grounded in the resolve that emerges in those moments in which we are overwhelmed by stress

(Semler), worry (Grove) and meaningless (Meyerson). For those who are in the stability of a rational mindset, contradiction is seen as something to be eliminated rather than as an energy that allows the new to emerge. In a rational mindset we tend to eliminate one arm of the contradiction. We, for example, ignore the demands of the body and work harder and harder. Yet for those of us who have had their lives disrupted, contradiction is the motor of change. As Kierkegaard says, contradiction is a challenge: "A contradiction is always the expression of a task, and a task is a movement..." (1980, p. 28)

As he embraced the contradiction, the absurdity of the old way of doing business came more and more into focus. To say that they were absurd is to say that they defied common sense. That they defy common sense means that we cannot take them seriously. They need to be overturned and new ways of being attuned put in their place. For example, a habitual assumption of work in the traditional model was that people should be formally attired when they come to work. Semler demonstrates the absurdity of this: "Why is it that when they come to work on weekends, people invariably dress in casual clothes? Because they feel more comfortable. Well why shouldn't they feel more comfortable everyday? So we told all our office workers and managers they could dress as they pleased. Period." (1993, p. 55)

What we see is that as the absurdity of the old way of doing business is crystallised so the principles and practices for a new way of being in organisations became clearer. Both a new form of thinking about organisations and new forms of organisational practice began to emerge and crystallise for him. Using the absurd to highlight the limitations of a way of seeing things and as the basis for opening up a new way of seeing things goes back to Socrates. In fact Semler is a master at creating a sense of Socratic perplexity. Just as Socrates incited people into thinking by showing them that their habitual way of seeing things was absurd, Semler brings us to think by highlighting the absurdity of current business practices.

Semler's questioning of traditional ways of doing things as a basis for developing new ways of doing things did not follow a predefined pattern. Rather Semler was following his nose, he was following a gut feeling or intuition that emerged out of his stress. This intuition only began to take shape as he committed himself to change. For example, Semler decided to end body searches of adults leaving the grounds of the organisation at the end of the day. On the new found assumption that workers were not items of machinery but adults, and that they liked to be treated as adults, he simply "decided to end the searches at Semco." No formula or procedure was involved: "It wasn't hard. I just had a sign posted at the gate that read, 'Please make sure that as you leave that you are not inadvertently taking anything that does not belong to you.'" (1993, p. 54)

Semler was surprised by the reaction from the workers. He expected them to feel empowered and trusted when he scrapped the body searchers. To his surprise, he found that they "demanded that searches be resumed." They were anxious that "they would be blamed if a tool disappeared." A plant-wide assembly was called to calm things down. He notes the contradiction in the workers attitude: "Imagine! Workers wanted to be searched to prove their innocence." (193, p. 55)

Although Semler was surprised at the workers response, it did not make him turn back but led to the refining of his new perspective. Workers wanted to reinstate the body searches because of a culture of mistrust. They believed that the best way to avoid management suspicion was to agree to being searched. Semler came to question workers assumptions that suspicion could only be dealt with by body searches at the end of the day. Rather there had to be a different way of dealing with mistrust in the work-place. This was not through any regulation but through a new philosophy or attitude towards theft: he gave up worrying about thefts. Semler realised that there were no conditions under which thefts could be eliminated, that no matter how sophisticated the monitoring in an organisation is, it will not eliminate thefts. But monitoring will create a culture of suspicion which would be bad for employee relationships. He would rather have a culture of trust than monitor threats: "Have thefts ... decreased? I don't know and I don't care." (193, p. 55)

Where theft is disregarded as an issue, workers do not have to worry about proving that they are not stealing. From Semler's perspective, moni-toring intensifies the problem that it intends to resolve. It entrenches a culture of suspicion, a feeling of being watched. Even if workers are relieved to be searched so as to confirm that it is not them that is found to be steal-ing, they are still in a paranoid state, a state of feeling watched. When the issue of theft is made insignificant, as it was by Semler, workers do not have to worry about being looked at as though they were stealing or about to steal. From Semler's perspective the traditional way of managing theft through monitoring reinforces the very problem it wishes to eliminate. It reinforces a culture of suspicion. To go beyond this we need to come to terms with theft in the workplace. Accept it and move beyond it.

Here we have a clear example of the way in which Semler reorganised his business practices by changing the assumptions in terms of which he thought about business. He questioned the traditional assumption about theft in the business. This allowed him to see theft and to relate to his workers in a new light.

From the outside it may appear as though Semler was taking many unnecessary risks. But stronger than any rational calculation of risk was a commitment to an intuition: "I couldn't help thinking that Semco could be run differently, without counting everything, without regulating every-one, without keeping track of whether people were late, without all those numbers and all those rules." Rational calculation was much weaker than the emotional power of this intuition. And this intuition, in turn got its strength from his experience of stress. The power of stress to paralyse him, his desire to go beyond stress and discover a new way of doing things underpinned his intuition. In his experience of stress he saw that it was precisely the counting of everything, the regulating of everyone, the keeping track of people's time, the preoccupation with rules and numbers that were the source of stress. The system was too busy monitoring itself in order to unleash its full potential and focus on its main job, production.

For Semler the only framework that could release both him and the organisation from stress and tension was a democratic framework. This is because it catered for the very tensions that surfaced in an autocratic system. In terms of a democratic mindset not only would managers be able to delegate work but they would also be able to tap into employees creative ability and their sense of know-how at the shop floor – contrast with scientific management where managers without being on the shop floor knew best, made decisions for workers without having a feel for the work. In terms of a democratic mindset managers are able to listen to the workers' appreciation of their feel for their work and managers are able to work with the suggestions that workers make. This is threatening to a traditional manager but is common sense from a perspective which treats the worker as an adult possessed of responsible judgement.

Instead of managers being concerned primarily with monitoring of work being done, in a democratic system, the role of management would be to allow the people to flourish, to express themselves. Instead of depriving them of their initiative and will the role of management would be to help them express their potential. Managers would become counsellors of potential. A democratic mindset is one that is able to entertain the kind of chaos and uncertainty that is required for innovation and enthusiasm. This form of democracy is crucial for allowing people to care for their work. In order to enable workers to work they must be allowed to care for their work and in order to care they must have responsibility for their work. They must own the work. Thus we need to give up the idea of controlling the workforce: "We are thrilled that our workers are self-governing and self-managing. It means they **care** about their jobs and about their company, and that's good for all of us."

Thus we see that, in the case of Semler, democracy emerges as a release from stress. It provides a framework in which the negative energy collected in the tensions and contradictions created by scientific forms of management can be released as a positive and creative force. It is not that democracy grew out of a detached or disengaged ideal of being democratic. Semler did not commit himself to democratic change because he was an ideologue who believed in democracy. In fact, as has been said, he did not have a firm sense of the direction in which he was taking Semco. He did not impose democracy on to it. It grew out of his commitment to change. Only well into the process could he see that it was a democratic culture that he was creating. Initially he used vague words such as " a natural business' to describe what he wanted. In a sense his democracy grew out of a pragmatic response to a situation of stress. It was a response to the unsustainability of the traditional practices of management at Semco. And as such it was a response to a sustainability crisis. It was not driven by the bottom line – although it did improve the bottom line. It was driven by the way in which a traditional concern with the bottom line undermines the life of those who are dominated by a concern with the bottom line.

III

However that democracy allows for individual empowerment does not mean that it promotes an atmosphere of "anything goes." Democracies are held together by values and by reflection on values. There is so much talk about values today and just as much scepticism about talking the language of values in organisation. Yet put in historical perspective, values have had a far longer history than regulations and rules in ensuring organisational cohesiveness and focus. In fact going right back to Plato's Republic, we see that a society is held together by a set of values and that the primary aim of educating the youth is to enable them to internalise the values that allow for social cohesiveness. For Plato the use of rules and regulations to maintain order in a society indicates a breakdown in the cohesiveness of society, that rules and regulations are used to attempt to patch up an already bad state of affairs. We also witness the same phenomenon in the politics of nationalism: people are prepared to fight to the death for a set of values. It unites people in a common purpose that does not require monitoring or policing from a management class.

How do values hold a modern corporation together? Responsibility is the basis of the values through which Semco is held together. Whereas in scientific concepts of management, managers are responsible for defining the work that needs to be done, determining how it should be done, constructing relations between workers and setting the salaries of employees in Semco employees are responsible for shaping their work practices. Under scientific concepts of management, workers are not responsible for themselves. Indeed because they are simply disembodied cogs in the machine, they, like machines cannot have responsibility for their actions. It is because accountability for self is not built into the scientific management concept of being an employee that workers do not see accountability as a standard in terms of which to behave. Again we see a double bind in scientific concepts of management: they deprive workers of responsibility for work and then wonder why they do not take responsibility for their work. But of course, as McGregor informed us, scientific managers are not for the most aware that they are projecting their own assumptions onto the workers.

At Semco everyone is responsible for their work. What does this mean? It means that rather than being able to blame the system when something goes wrong, they are accountable for the situation. They need to be able to come to terms with themselves in the face of criticism and where necessary they need to be able to change their way of doing things. The way in which accountability and responsibility work at Semco can be explained through what I have, following Sartre called the "gaze or look of the other." The gaze of the other refers to the way in which we look at ourselves in terms of the way in which others look at us. The example that was given early was that of Terry Anderson in Beirut who came to examine himself in the way that his colleagues examined him.

Semco has a number of practices which can be described in terms of the gaze of the other. In a traditional organisation salaries are usually private. They are not discussed in a public way. Furthermore they are usually set by senior management. Semco questioned both the privacy and the top down nature in which salaries were set. They believed that people should be responsible for setting their own salaries and that the salaries that were set should be publicly available and discussible. This gave people both the freedom to decide on their salaries but also ensured a mechanism through which the salaries people set for themselves could be held under check. For the salary that we set ourselves is always under the gaze of the other and needs to be justified before the other. There is no hiding but total transparency in this process. It is a process based on a person's own sense of his or her worth as an employee. If a person's sense of his/her own value was way out of line with the company's sense of his/her value this could be very hurtful and demoralising: "It was soon clear that if our executives were ashamed of their salaries, it might be because they felt they weren't really earning them, for if they merited their pay they could easily prove their worth. ... Executives should be proud of what they earn, and their salaries ought to provide everyone with an incentive to rise." (1993, p. 109)

From Semco's perspective, the issue is not whether executives can justify their salaries but whether they can listen to and respond to the way in which others think about their salaries. For to justify our salaries all we need is an agile analytic mind. But to listen to the way in which others see our salaries requires the willingness to digest ourselves from the perspective of others – just as Terri Anderson had to do in Beirut. Shame, to continue using the example of Semler, is that kind of experience in which we see ourselves being seen by others. We do not, as Sartre tells us, feel shame before ourselves. Just as we cannot feel embarrassment all by ourselves, so shame is the experience of ourselves before an other. When senior executives feel ashamed of their salaries they are thus seeing themselves through the experience of other employees.

If senior executives feel shame before others in response to the salaries that they receive, then this experience of being seen by the other serves as a way of checking our own sense of value or worth. In order to avoid being ashamed of the salary we set ourselves we will attempt to assess that it is in line with the way in which others see our sense of worth and value. Thus in setting our salaries we will not act only out of greed but will always check our self-assessment against the way in which we feel others are assessing us.

In this way instead of managers monitoring the company, people in the company begin to monitor their own performance and the worth of this performance. Through self-monitoring the company's checks and balances did not come from the top but were a natural process within the system. Workers did not have to fight managers for recognition. They needed to struggle with their own sense of self-recognition. They need to be able to assert their sense of self in public.

In general Semler found that people tended to under value themselves. They set salaries for themselves below that which the company thought they were worth. Not only is it difficult to form an accurate self-assessment, it is also difficult to take responsibility for what a person thinks he/she is worth. It takes much self-confidence to be sure of what one is worth. Indeed we live in a time period as psychologists keep on telling us that problems with self-worth are one of the main kinds of complaints dealt with in counselling, that many people seek therapy because they lack a sense of themselves. Furthermore, we live in a time period in which people are crying out for others to tell them that they are worth it. This is called narcissism. Semler is challenging people to develop and express their sense of self. The response has been an unleashment of creativity in which employees relish the opportunity of expressing their potential. This is because in Semler's terms they are adults being treated like adults.

In those cases in which people's sense of their worth to the company was out of line with the company's experience of their worth, these employees were invited to stay on in their existing positions with their existing salaries or leave the company. Semco did not feel the need to take on people at any price but at a price that would be agreed upon in dialogue.

From this example we see that freedom and responsibility form the basis of social cohesion at Semco, that is the freedom to choose and the responsibility before the other members of our team in the company. We also see that freedom and responsibility require a strength of character on the part of employees. We cannot just simply go through the motions of doing things or blame the system for our position. Rather we need to give account of ourselves and we need to be able to assess our own self-worth in the context of the company. We need to develop our sense of self in order to assess ourselves in this way.

We also see a movement away from explicit regulation to reflective relationship as the basis of cohesion in the company. But this requires the strength to work with reflection, that is, with the experience of your own way of seeing your worth being open to discussion by others. This is a theme that is being developed in other organisations.

Salaries are not the only practice under the gaze of the other. So too is performance. It is evaluated in a reflective space in which I see myself through the lens of the gaze of the other. In examining myself from the perspective of the other I learn to see things about myself that I cannot see on my own. Crucial to this experience is a willingness to see and experiment with myself in the terms that the other sees me – not to dismiss them out of hand but to examine myself in terms of these other ways. As an example Semler gives an experience in which he came to develop new habits of practice through the gaze of a secretarial assistant. Semler's secretary told Semler that she did not always tell him what his priorities were. At the time he was not aware of it. He did not refuse her insight but used it as the basis to develop " a system using labels of different colours to denote the importance of a task."

The practice of improving and changing through the gaze of the other has become part of the established practice at Semco. It is not always easy, often challenging people to change deeply ingrained habits. Semler gives examples of managers who had autocratic attunements, having in the face of the gaze of their subordinates to develop more open and flexible styles of management. His subordinates did not let him know in a kind and gentle manner what they thought of his autocratic style. Rather they were angry with him – and showed it. But instead of responding to the anger in a defensive way, he embraced their criticism of him and began to change his style to one that was more in line with the team based ethos that he had espoused.

In philosophy there are a number of different ways of interpreting the idea of the gaze of the other. Foucault, for example, sees the gaze primarily as a means of control. He believes that the gaze of the other is a transformation in the means of control. Instead of control coming from outside of us – as it did in scientific management, it now comes from within us. We are monitoring ourselves for the company. This is the way in which, for example, the voice of conscience works in the church. Instead of the priest monitoring our behaviour from the outside, we monitor it through the idea that God can see all of our actions. We monitor ourselves just in case God is seeing us. So too in Semler's organisation, we are monitoring ourselves just in case the other can see us.

A second version of the gaze comes from the philosopher Levinas who believes that the gaze of the other unleashes something in us that cannot be unleashed by ourselves. He calls this the "metaphysical desire." This is a form of desire that is not concerned with satisfying a need in ourselves. It is not about devouring or taking something in for ourselves rather it is a desire of going beyond ourselves, a desire that opens up new possibilities, in which we are excited in the strangeness of the world. In this desire we are held by the mystery of the world. We sense something but are not quite able to put our finger on it. It is the desire to create through exploring the unknown. It is through the gaze of the other that we are opened up to the unknown, to the mystery and thus to the creative. Reflecting this option Semler says: "A touch of civil disobedience is necessary to alert the organisation that all is not right. Rather than fear our Thoreaus and Bakunins, we do our best to let them speak their minds even though they often become thorns in our side." (1993, p. 134)

It is precisely by allowing the rebels to speak their minds that new possibilities are opened up in Semco. For rebels see things from another perspective. They see things in a way that is strange to common sense. Allowing them to speak enables the new, the exciting and the innovative to emerge. Initially through embracing them, we sense that something is there but we cannot quite put our hands on it. To follow this path is to be involved in the metaphysical rather than a physical desire.

These two options – the Foucauldtian and the perspective of Levinas – are not necessarily mutually exclusive. Semler did release the excitement of possibility in his employees through opening them up to the gaze of the other. At the same time the gaze of the other was a mechanism that ensured that people were monitoring themselves in terms of their relationships to others in the organisation.

Through the gaze much of the policing and motivating work of the manager is cut out. The manager does not have to waste time developing stringent rules and procedures, and does not have to spend time monitoring that these rules are obeyed and so avoids getting caught in a preoccupation with rules and regulations becoming an end in themselves. Similarly because workers are free to rely on their own initiative, external motivation is not the only source of motivation. Workers are motivated out of a sense of ownership of their work. They are motivated out of a sense of involvement in the work. Managers are wielders of neither the carrot nor the stick.

What we see then is that monitoring does occur at Semco but it is not a one way monitoring – that is, it is not only a top down form of monitoring but a bottom up one as well. In addition it is not a monitoring that is aimed at control or making workers tow the corporate line. Rather it is a form of monitoring that is aimed at both individual and organisational development. For we learn about ourselves through the way in which we accept and reject the perspectives that others have on us. This form of reflection is crucial to any relationship – whether it be partners in a family or business relationship. We need to be able to see ourselves through the way others see us. Furthermore, it is also not a monitoring based on suspicion or mistrust.

IV

Thus we see that Semler's philosophy did not precede the changes that he made but emerged out of the changes that he made. Through working in a creative way with the tensions and contradictions in the workplace he was able shift the philosophy of work and therefore the relationship between stakeholders in the workplace. Furthermore, we see Semler's intuitions emerge not out of a detailed formula but with an elegant simplicity; an innocence or self-evidence. He did not think long and hard about stopping searches. As he himself says, he just stopped them. In terms of his new intuition, he could see clearly what needed to be done and was able to act on it.

Yet the paradox of seeing clearly needs to be highlighted. For it was Semler's very lostness that promoted him to need to see things in a new way. In other words, it was by being lost in the "fog of reality," as John Seely Brown puts it, that he came to see clearly. This is the paradox that underlies so many new visions. They emerge out of the way in which visionaries grapple with being in the fog of reality. An example of this is the painter Vincent van Gogh who as a young man was so lost and confused, did not know what to do with his life, suffered from a life crippling depression yet as an artist produced a powerful and intense form of art. Similarly in the corporate context we have seen how Grove and Meyerson's sense of vision comes out of the way in which they battled with their lostness. We also see how their new vision emerges with an elegant simplicity.

Semler's new vision and practice of work emerged all the more clearly through the process of questioning the assumptions of the traditional way of working. He came to question the ethic of hardwork, moving to a notion of smart work, quality of work over quantity of work, giving up the idea of being orientated by clock time rather than time management – indeed he stopped wearing a watch altogether. Clock time was no longer a yardstick in terms of which he structured his activity. He began to question traditional accounting practices in the organisation and found that it had produced an uncontrollable spiral of number crunching activities in which nobody really knew what was going on, yet everybody played as though they knew what was happening: "And we had so many damn numbers, inside so damn many folders, that almost nobody was looking at them." (1993, p. 51)

Here again we see how traditional organisational practices prove to be self-defeating. Numbers create the very inefficiency that they intend to eradicate. We also see how the organisation failed, in Welch's terms to "face reality," that is face the reality that their traditional practices were not working for them. As Semler says: "Everyone just bluffed their way through meetings, pretending to be familiar with every little detail." (1993, p. 51) People went through the motions of doing things. It became more self-evident to him that the system needed overhauling. The more he questioned traditional organisational practices the more he found that they defied common sense. There was a rule for everything but he came to believe that there were certain kinds of activity that could not be formulated in terms of rules or regulations. The commitment that people required for work could not be put in a rule. Rules got in the way of people's sense of care and attunement to work: "One of my first acts at SEMCO was to throw out all the rules. All companies have procedural bibles. Some look like Encyclopaedia Britannica. Who needs all those rules? They discourage flexibility and comfort the complacent. At SEMCO we stay away from formulas and try to keep our minds open ... All that new employees at SEMCO are given is a 20-page booklet we call The Survival Manual. It has lots of cartoons but few words. The basic message: Use your common sense."

Again we see how he comes to believe that the very means that are thought of as sustaining work actually undermine work. Highly regulated organisations provide no room for common sense but people needed to be able to rely on their own sense and judgement in order to care for the work. The company had become so regulated that people needed to continually consult the manual before they acted. No one could act from their own initiative anymore. There was no room for common sense. Yet there was a certain dimension of organisational functioning that could not be put into a rule or regulation. This was the care vital to work.

In order to enable people to care for their work, they needed to be treated as adults – something that workers in the traditional workplace were not considered. Rather they were dehumanised and treated as cogs in the machine. Again we will see how Semler develops his perspective by pointing out contradictions and absurdities in the traditional view of management: "We simply do not believe our employees have an interest in coming in late, leaving early and doing as little as possible for as much money as their union can wheedle out of us. After all, these same people raise children, join the PTA, elect mayors, governors, senators and presidents. They are adults. At Semco we treat them as adults. We trust them. ... We get out of their way and let them do their jobs."

Just as in the example of Welch, it is through highlighting contradictions within the traditional system, that the assumptions in terms of which Semler critiques the traditional view begins to emerge with clarity and an elegant simplicity. As was discussed in the context of Welch, when we criticise something we always do so in terms of a set of assumptions which are not immediately explicit. What we see in both Welch and Semler is that they used the critique of the tradition to make their own assumptions explicit. Just as Welch refined his philosophy of differentiation, so Semler's philosophy of organisational democracy emerged with clarity. We need look only to his critique of control to see this: control of the work force on the traditional logic was the mechanism used by management to ensure that workers are working; yet from Semler's perspective such forms of control engendered the very resistance they were intended to overcome. They created a sense of apathy and indifference in the workplace.

From control to care – just as in the case of Welch, Semler allows a transition from the authoritarianism of scientific management to democracy to take place. This basic sense of trust is vital to work. It is what it means to be an adult and a human being. But this transition was frightening to managers who felt their paradigm, their identity and their basis of power to be eroded. And in the face of the uncertainty of the disruption to their paradigm a number of managers left. Others, like Semler were able to examine and rethink their function as managers. They were able to embrace the erosion of their traditional forms of power, secure enough in themselves to allow other possibilities to emerge. And what began to emerge is a new image and language in which to express the role of managers. Managers became counsellors, people who were able to see the bigger picture, were able to zoom in and out from the bigger picture to the immediate situation. The practices of dialogue in the workplace began to change. Instead of issuing orders or reprimanding each other, a reflective level of dialogue between employees was being encouraged. There was a move from regulations to values as the basis of organisational cohesiveness, one which respected the democratic context in which people lived. There was also a fundamental overhaul of the organisational architecture. Instead of thinking of the structure of the organisation in a traditional pyramid form, Semler began to think of it in terms of circles.

The process through which he came to think of the new form of organisational design is interesting. For we are accustomed to thinking of organisational design in rationalist terms. Yet for Semler the new view of the organisation emerged as an intuition in the least expected moment: "In the autumn of 1988 my soon-to-be-wife, Sofia, and I rented a house for two weeks on the Caribbean Island of Mustique. Our plan was simply to sit on the beach and relax. ... Even so, I spent most of my time thinking about Semco. ... Watching the clear, gentle Caribbean waves, **it suddenly** seemed so obvious. Why not replace the pyramid with something more fluid? Like a circle. A pyramid is rigid and constraining. A circle is filled with possibilities. Why not try to round the pyramid. We began sketching it out in Mustique. Sofia and I would find sticks and draw it in the sand, stepping back to ponder the implications of our handiwork. Back in Sao Paulo, I continued to refine the idea. After a few months I was playing with three concentric circles ... and some triangles. ... The circles and triangles signified the most radical changes we had yet contemplated at Semco" (193, p. 152)

What is interesting to note is the similar ways in which Semler's and Welch's idea for the structure of GE emerged. Welch's idea too emerged, as we shall recall from chapter 9, as an intuition on the beach. The contrast with scientific concepts of management is clear. They taught us that management especially in the context of corporate structure is a rational activity. Yet here we see that it emerges out of an intuition – just as the artistic process of creativity. First we have the intuition and then we allow it to be refined. It is also interesting to see that the intuition occurred to both when they least expected it – when they were not even thinking about work; when they had given up concentrating, their mind was free to roam and wonder. And in both cases, it emerged suddenly," in a "blink of an eye," as Heidegger would say. Yet in that blink of an eye both knew they had found something mind boggling, even though they did not have a fully developed justification for it. This would come as they wrestled with the intuition. This was the process underpinning the art of van Gogh. It was also as we have seen the process underpinning the scientific thinking of Newton. And it can even be found in the rational mathematics of Henri Poincare who while attempting to work in a rational way was overwhelmed by an intuitive insight into a new theory of mathematics: "For 15 days I strove to prove that there could not be any functions like those I have since called Fuchsian functions. I was then very ignorant; everyday I seated myself at my worktable, stayed an hour or two, tried a great number of combinations and reached no results. One evening, contrary to my custom, I drank black coffee and could not sleep. Ideas rose in crowds; I felt them collide until pairs interlocked, so to speak, making a stable combination. By the next morning I had established the existence of a class of Fuchsian functions, those which come from the hypergeometric series; I had only to write out the results, which took but a few hours." (Poincaré, 1946)

At best Poincare's rationality could help him unpack the details of his new intuition but it was not the basis of the intuition. It was not the basis of his seeing clearly. In this sense, as Einstein put it, rationality is a hand maiden to intuition: "The intuitive mind is a sacred gift and the rational mind is a faithful servant. We have created a society that honors the servant and has forgotten the gift."

The same process can be seen in Andrew Grove: it is when his attention was not focused on saving Intel that he was able to see Intel in a new light. It shall be recalled that Grove came to see Intel in a new light when he shifted his attention from analysing Intel to dreamily looking out of the window at the ferris wheel. In that moment he opened up another way of looking at Intel. And again, this new emerged in the blink of an eye.

V

What we see is that for Semler stress was not a problem to be coped with by attending stress reduction classes or by finding moments to soothe himself – and then getting on business as usual. Rather stress was a sign that business as usual needed to be questioned, that the system as a whole needed overhaul. It was an occasion on which to rethink his fundamental values and way of doing things in the organisation: "And you won't find a running track, swimming pool, or gym at Semco. Many companies build them to help their employees cope with stress. At Semco, we try not to cause stress in the first place." (Semler, 1993, p. 132) The way not to cause stress was to rethink organisational relationships. This was because stress from Semler's perspective is rooted in the structure of organisational relationships. The way it puts, as we have seen, everyone in contradiction with themselves and each other is the basis of stress. As we have seen in order to eliminate stress, we need to reframe organisational relationships. This is precisely what Semler has done. The democratic philosophy that underpins the practices at Semco is designed to move beyond stress and provide an environment in which everyone can express themselves in their work. It allows everyone to be an adult in their work.

17
Philosophical Narratives for Managers

The aim of this book has been to identify, describe, analyse and bring out the significance of philosophical experiences in the context of management. It has demonstrated that managers do have philosophical experiences, that these are central to their practices as managers. The book has claimed that there are two dimensions to philosophical experience: firstly there is the level of developing a business feel, a feel for the situation that we are involved in. This feel develops in a non-cognitive way through the ways in which we are involved in the world. As we are involved in the world we develop a sense of familiarity with the world. This sense of familiarity forms the basis of our feel for the world. Often we are not even aware of the fact that we are developing a feeling for the world. Furthermore, this feel is not something inside of us but is between the world and us.

The second dimension of a philosophical experience occurs when there is a disturbance or disruption in the feeling that develops out of our way of being involved in the world. This disruption is usually experienced as a heightened state of emotional arousal, as a shock or experience of self-doubt, frustration, confusion or stress. It is an experience in which we feel beside ourselves. This disturbance detaches us from our everyday experience of the world and calls us to put our world into perspective. As such the disturbance is the basis of the development of a "helicopter perspective" on our practices and experiences as managers. We come to stand outside of our own experiences or situation. However, disruption does not automatically lead to the development of a helicopter perspective. We need to embrace the disruption rather than defend against it. Embracing the disruption means embracing our own vulnerability in situations where we feel that we do not have ultimate control. This requires an act of being resolved which means the power to accept our own powerlessness in situations.

Three perspectives were used to develop the concept of a philosophical experience: Dru's idea whereby new visions are developed out of the disruption of existing conventions was the first model used to unpack the nature of a philosophical experience. His model was situated in terms of

Plato's metaphor of the cave. Plato was seen as providing the first idea for understanding the process of thinking outside of our boxes – or as he called it our caves. For him philosophy begins in that moment in which we are freed from the taken for grantedness of our own caves. In Heidegger, the philosophical experience is articulated as a disruption of our familiar and "average everyday" ways of being involved in the world. As our familiar ways of doing things are disrupted we are opened up to new possibilities. For Heidegger, disruption opens up the possibility of an authentic relation to our world.

The book has also suggested that in order to understand management in times of disruption, we need to move from a predominantly scientific understanding of management to a philosophical understanding of management. As management theory focuses more and more on "reframing" experiences, on "switching paradigms," on "abandoning perspectives," and on helicopter thinking there is more and more a need for an appreciation of philosophy and philosophical experiences. For it is a form of philosophy that is attuned to philosophical experiences that can enable us to bring out and describe the processes and practices involved in such management practices. Philosophy provides the language and skills of how to work under conditions of disruption. Science, especially the forms that have dominated management operate under times of routine and stability. A number of examples of leaders who function in a philosophical way were used to bring out the skills of philosophical thinking. We saw, for example, how Welch's experience of frustration enabled him to become philosophical, how Grove's experience of worry allowed him to become philosophical and how Meyerson's experience of despair brought out a philosophical attunement.

This would suggest that more work needs to be done on using the language of philosophy to articulate the experiences of managers under conditions of disruption – conditions which appear to be the norm today. The more that we can use the language of philosophy to understand how managers function under conditions of disruption, the more we can provide a framework for managers to understand their way of experiencing the world. Furthermore, the more we can do this, the more we will enable managers to understand the way they think about their practices of managers. Rather than imposing disengaged or abstract theories onto managers, we will enable managers to develop an understanding of their own frames or assumptions through their own experiences. To be philosophical from the perspective of this book does not mean to learn the theories of philosophers in abstraction from experience. It means to challenge our own way of experiencing the world as a means of exploring our assumptions about the way in which we see the world.

In this sense this book is advocating a form of philosophical education. In this form of education managers are encouraged to firstly highlight the assumptions underpinning their experience as managers, secondly, they need to be willing to challenge these assumptions and thirdly, they need to embrace both the uncertainty and excitement of new possibilities. Through challenging their assumptions in this way the possibility of developing what I shall call a philosophical narrative occurs. A philosophical narrative is the ability to make sense of things in a world that is in constant disruption. Today we can no longer rely on the system or a culture or even other people to make sense of the world for us. We have to make sense of the world for ourselves. Furthermore, the sense that we have of the world is constantly being challenged. For as things change our need to make sense is disrupted and changes. Changes in our circumstances often mean that we need to change the frame of reference in which we see things. We cannot take our sense of the world for granted but need to care for and be attuned to our way of making sense of the world – otherwise we will find that our sense is out of step with the changes in the world.

A philosophical narrative is a way of shining a light on the world. Just like a light allows things to appear out of the darkness, so a philosophical narrative discloses a world to us. It gives us a vantage point in terms of which to see things. It is more than a point of view. It is, as discussed in chapter 4, a point from which to view the world. It is not the dogmatic assertion of a set of principles but the opening up of a horizon in terms of which to see things. All of us have the potential to develop philosophical narratives. It presupposes the willingness to develop our business feel and to reflect on the sense that emerges through our business feel.

The notion of a philosophical narrative can be clarified by contrasting it with the idea of emotional intelligence. Both are concerned with feeling and reflection through feeling. However, they differ on the meanings of both feeling and reflection. From the perspective of emotional intelligence some one is seen as emotionally intelligent if they are aware of their own and others emotions and can manage these emotions. From the perspective of a philosophical narrative, there are moments of disruption in which we become confused, lose vision and are plunged into the fog of reality. What is crucial from the perspective of a philosophical narrative is the way in which we deal with our experience of being in the fog of reality: can we use our "Socratic ignorance" to open up a new world or do we become defensive and stay entrenched within the old world? Philosophical narratives allow for the movement between confusion and clarity rather than being concerned simply with being aware of our emotions.

Furthermore, it is often the case that in the development of a philosophical narrative we go through experiences of not being able to "manage" our emotions. For example, we saw Grove floundering, not able to manage his emotions. He in fact sees this as central to the development of a new vision: allow chaos to reign, he tells us – not as an end in itself but as the basis of making a transition to a new perspective. Again, it is how we work with not managing that is crucial to the development of a philosophical narrative. Sometimes we need to let go of "managing." Indeed it is when we let things be that the new is encouraged to emerge.

The more things change the more our sense of things is disrupted. We need to be able to work with our changing sense of things. Philosophical education is a process of being able to work with our changing sense of things. A philosophical educator is someone who is able to work with us in our changing sense of things. A philosophical educator does not operate in terms of a disengaged approach to philosophy. Rather he or she roots the process of philosophy in disruptive experiences. For it is these disruptive experiences that lead us to become philosophical. This means that a philosophical educator, like Socrates, moves from the experiential to the conceptual dimension and then back again. Philosophical education is the use of philosophy as a means of being able to make sense of our own experience. This does not mean that the texts of philosophy are not important. They are not important as ends in themselves but to the extent that they enable us to make sense of our experience they become partners in a dialogue with us. The role of the philosophical educator is to encourage managers to reflect on the assumptions that are implicit in their experiences. The history of philosophy is used as a means of doing this.

Bibliography

Argyris, C. and Schon, D.A. *Theory In Practice: Increasing Professional Effectiveness* (San Francisco: Jossey-Bass Publishers, 1977).

Bellah, R. et al. *Habits of the Heart* (NY: Harper & Row, 1985).

Benner, P. and Wrubel, J. *The Primacy of Caring: Stress and Coping in Health and Illness* (California: Addison-Wesley Publishing Company, 1989).

Blits, Jan, H. "Self-Knowledge and the Modern Mode of Learning" *Educational Theory* (Fall, 1989).

Bloom, A. *The Closing of the American Mind* (NY: Touchstone, 1987).

Boleman, G. and Deal, T.E. *Reframing Organizations: Artistry, Choice, and Leadership* (San Fransisco: Jossey-Bass, 2003).

Camus, A. *The Myth of Sisyphus* (Harmondsworth: Penguin Books, 1955).

Carlzon, J. *Moments of Truth* (New York: Ballinger Publishing Company, 1987).

Charan, R. and Useem, J. "Why companies fail" in *Fortune magazine*, May 27, 2002, http://www.fortune.com/fortune/information/Magarchive/1,16011,magarchive-11-18-02,00.html

Christensen, C. *The Innovator's Dilemma* (NY: Harper Collins, 2000).

Collins, J. "Level 5 Leadership: The Triumph of Humility and Fierce Resolve" in *Harvard Business Review*, January, 2001.

Covey, S. *The Seven Habits of Highly Effective People* (Australia: Simon & Schuster, 1989).

Dreyfus, H. *Being-in-the-World: A Commentary on Heidegger's Being and Time, Division 1* (Massachusetts: The MIT Press, 1993).

Dreyfus, H. "Heidegger on the connection between nihlism, art, technology and politics" in Guigon C. (ed.) *The Cambridge Companion to Heidegger* (Cambridge: Cambridge University Press, 1993).

Douglas, Mullen J. *Kierkegaard's Philosophy: Self-Deception and Cowardice in the Present Age* (U.S.A.: A Mentor Book, 1981).

Dru, J. *Overturning Conventions and Shaking up the Market Place* (New York: John Wiley & Sons, 1996).

Drucker, P. *Managing in a Time of Great Change* (Oxford: Butterworth-Heinemann, 1997).

Dunlap, A. *Mean Business* (NY: A Fireside Book, 1996).

Eagleton, T. *The Significance of Theory* (Manchester: University of Manchester Press, 1990).

Elliot, T.S. quoted in Bantock, G. *T.S. Elliot and Education* (London: Faber and Faber, 1970).

Farson, R. *Management of the Absurd* (New York: Touchstone, 1997).

Feinstein, B. "The Intelectual Capitalist" in *Strategy and Business 25, 2001* (Booz Allen Hamilton Inc.)

Finley, M. "The Reengineer Who Could" James Champy addresses The Masters Forum June 6, 1995 http://www.mastersforum.com/archives/champy/champy.htm

Flores, F. *The Impacts of Information Technology on Business Communications* Talk was given at ACM 97, http://research.microsoft.com/acm97/ff/

Foster, R. and Kaplan, S. *Creative Destruction: Why Companies That Are Built To Last Underperform the Market – And How To Succefully Transform Them* (NY: Currency, 2001).

Gabriel, Y. ISPSO 1996 Symposium on June 14, 15 and 16 at the New York City Marriott Financial Centre. http://www.sba.oakland.edu/ispso/html/gabriel.html)

Garten, J. *The Mind of the C.E.O.* (Basic Books/Perseus Publishing, 2001).

Gates, B. *The Road Ahead* (Harmondsworth: Penguin Books, 1996, p. 286).

Gellner, E. "Metamorphosis" in *Thought and Change* (London: Weidenfeld and Nicolson, 1964).

Gerstner, L. *Who Says Elephants Can't Dance? Inside IBM's Historic Turnaround* (Australia: Harper Business, 2002).

Grint, K. *Management: A Sociological Introduction* (Cambridge, UK: Polity Press, 1995).

Grove, A. *Only the Paranoid Survive* (Great Britain: Harper Collins Publishers, 1997).

Hamel, G. *Leading the Revolution* (Harvard: Harvard Business School Press, 2000).

Hanflig, O. (ed.) *Life and Meaning: A Reader* (Oxford: Basil Blackwell, 1988).

Heidegger, M. *Being and Time* (Oxford: Basil Blackwell, 1985).

Heilemann, J. "Andy Grove's Rational Exuberance" *Wired magazine* 9.06, June 2001 http://www.wired.com/wired/archive/9.06/intel_pr.html.

hooks, b. *Teaching to Transgress* (New York: Routledge, 1994).

Joss, B. www.e-coaching.org. 2001

Kierkegaard, S. *The Concept of Anxiety* (Princeton: Princeton University Press, 1980).

Kotter, J.P. *A Force for Change: How Leadership Differs from Management* (New York: The Free Press, 1999).

Kuhn, T. *The Structure of Scientific Revolution* (Chicago: The University of Chicago Press, 1970)

Lahav, R. "On Thinking Clearly and Distinctly" *Metaphilosophy* 23, 1 1992.

Levinas, E. *Totality and Infinity* (Pittsburgh: Duquesne University Press, 1985).

Locke, Weinberger, Searls & Levine *The Cluetrain Manifesto: The End of Business as Usual* Copyright © 1999, 2001 (NY: Perseus Publishing, 2000).

Meyerson, M. "Everything I Thought I Knew About Leadership Was Wrong" in *Fast Company*, April 1996.

Lowe, J. 'Neutron' Jack Welch *San Diego Metropolitan Magazine*, 1998 http://www.sandiegometro.com/1998/may/money.html

Lowe, J. *Jack Welch Speaks: Wisdom from the World's Greatest Business Leader* (USA: John Wiley & Sons, 2001).

Mandela, N. *Long Walk To Freedom* (Randburg: Macdonald Purnell, 1995).

Moodee, A.-M. Managerial Language: The Key to Communication, *Management Today*, April 2004.

Nagel, T. *The View from Nowhere* (Oxford: Oxford University Press, 1989).

Neff, T.J. et al. *Lessons from the Top: The Search for America's Best Business Leaders* (New York: Doubleday, 1999).

Nietzsche, F. *Thus Spoke Zarathustra* (Harmondsworth: Penguin Books, 1978).

Nishimura, K. *Worth Magazine* 2000.

Passagen hem.passagen.se/p47/rommel.htm–dok storlek: 6kB–engelska

Pasternack, B. "Dreamers with a Deadline" *Strategy and Business* 25, 2001.

Plato *The Republic* translated by Lee D. (Harmondsworth: Penguin Books, 1968).

Plato *Meno* (Harmondsworth: Penguin Books, 1976).

Poincaré, H. *Science and Method; The Foundations of Science* (Lancaster: The Science Press, 1946).

Roddick, A. *Business As Unusual* (London: Thorsons, 2000).

Roddick, A. *Let's Talk Business Network* 1996 http://www.ltbn.com/fame/Roddick.html

Rubin, H. 'The New Merchants of Light' *Leader to Leader*, 10 Fall 1998 http://www.pfdf.org/leaderbooks/L2L/fall98/rubin.html

Sartre, J.P. *Existentialism and Humanism* (London: Eyre Methuen Ltd., 1975).

Semler, R. *Maverick* (London: Century, 1993).

Schumpeter, J. *Capitalism, Socialism and Democracy* (NY: Harper Tourchbooks, 1955).

Shapiro, E. *Fad surfing in the boardroom: reclaiming the courage to manage in the age of instant answers* (Pymble, N.S.W.: HarperBusiness, 1995).

Sinclair, A. & Wilson, V. *New faces of leadership* (Melbourne: Melbourne University Press, 2002).

Spinosa, C., Flores, F. and Dreyfus, H. *Disclosing New Worlds: Entrepreneurship, Democratic Action, and the Cultivation of Solidarity* (Cambridge, MA.: M.I.T. Press, 1997).

Soros, G. *The Crisis of Global Capitalism: Open Society Endangered* (New York: Public Affairs, 1998).

Steers, R., Porter, L., and Bigley, G. *Motivation and leadership at work* (New York: McGraw-Hill, c.1996).

Stewart, C. "Perfect Pitch" *The Australian Magazine* (June 9–10, 2001).

Tichy and Sherman *Control Your Destiny or Someone Else Will* (Doubleday, 1993).

Watson, D. *Death Sentence: The Decay of Public Language* (Milsons Point N.S.W.: Random House Australia, c.2003).

Welch, J. quoted in *Washington Post,* March 23, 1997.

Welch, J. *Jack* (London: Headline Book Publishing, 2001).

Widlack, H. "Real-Life Shock: The Inapplicability of Theoretical Knowledge to Classroom Practice." *Education* 1980.

Wilshire, Bruce. *The moral collapse of the university : professionalism, purity, and alienation* (Albany: State University of New York Press, 1990).

Van Gogh, V. *The Letters of Vincent Van Gogh,* selected and edited by Ronald de Leeuw (Harmondsworth: Penguin Books, 1997).

Welch interview with Gottliebson, R. in article "World's greatest boss says it's no time for wallflowers" in *The Australian Wednesday,* June 18, 2003, p. 21.

Westfall, R. *The Life of Isaac Newton* (Cambridge: Cambridge University Press, 1994).

Woods, P. "Stress and the Teacher Role" in Cole M. and Walker S (eds) *Teaching and Stress* (Milton Keynes: Open University Press, 1989).

World of Strategy 2003 http://empires.world-of-strategy.com/abilities.php

Index